OBJECTING TO GOD

The growth of science, and a correspondingly scientific way of looking at evidence, have for the last three centuries slowly been gaining ground over religious explanations of the cosmos and mankind's place in it. However, not only is secularism now under renewed attack from religious fundamentalism, but also it has been widely claimed that the scientific evidence itself points strongly to a universe deliberately fine-tuned for life to evolve in it. In addition, certain aspects of human life, like consciousness and the ability to recognise the existence of universal moral standards, seem completely resistant to evolutionary explanation. In this book Colin Howson analyses in detail the evidence which is claimed to support belief in God's existence, and argues that the claim is not well founded. Moreover, there is very compelling evidence that an all-powerful, all-knowing God not only does not exist but cannot exist, a conclusion both surprising and provocative.

COLIN HOWSON is Professor of Philosophy at the University of Toronto, and Emeritus Professor, London School of Economics and Political Science. He is the author of *Hume's Problem: Induction and the Justification of Belief* (2000), *Logic with Trees* (1997) and, with Peter Urbach, *Scientific Reasoning: The Bayesian Approach* (3rd edition, 2006).

OBJECTING TO GOD

COLIN HOWSON

University of Toronto

CAMBRIDGE UNIVERSITY PRESS
Cambridge, New York, Melbourne, Madrid, Cape Town,
Singapore, São Paulo, Delhi, Tokyo, Mexico City

Cambridge University Press
The Edinburgh Building, Cambridge CB2 8RU, UK

Published in the United States of America by Cambridge University Press, New York

www.cambridge.org
Information on this title: www.cambridge.org/9780521768351

First published 2011

Printed in the United Kingdom at the University Press, Cambridge

A catalogue record for this publication is available from the British Library

Library of Congress Cataloguing in Publication data
Howson, Colin.
Objecting to God / Colin Howson.
p. cm.
Includes bibliographical references and index.
ISBN 978-0-521-76835-1 (hardback) – ISBN 978-0-521-18665-0 (paperback)
1. God – Proof. 2. Religion – Controversial literature.
3. Science and religion. I. Title.
BL200.H69 2011
211′.7 – dc22 2011013514

ISBN 978-0-521-76835-1 Hardback
ISBN 978-0-521-18665-0 Paperback

The fool hath said in his heart, There is no God.
Psalm 14:1

Contents

Preface

As its title suggests, this is a book about God. More precisely, it tries to answer two highly topical questions about God. One, to which I have devoted the most space, is whether the arguments in the contemporary literature for believing in an all-powerful, all-knowing and all-loving Creator of the universe are good ones. The question isn't of merely theoretical interest: there is a widespread preoccupation that morality cannot survive a loss of religious faith, with many echoing Ivan Karamazov's famous claim in Dostoevsky's *The Brothers Karamazov* that without God everything is permitted. So the other question is: was – is – Ivan Karamazov right? Despite an understandable reluctance to give anyone an excuse for not reading further, I will compromise and reveal now that my answers to these two questions will be 'no' to both, but leave it to the rest of the book to explain why. If you want to find out more, start at Chapter 1 and keep going.

At the end of each chapter there is a little section marked 'Exercise' (not compulsory!). This consists of a quotation from an actual person of a certain standing, either academic or theological, among them one the latchet of whose shoes I, like John the Baptist, am not worthy to stoop down and unloose. Each quotation consists of a claim or argument to which the material in the chapter is relevant, and the reader is invited to consider how they would respond to it.

Acknowledgments

I have received much help in writing this book from various people. More than anyone else I would like to thank my wife Margie Morrison for providing me with many and invaluable suggestions for improvement, both in style and content. While she did her best, she was dealing with recalcitrant material and I must take final and full responsibility upon myself. Matt McCormick also gave me invaluable help in the way of friendly criticism of the manuscript. I am also grateful to Adam Harmer for his hard work editing the final draft, and compiling the bibliography and index. Others to whom I am indebted are Sorin Bangu, Pierre Bouffier, Hao Hu, my old friends and erstwhile collaborators Allan Franklin and Peter Urbach, and the members of TBB 199, my first-year seminar on God and science at the University of Toronto, all of whom did so much to help me get my own ideas straight (if they are straight). My thanks also to the Department of Philosophy at the University of Toronto for financial assistance in the form of an SSHRC Institutional Grant.

I would also like to express my gratitude for their constant encouragement and help to Hilary Gaskin, Joanna Garbutt and Anna Lowe of Cambridge University Press, and to thank Rose Bell for her extremely scrupulous copy-editing, as well as two anonymous reviewers for that Press and last but not least Tom O'Reilly of the Press for his remarkable efficiency during the production process. Other press personnel whom I would like to thank are the translators of the King James Bible. All the Biblical quotations are from their translation on which, like most people of a certain age in the UK, I was brought up. The Devil doesn't always have the best tunes.

I would like to give special thanks to Nicholas Beale. He and I were jointly going to write a book about God and science, and in particular the way Bayesian ideas illuminate the discussion. It is well known, however, that Bayesian methodology depends to some extent on prior probabilities, and unfortunately for Nicholas's and my joint project it quickly became evident that ours were pulling us too far apart for there to be any realistic hope of an agreed final manuscript. But Nicholas did provide me with a great deal of insight into the questions addressed in this book, and at all the points where I have gained from it I have, I hope, given him full acknowledgment.

Finally finally, as a recent incumbent of the US Presidency might have put it, I am grateful to Dr Jill Marrington and my Toronto colleague Professor Brad Inwood for improving my understanding of what 'telos', or rather 'τέλος', meant to Aristotle.

CHAPTER 1

Of human bondage

'Thy will be done.'

1. THE PERILS OF PROPHECY

That the faith of his forebears had passed the flood-tide was sensed with apprehension by the Victorian poet and critic Matthew Arnold, who developed the metaphor in some of the most beautifully elegiac lines in the English poetic canon:

> Listen! You hear the grating roar,
> Of pebbles which the waves draw back and fling,
> At their return, up the high strand,
> Begin, and cease, and then again begin,
> With tremulous cadence slow, and bring
> The eternal note of sadness in.
>
> -
>
> The Sea of Faith
> Was once, too, at the full, and round earth's shore,
> Lay like the folds of a bright girdle furled.
> But now I only hear
> Its melancholy, long, withdrawing roar,
> Retreating, to the breath
> Of the night-wind, down the vast edges drear
> And naked shingles of the world.[1]

Coincidentally, in the very same year (1867) that Arnold was posting the decline of one millennial faith, another was born: Karl Marx, a second Messiah promising salvation to the poor and powerless, published *Das Kapital.* As did his illustrious predecessor (or more precisely his predecessor's apostles), Marx also foretold that a final apocalypse would precede

[1] Matthew Arnold, 'Dover Beach' in *Poems* (London: Macmillan, 1923).

mankind's rebirth into a new world. Marx's was, of course, purely terrestrial, a cooperative of mortal men and women. His apocalypse, once it had commenced, in 1917 in Russia, became one of terror, persecution and death.

But capitalism inconsiderately failed to heed Marx's prognosis and succumb to its internal contradictions. On the contrary, it still seems to be in rude health, and paradoxically at its most exuberant in one of the few countries where Marxism remains part of official dogma, thriving under the benign gaze of the Chinese Communist Party. Arnold's threnody was also at best premature. Whether he would have liked its modern manifestations or not (and I strongly suspect that the author of *Culture and Anarchy* would not), religious faith is resurgent throughout the world, not only in the areas peripheral to western culture but in its heartland: it is probably political suicide for a presidential candidate in the United States to allow any doubt that he or she is a Believer. It is also in the process of effectively immunising itself from criticism: to engage religion in critical debate is suicidal in several countries, verges on illegality in others, and has now been condemned by no less a body than the United Nations. In March 2009 the UN passed a resolution, 62/154, 'Combating the Defamation of Religion', urging member states to limit by law any expression of opinion which is not respectful to religion(s).[2] The resolution specifically seeks to protect Islam from criticism (paragraph 5), but officially all religions are in its scope.

Publication of this book would arguably be illegal in any country which incorporated that resolution into its law. Fortunately only Security Council resolutions are binding on member states, but UK law already seems to go quite a long way in the direction intended by the authors of 62/154, to judge by what happened to a pair of innocent hotel-proprietors recently in Britain. I quote a newspaper report of what happened after a complaint to police in the UK by a Muslim woman who, while staying at a hotel in Liverpool, engaged in a conversation with the hoteliers about their respective faiths:

> It is understood that among the topics debated was whether Jesus was a minor prophet, as Islam teaches, or whether he was the Son of God, as Christianity teaches. Among the things Mr Vogelenzang, 53, is alleged to have said is that

[2] Article 9 of the text 'stresses the need to effectively combat defamation of all religions' (but singles out Islam for particular mention). Article 10 'Emphasises that everyone has . . . the right to freedom of expression [but] the exercise of [that] right . . . may therefore be subject to limitations as are provided for by law and are necessary for [among other things] respect for religions and beliefs.'

Mohammed was a warlord. His wife, 54, is said to have stated that Muslim dress is a form of bondage for women. The conversation, on March 20 [2009], was reported by the woman to Merseyside Police.[3]

The hoteliers were duly charged with a criminal offence under the Public Order Act of 1986 and the Crime and Disorder Act of 1998. The case went to court and was summarily thrown out by the judge. The Crown Prosecution Service nevertheless insisted that it had acted in the public interest in bringing criminal charges against the hoteliers, who have since been forced to sell their once-flourishing business. In dismissing the case, the judge remarked that it was probably wise not to discuss religion in public.

2. NEW ATHEISM

Adding to the protective cordon of criminal law is a large cohort of *bien-pensants* who think that any vigorous criticism of religion is distasteful and somehow unworthy: 'not quite cricket', as the British colloquialism puts it. A recent focus of their displeasure[4] has been Richard Dawkins's best-selling book, *The God Delusion*. Though written by a distinguished scientist whose ideas have been seminal, who occupies an endowed Chair at one of the UK's leading universities, and whose seriousness of purpose can hardly be in doubt, the book is frequently described as 'rant' in the journalism of the UK and North America,[5] and Dawkins-bashing has transcended its national boundaries to become something of an international blood-sport.

But if Dawkins offends against what is regarded as good taste, his Fourth-Estate detractors need even fewer lessons in the art. In an article in the British daily newspaper *The Times* on 16 November 2009, Dawkins is referred to as a 'fundamentalist atheist', while in the London *Evening Standard* on 31 August 2010, a columnist called Rosamund Urwin wrote: 'Dawkins and his ilk make no attempt to engage or debate: they simply seem to enjoy castigating and poking fun.' Even a cursory inspection of

3 *Sunday Telegraph*, 19 September 2009. The British press has developed an obsession with age, and it is now *de rigueur* to state the age of anyone mentioned in a newspaper report.

4 An even more recent one is Stephen Hawking, whom Baroness Greenfield accused of displaying a 'Taliban-like' presumption of omniscience when he merely commented that physics no longer needs God (*Daily Telegraph*, 8 September 2010).

5 The scientists are naturally a different matter. The eminent evolutionary biologist Robert Trivers wrote the Foreword to *The Selfish Gene* (and generously pointed out that Dawkins corrected a mistake that he, Trivers, had made). A recent tribute to the fertility of Dawkins's ideas comes from the distinguished physicist Leonard Susskind, in *The Cosmic Landscape* (New York: Little, Brown and Co., 2006), p. 344.

Dawkins's activities would have shown this to be false. I have seen and heard Dawkins debate several times, and on each of those occasions he was measured and rational. Ms Urwin's sally seems to be an example of what psychoanalysts call *transference*: the imputing to others of one's own deficiencies.

One might feel entitled to expect a somewhat higher standard from academics. And one might be disappointed. The following passage appeared in a newspaper book-review by John Gray, Emeritus Professor of European Thought at the London School of Economics:

> Just like the monotheists they obsessively attack, Dawkins and his followers believe that consciousness makes humans categorically different from their animal kin. To be sure, these ideologues insist (they always insist) that consciousness emerged without any kind of supernatural invention. Now that consciousness has appeared among humans they – or at least the most advanced members of the species, the self-styled 'brights' as Dawkins and his followers describe themselves – can master the blind forces of evolution.[6]

It is not entirely clear what that last sentence is intended to mean. But here, for the record, is what Dawkins said about consciousness in the book that propelled him to popular fame, *The Selfish Gene*:

> When we watch an animal 'searching' for food, or for a mate, or for a lost child, we can hardly help imputing to it some of the subjective feelings we ourselves experience when we search.... Each one of us knows, from the evidence of his own introspection, that, at least in one survival machine, this purposiveness has evolved the property we call 'consciousness'. I am not philosopher enough to discuss what this means ...[7]

And here is something more recent:

> we don't know which animals are conscious. We don't actually, technically, even know that any other human being is conscious. We just each of us know that we ourselves are conscious. We infer on pretty good grounds that other people are conscious, and it's the same sort of grounds that lead us to infer that probably chimpanzees are conscious and probably dogs are conscious.[8]

Thus is a very distinguished thinker mocked, judged and – metaphorically – crucified by an academic for whom a lively canard trumps the truth. Dawkins may be something of a latter-day Darwin's bulldog – as Darwin's

[6] Review of Marilynne Robinson, *Matters of the Mind*, *Toronto Globe and Mail*, 21 May 2010.

[7] Richard Dawkins, *The Selfish Gene*, 30th Anniversary edn (New York: Oxford University Press, 2006), p. 53.

[8] From a recorded interview, 21 October 2009.

great Victorian defender, T. H. Huxley, called himself – but like Huxley himself he is a scientist and a tireless and gifted campaigner on behalf of an increased public understanding of science. Ironically, the main charge against him that is not entirely polemical is that his assault on religion goes well beyond what science and the standards of scientific reasoning justify: in particular, that he has not bothered to understand enough about what he is attacking. I myself think that Dawkins understands quite enough to form a reasoned and – as far as I am concerned – entirely convincing judgment. I hold no brief for him, however, and later I will argue that some of his own arguments are radically unsound, including the centrepiece-argument of *The God Delusion*.

Another cause of the widespread resistance to Dawkins's philippics is what is seen as a particularly intransigent way in which he and the 'new atheists', as they are called,[9] state their case. Religion is still so respectably entrenched even in western liberal societies that any overtly critical assault is regarded as suspect. Many people will never be convinced however good the arguments, because arguments in themselves have only a very limited power to persuade; but it would anyway be very surprising if a belief-system that has been so dominant politically, socially and spiritually for nearly two thousand years, and still exercises a powerful hold on billions of minds, would yield either suddenly or easily. Many people – myself among them – believe that the intellectual case against God was actually made over two-and-a-half centuries ago, by the Scottish philosopher David Hume – of whom more later – in his *Dialogues Concerning Natural Religion*.[10] Others have made the case for themselves without Hume's assistance. But to little avail: God is showing no inclination to quit the scene. Indeed, the number of adherents of two of the three big monotheistic religions, Christianity and Islam, has increased roughly in step with the increase in the world's population and each of them numbers more than a billion followers, and they are still growing, Islam very rapidly. And of course there are many more religions than just these. Hinduism also numbers many millions, so does Buddhism, while if a count were taken of all those who follow one

[9] This intellectually distinguished group includes, in addition to Dawkins himself, the particle physicist Victor Stenger, the chemist Peter Atkins, the neuroscientist Sam Harris, the philosophers Daniel Dennett and Michel Onfray, the mathematician Piergiorgio Odifreddi and the writer and journalist Christopher Hitchens. If I have omitted anyone of note I apologise.

[10] Paul Davies notes that this remarkable work even contains the first suggestion that we might inhabit a multiverse (*The Goldilocks Enigma: Why is the Universe Just Right for Life?* (London: Allen Lane, 2006), p. 96).

or other of the active religions that currently exist it would amount to a sizable proportion of the world's population.

3. GOD OF OUR FATHERS

The anthropologist Pascal Boyer, in his book *Religion Explained*, makes a plausible case that religions arise and persist because they answer a variety of human needs, emotional and intellectual. Because the needs persist so does religion, even when it is assailed by what might seem to the scientific mind to be overwhelmingly adverse evidence. Unfortunately, the way it accommodates those needs has often come with a considerable cost, sometimes highly visible, sometimes more insidious. I know of no reliable record of the number of lives lost, to say nothing of serious physical and mental injuries also sustained, on behalf of some of the world's principal religions, but to put it at several million is probably not an overestimate.

Not all religions are inherently toxic, and there is no doubt that some of the violence perpetrated in religion's name is often mixed with more worldly causes. But by no means all of it. Though they may not all contribute in a significant way to violence and intolerance, some religions, unfortunately those with large world followings, nevertheless have a special mix of ingredients which predisposes them strongly in that direction. Foremost among them are the Abrahamic religions, Judaism, Christianity and Islam. The ingredients are set out in the foundational narrative those religions share: an absolutist morality based on the command of an all-powerful creator of heaven and earth, better known as God. God will tolerate no disobedience or any challenge to, or even *doubt* about, his authority. God needs no informers and secret police to inform him of even contemplated deviance,[11] because he knows every detail of your thoughts ('I know that thou canst do everything, and that no thought can be withholden from thee', conceded Job,[12] after being treated to a first-hand recital of God's limitless powers). Against God's verdict there is no appeal, and his punishments and rewards are so extreme that one of Europe's foremost mathematicians, Blaise Pascal, who was also a Christian mystic, claimed that only mathematical infinity could represent their magnitude.[13] Even the New Testament, though incorporating the Sermon on the Mount, is not without hints, and sometimes

[11] It is entirely appropriate if this observation brings Stalin to mind. Stalin had personality traits very similar to those of the Old Testament God.

[12] 42:2.

[13] Pascal developed a famous prudential argument for belief in God based on that 'number' which we shall look at more closely in Chapter 3.

more than hints, of the older methods of persuasion. There is gentle Jesus, the Lamb of God, threatening eternal damnation to the wicked ('Depart from me, ye cursed, into everlasting fire'[14]), and his apostle – and some claim dearest disciple – St John the Divine condemning the merely 'fearful and unbelieving' to Hell.[15] The New Testament signally failed to temper the ferocity of the Counter-Reformation, and atheism could be punished by death even in eighteenth-century England and Scotland.

The extremity of God's enduring wrath is dramatically illustrated in the story of the Fall in Genesis: for a single act of disobedience Adam and Eve were driven out of Eden and the stigma of sin stamped on all their posterity, together with the certainty of – to hijack some famous words of the seventeenth-century philosopher Thomas Hobbes – a life nasty, brutish and short. The regime pictured in this piece of sacred mythopoeia is a *totalitarianism*, but a totalitarianism more thoroughgoing than any earth can offer, even Stalin's, with no detail of quotidian life or thought escaping the attention of a punitive God.[16] But it is not just a fear-inspiring totalitarianism. If it were it would not have exerted the peculiar attachment that it has done and continues to do. Its grip on the human psyche is arguably as powerful as it is because, in a beautifully Orwellian turn, between the beatings (remember that mankind is inherently sinful), God professes to love his people, asking for their love and worship in return. According to Christianity, he even sacrificed his own son to mitigate the savage punishment he had meted out to the whole of humanity for the disobedience of Adam and Eve. Beaten wives, tortured prisoners, unhappy victims of systematic bullying, can all attest to the peculiar psychological efficaciousness of this sort of equivocal treatment. I said 'Orwellian' because whether George Orwell intended it or not (and it is very difficult to believe that he didn't), his chilling novel *1984* reads as an allegory of the Inquisition, with God the invisible Big Brother and O'Brien, the friend-turned-inquisitor and torturer, a latter-day Torquemada. At the end of the novel Winston Smith, a broken man, has learned to love Big Brother.[17]

14 Matthew 25:41.

15 Revelation 21:8. Together with 'the abominable, and murderers, and whoremongers, and sorcerers, and idolators, and all liars', these sinners will 'have their part in the lake which burneth with fire and brimstone: which is the second death'. The Koran employs a similar rhetoric of hatred in consigning unbelievers to the same fate.

16 A contemporary Muslim philosopher, Abdennour Bidar, has actually had the considerable courage to describe Islam as totalitarian – 'archaic, violent and totalitarian' ('La lapidation, preuve extréme de la logique de violence de l'Islam', *Le Monde*, 31 August 2010). Totalitarian *all* the Abrahamic religions are, not just Islam.

17 One of the Jewish prisoners who survived Auschwitz, rabbi Hugo Gryn, said that when he once broke down weeping he believed that God was also crying. Then, Gryn reported, 'I seemed to

This highly potent mix of foundational doctrine is stiffened with the addition of the claim of the two proselytising religions, Christianity and Islam, that they represent God's law for all mankind, giving themselves licence to convert disbelievers – and each other – and if necessary to wage holy war. Torah, Bible and Koran, and their accompanying commentaries and additions, all claim to be literally God's truth, but unfortunately they are mutually contradictory. All the ingredients are now here for a recipe for discord, intolerance and the infliction of suffering. The possibility of inviting God's displeasure becomes an issue of concern even for those whose personal loyalty is unquestioned but who are anxious not to be seen to be condoning dissent, or corrupting his Word. Theologians, employed to determine exactly what that word is, often led hazardous lives and some still do. Arius, an Alexandrian priest of the third and fourth centuries CE, achieved theological notoriety for claiming that God and Jesus were not of the same essence, but he was merely anathematised and exiled for his heresy and subsequently readmitted to the fold (at which point he dramatically died). Many centuries later, under the Inquisition, the penalty for heresy was death, after torture. It was a remedy widely copied. William Tyndale, the sixteenth-century Protestant scholar who gave us the first English translation of the New Testament, and parts of the Old, from the Greek and Hebrew originals was condemned and executed by being strangled and then burned.

You might object that no mere collection of myths or texts by itself amounts to totalitarianism. *People* make totalitarianisms. That is true, but people can easily be roused to the noblest of actions, and also to the most depraved, by 'mere' writings. A book on economics written in the second half of the nineteenth century inspired not one but several earthly totalitarianisms, more than one of which still thrives. The crucial factor which causes an otherwise inert collection of myths and texts to become potent is, of course, *belief.* The most nightmarish of fairy stories will remain fairy stories if they are not believed, as the bizarre but harmless rituals of Halloween bear witness. We are talking about active *belief*-systems, and the sacred scriptures of the three monotheisms, plus the extensive bodies of theology accompanying them, currently support the beliefs of billions of people, inspiring them in various places and times (which unfortunately

be granted a curious inner peace . . . I found God' (*Chasing Shadows* (London: Allen Lane, 2001)). Note that this occurred on the day that Jews atone to God. In making the comparison with Orwell's novel I do not in any way intend to belittle the ineffable enormity of what Gryn and others went through in the death camps.

include the present) to recreate God's totalitarianism on earth, under the proxy-governance of priests.

4. CLEAR AND PRESENT DANGER

Though often sharing the opinion of atheists and agnostics ancient and modern that those beliefs are very probably untrue and the regimes based on them repugnant, the *bien-pensants* still manage to disapprove strongly of vigorous frontal assaults on them. They may or may not be true, a typical objection runs, but what virtue is there in trying to destroy the faith of billions of people together with the inspiration those beliefs provide to do good, help the weak and sick, etc.? Why not tolerate the edifice of faith as one more, and probably the most powerful, support of public morality and social benefit? Judged in terms of its practical outcomes – for example in the extensive charity work undertaken by religious organisations – religious belief is on record as having promoted and continuing to promote a great deal of good, while in basing itself on the presumed love of God it is the least likely to promote harm. Admittedly, there is the regrettable fact that from time to time there are outbreaks of religious intolerance, with violence at the extreme, but given time, increasing education and 'globalisation' will hopefully cause them, if not to disappear entirely, at least be marginalised and contained.

It's a reassuring story. It may even be true in the long-enough run. But it is not true now, nor in the near future. Quite the contrary: we are witnessing a marked and rapidly increasing renewal of religious intolerance, sometimes very violent and always drawing its inspiration from holy scripture. Even in formerly tranquil areas of the world security services work day and night to prevent what has every appearance of being Islamic-inspired terrorism from following up the destruction of the World Trade Center in New York, the Madrid and London bombings and the guerrilla attack in Mumbai, with new attempts to turn the world into a single Islamic state. Faisal Shahzad, a US citizen, condemned to life-imprisonment in October 2010 for attempting to detonate a car-bomb in Times Square, warned the court: 'Brace yourselves, the war with the Muslims has just begun', adding generously 'If I'm given 1,000 lives I will sacrifice them all for Allah.'

The same uncompromising message is conveyed on the numerous jihadist websites urging believers everywhere to enlist in the war against the enemies of Allah, with the Koran and hadiths cited in support. In the so-called 'sword verse' (9:5) of the Koran, the Prophet appears to include murder in his God's list of punishments of idolaters once the four 'forbidden months' are over. Sura 5:33's tone is equally menacing:

> Those who wage war against God and his Messenger and strive to spread corruption in the land should be punished by death, crucifixion, the amputation of an alternate hand and foot, or banishment from the land: a disgrace for them in this world, and then a terrible punishment in the Hereafter, unless they repent before you overpower them – in that case bear in mind that God is forgiving and merciful.[18]

Such passages are frequently glossed over by modern Muslim editors, who cite the contemporary context of local wars against specific opponents. That is all very well, but the Koran is nevertheless regarded by all Muslims as the unedited word of God valid for all times and all places, and it seethes with hatred of unbelievers, expressing God's loathing in language of graphic violence.

This is not to deny the (undeniable) fact that there is a large social and political dimension to the current wave of Islamic violence. A powerful source of grievance was undoubtedly the implantation of Israel into Palestine and its subsequent support by some western countries and particularly the United States. The recent invasion of a sovereign Muslim state, Iraq, by a coalition of western countries, on what even then were clearly trumped-up charges, simply added fuel to the fire.[19] Traditional Muslim societies also see themselves threatened by a secularism widely thought to be promoted by western countries, which is not only a threat to their religion as such but also to the social structures it supports and sanctifies. It hardly needs saying that those who benefit most from the distribution of offices and influence traditionally 'due' to them do not generally welcome the invasion of an alien culture threatening those privileges. Men certainly enjoy great power over women in traditional Muslim societies and the sexual privileges that go with it. But to see religion itself as causally innocent in the current wave of religious violence is simply a refusal to face reality.[20] Many Muslims among the world's one and a half billion see their shared religion as their ultimate loyalty, and it is the fact that it is *Muslim* territories that are being threatened, invaded and more generally desecrated by the West that is at the heart of the militancy. Osama bin Laden's dramatic communiqués are peppered with minatory quotations from the Koran, and I think that one can reasonably assume that he believes that he is conveying the will of God.

[18] The highly conditional nature of God's mercy is common to all three monotheisms.

[19] It was on the basis of similarly trumped-up charges that Hitler invaded Czechoslovakia in 1938, and forged Britain's and France's determination to resist any further invasion. The result was the Second World War.

[20] This point is made forcefully in Ayaan Hirsi Ali, *Nomad* (Toronto: Knopf Canada, 2010).

Hezbollah, the paramilitary Islamic organisation in Lebanon, supported by among others the theocracy in Iran, is the 'Party of God', its website announcing that 'we are an ummah [Muslim community] linked to the Muslims of the whole world by the solid doctrine and religious connection of Islam'.

But Islam isn't the only culprit. Far from it. Christianity in its time has been responsible for much greater destruction, persecution and death. It might conceivably be again, for fundamentalism is once more on the march as far as all three religions are concerned. Every day American Christian TV stations spew out bilious condemnation of evolutionary theory, atheism, homosexuality, abortion, same-sex marriage, 'liberalism', etc. The Christian apologist William Lane Craig argues that the Canaanites, slaughtered man, woman and child by the Israelites on the instructions of God, were irremediably wicked and that God had already held off 400 years from punishing them as they deserved: 'Israel was merely the instrument of his justice', he observes.[21] Many unhappy Christians still see God's commands all too regularly flouted, so unhappy that

> [i]f push comes to shove, some of them are prepared to lie and even to kill, to do whatever it takes to help bring what they consider celestial justice to those they consider the sinners.[22]

The killing started in the 1990s, with a spate of murders of doctors in America and Canada who performed abortions. After being sentenced to life imprisonment, one of those convicted, Scott Roeder, observed that God's judgment 'will sweep over this land [the United States] like a prairie wind'.

> And what rough beast, its hour come round at last,
> Slouches towards Bethlehem to be born?[23]

What rough beast indeed?

5. APOSTASY, WOMEN AND OTHER PROBLEMS

There is one large difference between the older outbursts of religious intolerance and the intolerance of contemporary fundamentalism: the principal enemy has ceased to be a different religion or doctrinal differences within a

21 W. L. Craig, *Reasonable Faith: Christian Truth and Apologetics*, 3rd edn (Wheaton, IL: Crossway Books, 2008). 'Reasonable'?

22 Daniel C. Dennett, *Breaking the Spell: Religion as a Natural Phenomenon* (New York: Penguin, 2006), p. 338. Dennett is specifically referring to the religious right in America.

23 W. B. Yeats, 'The Second Coming'.

religion, and has now mostly become the lack of any religious belief at all. Secularism, decadence, blasphemy, profanity: the work of Satan is being performed daily in full view of the faithful and, even worse, often carried out in holy places, and – as many see it – is deliberately seeking to subvert the faith. Drawing nourishment from its primitive roots, resurgent fundamentalism has in its sights the ideals of tolerance, equality between men and women, freedom of expression and thought and the freedom to reject religion, not just one religion but any at all. In parts of the United States exercising that last freedom too publicly can put you in danger of your life, while in several of the jurisdictions incorporating sharia law, including Iran, the rejection of Islam is punishable by death.[24] In September 2008, with a majority of 196–7, the Iranian Parliament extended the death penalty to any Iranian male who renounces Islam; apostate Iranian women were more fortunate, at least in this respect, inviting only a life sentence.[25]

Sharia law is implemented in different ways in different places, some more lenient than others. In some the penalty for adultery is a fixed number of lashes of the whip, the number laid down in the Koran. In others it is death by stoning. The Associated Press reported on 18 November 2009 that in Somalia a woman had been stoned to death in front of 200 onlookers, after being sentenced to death for adultery by a local sharia court. A woman in Iran recently escaped the same fate, but only after a concerted campaign in the western media. In general women have inferior status in Islam. Muslim women can only marry Muslim men, but Muslim men can marry any of the 'People of the Book' (i.e. Muslims, Christians and Jews; 'the Book' is the body of scripture common to all). Women's testimony in courts is weighed at one half that of men. The Koran authorises a man to strike his wife if he merely suspects her of undermining his authority (4:24). In the hadith literature the Prophet is reported as saying that a woman has to agree to her husband's request for sex whatever she may be doing, or however she may feel. The President of the Sharia Council of Britain recently stated (14 October 2010) that rape in marriage is not recognised in sharia law.

Women who oppose the teachings of the Koran and Sunna on the status and role of women have been reviled in mass demonstrations and threatened with execution in those countries where it is strictly observed. And not only in those. Western countries now harbour substantial numbers of Muslims, some of whom (usually males) also strongly resent 'their' women

[24] Hadith 260 of Sahih Bukhari is invoked: 'The Prophet said "If somebody (a Muslim) discards his religion then kill him."'

[25] The right to freedom of religion is an article (Article 23) of Iran's constitution.

failing to play their traditional role, particularly where dress and marriage are concerned (and I think one does not need to add, sexual orientation). Ayaan Hirsi Ali, who repudiated Islam and wrote the screenplay for a provocative film with the Dutch film-maker Theo van Gogh on the status of women under Islam, has lived with death-threats ever since. Van Gogh was murdered for his pains, though the murderer took care to indicate that Ali was the principal offender. The dissident poet and writer Taslima Nasrin has been forced into exile after being expelled from Bangladesh, and remains under constant threat of death. She is about to be expelled now from India, her temporary refuge, after prolonged and violent protests by Indian Muslims.

Christianity and Judaism also contain more than a strain of misogyny. A Jewish prayer recited by Orthodox men is 'Praised be God for not creating me a Gentile. Praised be God for not creating me a slave. Praised be God for not creating me a woman.' The apostle Paul told wives to 'be in subjection' to their husbands,[26] and issued the following injunction to the Corinthians:

> Let your women keep silence in the churches: for it is not permitted unto them to speak: but they are commanded to be under obedience, as also saith the law. And if they will learn any thing, let them ask their husbands at home: for it is a shame for the women to speak in the church.[27]

Paul's words still have plangent echoes. The Reverend Angus MacLeay, a member of the General Synod of the Church of England, issued a letter to parishioners citing Biblical authority for demanding that women 'submit to their husbands in everything'.[28] Priests in the Catholic Church are of course male and celibate: the nearer to women, the farther from God. Christ had no female disciples so, by impeccable logic, there can be no women priests. Once the possibility of ordaining women became a serious issue in the Church of England, 'traditionalist' brethren have been decamping in droves to Rome where this important point of principle remains observed.

The God of Abraham is notoriously a principled homophobe, and indulgence in homosexual behaviour is duly deplored as one of the gravest sins by the main branches of the monotheisms. The condition, for want of a better word, is increasingly recognised as something some people can't help. But what if they could? What is wrong with that? If like mine your answer is 'nothing', you contradict the word of God, and homosexuals are in more or less grave danger wherever fundamentalism is rooted. In possibly jocular

[26] 1 Peter 3:1. [27] 1 Corinthians 14:34. [28] Reported in the *Daily Telegraph*, 11 February 2010.

vein the Iranian President Mahmoud Ahmadinejad remarked that there were no homosexuals in Iran. That is because in Iran homosexuality is punishable by death (it is estimated that 4,000 people have been executed for this reason since 1979), as it is also in Afghanistan, Pakistan, Saudi Arabia, Yemen, Mauretania and Sudan. Homosexual feelings may be just a 'disorder' according to modern Catholic doctrine, but engaging in homosexual acts remains a grievous sin. With the weight of religious authority behind it, it is small wonder that homophobia remains such a potent force even in 'liberal' western societies, let alone Muslim ones. Same-sex marriage also gets a strong thumbs-down, implicitly defying as it does the 'fact' that according to God the purpose of marriage is procreation. Recreational sex ('fornication') is condemned for a similar reason. It is also the most widely broken of God's laws by the devout. From the point of view of the principle of individual autonomy, choosing to abstain from or engage in any of these activities is the business of no-one but the individual or individuals concerned. But that principle is of course emphatically denied in God's universe.

While all the Abrahamic religions remain a potential, and sometimes actual, threat to human freedom, Islam exceeds the other two in menace because not only is freedom of expression when it comes to religion usually strongly proscribed in Islamic jurisdictions, but it is punished in some with a degree of savagery that is almost unthinkable in liberal societies. In Pakistan and some other Muslim countries the death penalty can be imposed for blasphemy; at the time of writing a Christian woman in Pakistan is under sentence of death for allegedly defaming the Prophet. Nor is the threat confined. Muslim *fatwah*s are issued against authors and publishers of offending material wherever they may be domiciled, and also to those in the electronic media who broadcast it. The worldwide riots after the publication in 2007 of cartoons of the Prophet in a Danish newspaper were a coordinated Muslim response, as was the excoriation of Salman Rushdie, sentenced to death by the Ayatollah Khomeini for the crime of – *writing a satirical novel*!

The fact that people in non-Muslim countries are under a very genuine threat to their lives because they have infringed a Muslim religious taboo quite understandably sends shivers up many people's spines. Some western religious 'leaders' do of course lament the fact that their own congregations seem to display less enthusiasm for taking the Word of God to heart. The rest of us can only feel lucky to be where we are. The liberal countries have slowly and often painfully constructed over the years legal and moral systems guaranteeing, or so it seemed, the freedom of the individual to express his or her views, subject to certain relatively mild conditions. Sadly, that freedom is now being eroded by fear: the signs are all around us in cancelled meetings, films, TV documentaries, book-contracts, even the readers' comments sections in some newspapers. UN Resolution 62/154 is just the latest in the accumulating threat to hard-won liberties.

6. EDUCATION FOR BELIEVERS

A striking and at first sight puzzling fact is that several of the Muslims convicted of terrorism are far from poorly educated, having university degrees, and sometimes higher degrees, in engineering, the sciences and even medicine. What, it may well be asked, is a healer of the sick doing trying to kill and maim thousands of people? There is however a profound sense in which those educational accomplishments by themselves do *not* amount to an education, if we understand by that word not only the inculcation of factual knowledge but also the development of an impartial critical faculty. There is an old joke that the ancient Greeks knew a lot about knowing but didn't know much about anything else. This is funny but untrue. With meagre technology by today's standards, and starting from a low baseline, they made enormous strides: they knew that the earth was roughly spherical, and even measured its diameter; they knew that the moon was not a source of illumination in its own right but merely reflected sunlight; and they came to within an epsilon, so to speak, of inventing the calculus. But above all they were the first in recorded history to undertake a systematic investigation of logic, the theory of valid reasoning itself, and to construct mathematics and to some extent other disciplines on a systematic deductive basis where the *justification* of each claim was transparent.

Cultivating a critical and enquiring attitude was a central part of their conception of understanding, as it should be of ours. And the biggest impediment to that is indoctrination into the belief that a higher, infallible 'knowledge' is revealed by scripture and its officially accredited interpreters. For too many, Jew, Christian and Muslim alike, suitably authenticated religious dogma trumps a critical, evidence-based evaluation, and where such an evaluation is in any tension at all with dogma it is to be condemned not merely as false but dangerously false. It was through eating the fruit of the tree of knowledge that Adam and Eve were dispatched from Paradise, and the condemnation of free thought that in any way threatens the authority of scripture remains undiminished in Islam and Catholicism. Though the Catholic Index of Proscribed Books now lacks ecclesiastical enforcement, it remains as a 'moral force', as the current Pope (then Cardinal

Ratzinger) insisted in a letter in 1985 to Cardinal Giuseppe Siri. Among the authors whose works are on the index are such distinguished scientists, mathematicians and philosophers as Copernicus, Galileo, Kepler, Francis Bacon, Descartes, Kant, Hume, Berkeley, Locke, d'Alembert, J. S. Mill and Comte. One can only infer that for Ratzinger these authors are a moral danger because they represent *par excellence* the spirit of free, dispassionate enquiry.

The theory of evolution remains a proscribed theory for many Jews, Christians and Muslims, who refuse to have it taught to their children because it conflicts with the assertion of Torah, Bible and Koran that humanity was a special act of creation by God.[29] And so we have the apparent paradox of highly trained healers manufacturing bombs to kill and maim enemies of Islam. But it is no paradox: knowledge that in most western democracies is, at any rate officially, held to be an end in itself is for others merely a technical instrument subservient to the demands of religion. The Islamic theocracy in Iran has recently proscribed the teaching of philosophy, together with other humanities subjects, in Iranian universities: 'such teachings will lead to the dissemination of doubt in the foundations of religious teachings', Ayatollah Ali Khamenei is reported as saying.[30]

7. THE IMPORTANCE OF BEING SELECTIVE

It is of course a familiar tactic of religious apologists, confronted with the many inflammatory, unpleasant or simply absurd claims and exhortations to be found in their respective bodies of sacred writings, to urge a non-literal reading of them. They are metaphorical, or they are taken out of context (as it has been claimed that 9:5 of the Koran was a specific order in a particular time of war), or they incorporate mythic or allegorical features which are taken literally only by the ignorant or in a spirit of *parti pris*, or . . . (one could go on for quite a long time). It is quite usual for more liberal imams, appalled by yet more suicide bombings, or by the stoning to death of women convicted of adultery, to claim that such actions lack textual authority.

Most educated Christians probably reject a literal interpretation of that story, though amazingly forty-five per cent of the citizens of the US do not,

[29] It took the Catholic Church a century and a half to accept it. Nidhal Guessoum, Professor of Physics and Astronomy at the American University of Sharjah in the United Arab Emirates, recently estimated that only fifteen per cent or so of people in Tunisia, Egypt, Pakistan, Turkey and Malaysia believe that the theory is true.

[30] *Daily Telegraph*, 24 October 2010.

and believe that God created human beings 10,000 years ago. The claim that the earth is fixed and that the sun moves is made in several places in the Bible (e.g. Psalms 93:1 and 104:5), and Galileo's apparent denial of it in the heyday of militant Christianity notoriously brought him into open conflict with the Roman Catholic Church, to his extreme peril (he was lucky to escape with his life). But in our own perforce mellower times Francis Collins, a geneticist and ex-Head of the Human Genome Project in Washington, together with many other committed Christians denies that there was any genuine conflict of claims:

> The claims that heliocentricity contradicted the Bible are now seen to have been overstated, and the insistence on a literal interpretation of those particular scripture verses seems wholly unwarranted.[31]

It is of course rather easy to disclaim responsibility for awkward facts in this cavalier way. The claims that heliocentricity contradicted the Bible certainly weren't 'seen to have been overstated' during the long deliberations that preceded Galileo's arraignment, and Collins's verdict that the literal interpretation 'seems wholly unwarranted' is made at a safe temporal distance from the contemporary events, and with the hindsight afforded by a more reliable source of knowledge. But for the committed believer there is of course no alternative to such bland dismissals of what previous generations of believers had taken for granted. The fact is that many of the passages in sacred literature are unacceptable to a contemporary readership because they are rather obviously the production of primitive, pre-scientific societies. As a consequence many are in conflict with liberal codes of conduct and law. In many jurisdictions that does not matter so much because those codes are dominant and enforced by the state, but there are some jurisdictions, like Iran, that have deliberately regressed to a primitive state, and some that have never emerged from it.

It is an ironically convenient fact that the multitude of contradictory claims in all the sacred books implies that there simply has to be selectivity unless one is to dismiss most of it out of hand. The Old Testament has inconsistencies liberally scattered throughout its length, while the New Testament is a veritable tissue of them, with its various books contradicting not only each other but each itself. Despite the claim (of the Koran!) that because the Koran is all true, being the unedited word of God himself, it must be consistent (4:82), it is nevertheless a frequent occurrence for something to be stated without qualification on one page and denied on

[31] Francis Collins, *The Language of God* (New York: Free Press, 2006), p. 156.

another.[32] All these texts are luxuriously inconsistent: God is all merciful, God is implacable; God loves us, God dislikes us so much that His only Son, Jesus Christ, had to die for our sake before God would consider changing His mind. And so on.

This sort of pick'n'mix policy may be practically workable, at least temporarily, and leave more sophisticated votaries free to reject the excesses of a primitive morality reflecting the harshness of the desert in which it was born. But nobody outside the ranks of the faithful, or even within for that matter, should believe that this represents a satisfactory state of affairs. In the first place, there is an issue of elementary logic. The conjunction 'A and B' of two assertions A and B logically implies each of A and B, even if B happens to be the negation of A. If God demands that his followers punish dissidents and unbelievers with all force, and then states that the dissidents and unbelievers are to be shown mercy, it still follows that he has demanded that his followers punish dissidents with all force, and those who find the idea congenial certainly have logic on their side when they appeal to scriptural authority for such action. An infamous *fatwa* issued by the fourteenth-century scholar Ibn Taymiyya, declaring that all those not adhering to classical Islamic law could be killed, is invoked by Osama bin Laden and other militant Muslims. Another *fatwa*, issued by the Pakistani scholar Muhammad Tahir-ul-Qadri in 2010, declared just the opposite, adding that terrorism is counter to Islam. My *fatwa* against your *fatwa*.

Secondly, there is an issue of moral honesty and courage. Trying to find a 'nice' bit of the Koran, or the Bible, to counter a nasty one, is implicitly conceding the primacy of one's own intuitive ethical judgment, but then in effect betraying it by looking for an appropriate bit of dogma to 'authorise' it. Mildly inclined Muslims, desperate to disown the bloody deeds that the radical imams enjoin pleading the authority of the Koran, can find suitably eirenic quotations from the Koran to support their case that the imams do not speak for God. But the mere fact that they have to mine the Koran in this way shows that they know full well that those acts are wrong whether the Koran says they are or not. No matter: the Koran still has to say so. These people have been so schooled into thinking that it is the sole source of authority that they cannot believe in any other, including themselves. Christians and Jews of course do the same thing. *These people have lost their intellectual and moral integrity.*

[32] Michel Onfray provides a long list of examples in his recent book *In Defense of Atheism: A Case against Christianity, Judaism, and Islam*, Jeremy Leggat (trans.) (Toronto: Viking Canada, 2007), pp. 170–4.

8. YOUR LIFE ISN'T YOUR OWN

Not even the secular totalitarianisms of Nazism or Marxism–Leninism, dreadful as they were, went so far as to claim literal ownership of one's body. Yet that is precisely what the Abrahamic monotheisms do. Human life (but only *human* life), they agree, is sacred to God, because God created it, made it in his image, and most importantly *retains ownership*. Practitioners of these religions often say that it is a gift from God, but it is not a gift in the sense in which we usually understand a gift, as a transference of ownership. That it most certainly isn't. Our lives are not our own. We are merely leaseholders – or as the Roman Catholic catechism 2280 rather daintily puts it, '*stewards*' – of lives which belong to God:

> It is God who remains the Sovereign Master of Life... We are stewards, not owners, of the life God has *entrusted* to us (my emphasis).

St Paul gave a less nuanced interpretation of the contract:

> What? know ye not that your body is the temple of the Holy Ghost, which is in you, which ye have of God, and ye are not your own?
>
> For ye are bought with a price: therefore glorify God in your body, and in your spirit, which are God's.[33]

'Bought with a price'! We are not only owned by God; *we are also slaves of God*. Small wonder the churches failed to condemn slavery – until sufficiently many other people did.

9. ASSISTING A CRIME

Another corollary of God's ownership of us is that suicide is a *theft* from God, while the assistor of a suicide is an accessory to the crime as well as – if you are a Christian – prejudicing the destination of the sufferer's soul. Unsurprisingly, to assist a suicide is a mortal sin in the Catholic catechism. The Church of England also vigorously opposes relaxing the UK law prohibiting assisted suicide, despite a large and stable majority (over 70%) of the population being in favour. In a telephone poll conducted by Populus Surveys in July 2009 of a random sample of 1,504 British adults, 74% were in favour of changing the law on physician-assisted suicide. But the Upper House of the UK legislature, the House of Lords, has 26 seats reserved for Church of England bishops. Despite a full awareness of the extent of

[33] 1 Corinthians 6:19–20.

the popular feeling, and the fact that regular Church of England attendees make up currently fewer than 3% of the population (with an average age of over 50),[34] the bishops in the Upper Chamber under the leadership of the head of the Anglican Church,[35] Dr Rowan Williams, have worked indefatigably in the (successful) cause of defeating every Private Members' Bill to change the law.

Rowan Williams was recently at work again, this time in concert with the Chief Rabbi and the Roman Catholic Archbishop of Westminster, opposing an amendment to a parliamentary bill which would have legalised assisting terminally ill people to travel to countries where assisted suicide is legal. A letter sent by these three dignitaries to a large-circulation daily newspaper (*Daily Telegraph*, 29 June 2009), stating their opposition, notes that a Bill asking for the legalisation of certain forms of assisted suicide was defeated in the House of Lords. It fails, however, to mention that a substantial proportion of the opposition's vote was that of bishops under the leadership of Rowan Williams. The letter notes that vulnerable people might be put at risk, but fails to mention those in terrible pain and indignity who cannot travel by themselves and the appalling dilemma in which the existing law places their friends and relatives if they choose to help them. It raises a patriotic cheer on behalf of the British hospice movement but carefully avoids saying *whose* opinion it is that dying in a hospice is a 'better' (I am quoting) option than assisted suicide: there is no evidence that it is the opinion of the dying, and it is certainly not that of the very large majority of the population in favour of assisted suicide. Notable also is the omission by Rowan Williams *et al.* to mention that assisted suicide is a mortal sin, or the equivalent of one, in their religions. *Thou shalt not kill*! One might have thought fundamental doctrine would be an important consideration for these spiritual leaders: at the very least, worth a mention. Not so, apparently. Might it be that a candid statement of doctrine would risk alienating a broader public opinion indifferent or hostile to religion? A spokesperson for the Church of England has stated that the bishops bring 'an important independent voice and spiritual insight to the work of the Upper House'.[36] 'Pull the other one' is the only appropriate response to that. Jonathan Sacks has told us that he

[34] Its substantial *ex officio* representation in the legislature makes it the last rotten borough in the UK (the 'rotten boroughs' in the nineteenth century were those which returned Members of Parliament even though their populations were a minute fraction of those of the growing cities denied parliamentary representation).

[35] Always the Archbishop of Canterbury.

[36] *Daily Telegraph*, 2 January 2010.

will continue to believe that God who created one or an infinity of universes in love and forgiveness continues to ask us to create, to love and to forgive.[37]

Nice words from a man who wishes it to remain a criminal offence punishable by up to fourteen years in prison to help an incapacitated person to a clinic in Switzerland where they can end their lives in peace. By their fruits ye shall know them.

Shortly after Williams *et al.* penned their letter, some UK newspapers reported a local Health Authority whose staff had denied additional morphine to a man dying in terrible pain of leukaemia. The Authority reported with satisfaction that it had remained within the demands of the law, since to administer additional morphine might have shortened the man's life. What chilling indifference. In prolonging suffering to avoid a clash with the state there is little difference between what the people responsible in that case did and what those 'merely carrying out orders' did in Majdenek or Bergen-Belsen. In a recent move the Director of Public Prosecutions in the UK has relaxed the automatic charging of anyone offering any help at all – this includes merely travelling with them to an assisted suicide clinic outside the UK – to those seeking assistance in bringing about a dignified death on their own terms, and has embarked on a public consultation on the matter. The Christian Medical Fellowship, numbering over 4,000 doctors, refused to participate.

It is true that the opposition to assisted suicide extends beyond the churches. But the churches continue to muddy the waters to obscure the fact that what is at issue is a simple principle of self-determination – up to death itself. A communiqué from the Bishops' Conference of England and Wales, *à propos* new guidelines issued by the Director of Public Prosecutions seeking to clarify the circumstances under which the Crown would not prosecute anyone assisting a terminally ill person to end their life, states that 'it seems to imply if the victim is disabled or terminally ill, then his or her life does not merit the same degree of protection by law' (reported in the British press on 20 November 2009). The claim is preposterous: the guidelines imply no such thing.

But the propaganda machine grinds on, as it has ground on for centuries, in a way of which Goebbels himself might have been envious. Welcoming the addition to the Church of England's website of a statement of the Church's opposition to assisted suicide, the Bishop of Winchester wrote:

[37] *The Times*, 3 September 2010.

This is especially important as distinguished voices are suggesting that dependent sufferers are 'wasting the lives of those who care for them, and have a duty to die to stop being a burden on others'.

No attribution for those 'distinguished voices' is provided, and one might well be puzzled why they spoke in unison. Pure Goebbels. Slogans like 'the sanctity of human life', 'the precious gift of life' [but only human life], 'playing God', together with newer ones like the 'Culture of Life versus the Culture of Death', are wheeled out to do their usual service as argument-substitutes. They have achieved their apotheosis in surely one of the most ridiculous pieces of hyperbole ever produced, by Edmund Adamus, an adviser to the Archbishop of Westminster, who blamed the British Parliament for allowing the country to become 'the geopolitical epicentre of the culture of death'.[38] Ironically, 'The Culture of Death' is a very appropriate description of the activities of these ghoulish, dissembling clerics intent on keeping alive to the bitter end of their ordeal people who, judging by the opinion poll statistics, would rather shuffle off their mortal coils peacefully in the manner of their domestic pets. But those urbane torturers are probably aware of what another Victorian poet, Arthur Hugh Clough, wittily pointed out:

> And almost everyone when age,
> Disease or sorrow strikes him,
> Inclines to think there is a God,
> Or someone very like Him.

10. A MORAL HEALTH WARNING

Enjoying the weight of historical precedent and the respectful attention that they command almost everywhere, the churches are still widely believed to be beacons of light in a surrounding moral darkness. I hope that the preceding discussion has at least suggested that the belief is erroneous. Yet few people seem to be able to bring themselves to acknowledge how unpleasantly intolerant a good deal of the moral 'teachings' of the monotheisms actually is, rooted as it is in scripture reflecting a primitive appreciation of the world and its doings. Even in the more liberal spiritual jurisdictions of modern Christianity the churches play a major role in sustaining inhuman and illiberal laws and placing obstacles in the way of reform. In the areas of both factual enquiry and ethics they continue to play the catching-up

[38] *Daily Telegraph*, 1 September 2010. He seems to have forgotten that Parliament is elected by the people.

game they have been doing for centuries. They eventually give way, but only after they have caused a great deal of human damage. The Roman Catholic Church still will not acknowledge that homosexual acts are anything but sinful, contrary to Natural (i.e. God's) Law, or that contraception is not a worse sin than the production of too many people in areas of the world which cannot support existing populations, or than the spread of HIV and AIDS.

But apologists will still say – do still say – that it is all a question of *balance*. Religion, they claim, particularly Christianity, has inspired and continues to inspire a great deal of good. And it is probably true that for every religious radical prepared to bomb civilian targets[39] and kill unbelievers, there is someone helping to assuage the ravages of hunger and illness under the auspices of a church or religious belief. But the churches' contribution to major social reforms, like the abolition of slavery, the extension of state-funded welfare, the emancipation of women, has been very much exaggerated. St Paul himself enjoined slaves to obey their masters gladly, even bad masters,[40] and slave-owners in the southern states of the USA and the British and French West Indies took him at his word. Devoutly Christian and Muslim slave-traders pursued their profession for centuries; the extension of state welfare to the poor was opposed for a long time by Christians, and still is even in the Christian heartlands of the United States; female emancipation is vigorously opposed by a large number of Islamic teachers, and a large part of the Christian fellowship maintains barriers against the ordination of women. Christian aid to developing and stricken countries is often far from an unmixed blessing, and often not a blessing at all. Much-needed help might be, in fact notoriously has been, accompanied by a list of prohibitory conditions forbidding the use of contraceptives and of abortion where curbing population growth not only offers a long-term benefit to those regions, but is probably a necessary condition for the survival of humanity at all.

The fact that the major faiths often do good work is analogous to the logical fact that every falsehood deductively implies a truth. But the converse is not true: one can have truth without falsehood. So why follow the injunctions of religion, which often gets it very wrong indeed on moral matters, when we can follow our own consciences and more often get it

[39] Bombing civilian targets is not, unfortunately, by any means a monopoly of religious fanatics, as any cursory examination of the records of the Second World War, and subsequent 'liberating' wars, will reveal. One of the most appalling offences ever committed against humanity was the dropping of atomic bombs on two unprepared Japanese cities in 1945.

[40] Ephesians 6:5–8; Colossians 3:22–5; 1 Peter 2:18.

right? We certainly can do good, and want to do good, without having to be directed to do so by a presumptive God whose moral directives are frequently unpleasant and *immoral*. The great Enlightenment philosopher Immanuel Kant pointed out that *no* action taken in deference to the wishes, or perceived wishes, of any external authority (and he included God in this category) ought to be regarded as truly moral. And he is surely right: no deed performed under duress, or to please a powerful individual, deserves to be judged as virtuous.

II. THE GOOD, THE BAD AND THE HOLY

Many people nevertheless still think that work done in the name of religion is morally superior to that done for any other reason. That this continues to be believed when included in the numbers of those acting in the name of God were people who prescribed torture and execution for the slightest doctrinal deviance shows a dangerous naivety: still dangerous because it promotes a belief that civic oversight of ecclesiastical activities can be relaxed. A chilling counterexample is the recent evidence of widespread, long-term sexual abuse of children in Catholic orphanages and schools under the control of Catholic clergy, in the United States, Spain, Canada, Ireland, Germany, Brazil, the Netherlands, Switzerland and Mexico. At the time of writing, the Catholic Church has already paid out 2.5 billion dollars in compensation since 1950, but for long there were systematic attempts to conceal the evidence, sometimes with the police deliberately not being informed and sometimes where the victims were even paid for their silence. The leader of the Roman Catholic Church in Ireland, Cardinal Sean O'Brady, admitted being present when two teenage boys were persuaded by Church authorities to sign oaths of silence after testifying against Father Brendan Smyth, later convicted of a multitude of sexual offences' assaults on children over the course of twenty years.

More evidence is coming forward that what happened in Ireland also happened in other Catholic jurisdictions. Investigators, working with the support of the Belgian Catholic Church, received 475 complaints of child abuse committed in the 1950s through to the late 1980s by Catholic clergy. 'We can say that no congregation escapes sexual abuse of minors by one or several of its members', the commission concluded.[41] *No congregation, in the whole of Belgium*. Meanwhile, hotlines established in Germany and

[41] *Daily Telegraph*, 10 September 2010.

Austria to deal with people claiming to be victims were inundated with calls: in Austria the system crashed on its first day, unable to cope with the more than 4,000 calls it received. Holger Eich, a psychologist with an Austrian support group, remarked: 'We are learning daily about the methods of education in Catholic institutions in Austria during the 1960s and 1970s. They can be summed up in one word: sadism.'

The terrible damage to very large numbers of vulnerable young people seems, however, to have been of less concern to the upper reaches of the current Catholic hierarchy than the ensuing damage to the Church itself. The current Pope, when as Cardinal Ratzinger he was in charge of the Congregation for the Doctrine of the Faith,[42] asserted the Church's sole judicial authority during the ten years after the eighteenth birthday in cases involving accusations of rape and torture of erstwhile juveniles in its care.[43] All preliminary investigations were to be conveyed to Ratzinger's office and be subject to the so-called Pontifical Secret, breaches of which carried a variety of penalties up to and including excommunication. Benedict, to call him now by his Papal moniker, is fond of blaming the ills of society on secularism. But it is the secular authority that was prevented, by his Church and apparently on his orders, from acting to protect these victims.

There are models of how large organisations behave when threatened, in which they retaliate with whatever weapon comes most easily to hand, usually at first the law. The Roman Catholic Church, a very large multinational organisation, is no exception. It has responded to the well-founded accusations of child rape, torture and evasion of justice by denying liability and even declaring diplomatic immunity (the Vatican has stated that the Pope as head of a sovereign state cannot be convicted of offences against the civil law in the US, where a charge of obstructing justice has been laid). It has even claimed that the Church itself is a victim of hostile forces, which include the national presses of many countries, on one occasion comparing the unfavourable comments with anti-semitism.[44] One might think that after that at least non-Catholic countries would for the time being keep their distance from the Holy See. Not so. Such is the power of the brand, as the advertisers say, that in 2010 British taxpayers paid millions of pounds sterling for a state visit by the Pope.

[42] The same body that oversaw the Inquisition.

[43] The British *Guardian* newspaper has a copy of the letter, written in 2001.

[44] The preacher to the papal household was reported as saying that the criticism of the Church reminded him of 'the more shameful acts of anti-semitism'.

12. DO AS YOU'RE TOLD

It is no understatement that mankind faces very grave threats to its survival: from overpopulation, over-exploitation of natural resources, destruction of supportive ecosystems and potentially catastrophic climate-change. The threats are magnified by the fact that a very substantial proportion of the world's population is in thrall to belief-systems that cause it to enhance these dangers. The major components of each of the three Abrahamic religions regard procreation as a command of God and any artificial inhibition of it as wicked; they regard the earth and its other species as merely a source of sustenance for human beings; and any indication that mankind is in peril through its own activities or otherwise is usually either condemned as a mischievous falsehood, or viewed as retribution for sin, or alternatively as a preparation for a Divinely planned end of the world: in any of these cases it is not something that mankind should or could attempt to prepare itself against. A certain amount of the widespread resistance to acknowledging the threat from climate-change, and even climate-change itself, comes from vested economic interests, but a good deal is certainly religiously inspired, particularly in the United States. In 2009, in a congressional hearing on proposed legislation to limit carbon emissions, John Shimkus, a Republican evangelical Christian, quoted God's postdiluvian promise in Genesis 8:26:

> Never again will I curse the ground because of man, even though all inclinations of his heart are evil from childhood and never again will I destroy all living creatures as I have done.

Mr Shimkus added: 'I believe that's the infallible word of God, and that's the way it's going to be for his creation.'

The churches' views of what are serious threats are summed up in one word: *sin*. Sin takes centre-stage. In all its multifarious forms, sin threatens God's disapproval not only of the sinner but of any complicity in the sin – which in practice means a tolerance of lifestyles in conflict with the injunctions of the churches and mosques. The current Pope observed in December 2009 that saving humanity from homosexual or transexual acts was as important as saving the rainforests. Visiting Portugal a week before the Portuguese Parliament was due to legalise gay marriage, he further observed that legitimising gay marriage poses one of the most insidious threats to the fabric of society. Coming on the heels of the revelations of systematic child abuse within his church, this was a bit rich. But such is the religious perspective. His Holiness's observation was made on a visit to the shrine of Fátima in Portugal, where in 1917 three shepherd children saw the Virgin Mary. Shortly after that, many thousands of people who had been commanded to look at the sun from that spot saw it changing colour and dancing in the sky. This is apparently a common effect of prolonged staring at the sun. 'We delude ourselves if we think that the prophetic mission of Fátima has come to an end', Benedict added. There are other delusions.

The Pope's view of a morally healthy society is, it need hardly be said, a society obedient to God. Dominating all the specific sins to which errant humanity is prone is that of *disobedience*. God's favourite archangel, Lucifer, was disobedient and was hurled out of heaven for it. Adam and Eve were disobedient and were cast out of Eden. 'For as by one man's disobedience many were made sinners, so by the obedience of one shall many be made righteous', the apostle Paul helpfully informed the Romans.[45] In this view, being moral *means* being obedient to God's commands and wishes, as the gospel of John makes explicit: 'sin is the transgression of the law'.[46] Centrally directed economies are called *command economies*. The Abrahamic religions are *command religions*.

But what is wrong with being obedient to God? one might ask. Surely the fact that God created us and indeed literally everything (including himself in a way that theologians believe to be both the greatest mystery and the greatest wonder) confers on him an automatic right to command, and a corresponding obligation on us to submit.[47] Someone who gave that claim more than a second thought, and presented the conclusive argument for dissenting that still reverberates through the philosophical world,[48] was the great eighteenth-century Scottish philosopher David Hume. The argument appears in a short passage of his *Treatise of Human Nature*, one of the great classics of western philosophy, a passage so deservedly much-quoted that I shall quote it again:

[45] Romans 5:19.

[46] John 3:4. There is a centuries-long debate inspired by a question Socrates posed in Plato's dialogue *Euthyphro*: 'Is something good because God commands it or does God command it because it is good?' It impales the theist on the horns of an unpleasant dilemma: if the former disjunct is correct then God could in principle decide that murder was good and we would be morally obliged to act accordingly. William of Ockham reluctantly took this view, but only because he recognised that the alternative undermines theism completely: if God commands something because it is good then there is a standard of goodness independent of God, who then faces dismissal from one of the two central roles in which scripture cast him: creator of the universe and arbiter of good and evil. Aquinas tried to avoid the dilemma by asserting that God only enjoined us to do what is good *for us* given our natures, but this is just a disguised way of opting for the first horn since God himself endowed us with those natures.

[47] 'Islam' means 'submission'.

[48] And largely unknown outside, it need hardly be added.

I cannot forbear adding to these reasonings an observation which may perhaps be found to be of some importance. In every system of morality which I have hitherto met with I have always remarked that the author proceeds for some time in the ordinary way of reasoning, and establishes the being of a God, or makes observations of human affairs; when of a sudden I am surprised to find, that instead of the usual copulations of propositions, is and is not, I meet with no proposition that is not connected with an ought, or an ought not. The change is imperceptible; but is, however, of the last consequence. For as this ought or ought not expresses some new relation or affirmation, it is necessary that it should be observed and explained; and at the same time that a reason should be given for what seems altogether inconceivable, how this new relation can be a deduction from others that are entirely different from it.

Hume might seem to be simply making a logical point,[49] but as so often with him – and as he intended – there is a profound implication to be drawn from it, of which many theologians still seem to remain, by and large, unaware. Just because God did what he did, exhibiting his infinite power and knowledge, etc. etc. (you can pile on as much infinity as you like here), it simply does not follow that we are *morally obliged* to do what he wants. If you want that to follow you will have to add as a new premise that we ought to obey God's will because he created us and the universe (such a 'new relation or affirmation . . . should be observed and explained'). But that, of course, is begging the question. It is no defence to say that God gave us a free will to *freely choose* whether to follow the moral norms he laid down for us.[50] The relevant fact is that he did not give us the freedom to *dissent* from his own view of their obligatory nature. On the contrary: he made it very clear that if we violate them we are liable to more or less severe punishment. Embellishing the account with declarations of his love for us, or with the promise of rewards for compliance, does nothing to change the fact that this is a morality imposed on a captive people.

But what, you may ask, about God's *love*, manifest (if you are a Christian) in his son Jesus Christ, who died to save us all? Though an originally jealous and punishing God managed – at any rate in the Christian Church – to modulate himself into a tender and loving one, the former was never extirpated, often imparting a discordantly sinister tone to the exhortations of the latter. Even though Christ was the incarnation of the phase-two,

[49] There have been many attempts to prove him wrong: the task is almost a rite of passage for philosophers. I examine them in my book *Hume's Problem: Induction and the Justification of Belief* (Oxford University Press, 2000).

[50] 2 Corinthians 9:7 is usually produced to emphasise that God doesn't want us to feel *compelled*.

tender and loving God, some of his warnings of divine retribution are strongly reminiscent of the sterner phase-one individual (this composite character seems less a Holy Trinity than a good cop–bad cop act). And even though Christ is supposed by his death to have atoned for our sins, we have it on the authority of the apostle Paul that we all still suffer from the Original Sin which persists like a lingering disease that can never be quite shaken off, and which together with Death is our collective punishment for the disobedience that dispatched Adam and Eve out of Paradise.

13. NONE SO BLIND . . .

It is a tribute – if that is the right word – to the extent to which people can willingly blind themselves to what they know instinctively is wrong, that the Biblical story of God's command to Abraham to sacrifice his only son Isaac is still widely seen as conveying a deep moral lesson. When the Lord, through his Angel, stays Abraham's hand at the last second from cutting Isaac's throat it is with the acknowledgment that 'now I know that thou fearest God, seeing that thou hast not withheld thy son, thine only son from me' (Genesis 22:12). The Lord of Hosts benignly concludes his message by granting Abraham the favour that 'in thy seed shall all the nations of the earth be blessed; because thou hast obeyed my voice' (22:18). The Old Testament contains quite a bit of this sort of thing. The story of God's faithful servant Job is very similar in tone. God is a *person* according to Richard Swinburne,[51] and according to a theory of ethics that originated with Aristotle and is still highly influential, the moral character of a person's act is dependent on the motive behind it (the theory is called *virtue-ethics*). In that case the Abraham story casts strong doubt on God's own morality, and it says a great deal about human credulity that generations of people have read that passage in the Bible without drawing the reasonable conclusion that the God of Abraham is a psychopath. It is curious, to say the least, that people can worship a deity whose standards of behaviour they would rightly condemn in any other person. Obeying the word of God is all-important, no matter how harsh and inhumane the order it conveys is. We saw the same deference to authority in the churches' opposition to legalising physician-assisted suicide. *This* is the Judaeo-Christian moral heritage for which, we are frequently told, we should be eternally grateful.

[51] Richard Swinburne, *The Existence of God*, rev. edn (Oxford: Clarendon Press, 1991), p. 7.

It should, I believe, by now be reasonably apparent that we should definitely *not* accept the widespread view that undermining the authority of religion will result in a collapse of public morals. On the contrary: most of us have a moral standard according to which punishing people for events over which they had no control (Original Sin) is wicked. Most of us feel an impulse to do good according to this standard, some admittedly more than others (the Latin poet Ovid said that he saw and approved the better and followed the worse[52]). Secular charities still manage to thrive: generosity and kindness are far from being a monopoly of the religious. But what is needed is a confident assertion of a wholly secular but clearly compelling ethics to refute the propaganda of the churches that no such thing is possible, or if possible in theory, carries no force. Though exploded by Hume (and also Kant) in the eighteenth century, that claim is still repeated like a mantra, and not only by the churches, but also by those still too inured to think of good behaviour as the response to a divine command that they simply cannot imagine a more mature foundation for morality.

14. BACK TO THE FUTURE

Perhaps surprisingly, such a foundation was provided over two millennia ago. The place was Hellenistic Greece, in the fourth century BCE, most notably – in terms of what has survived – in the *Ethics* of Aristotle. The Greece of Aristotle was a very mixed society, or societies, engaging in a great deal of primitive god-worship. But at the same time, for reasons that have never been fully explained and probably never will, those societies were the origin of arguably all that is best in our contemporary world but is every day in danger of being lost: a spirit of free enquiry and a thirst for knowledge, coupled with the keen cultivation of a critical and analytical temperament. These found their expression not only in Greek science and mathematics, but also in its literature and drama. Nothing approaching that level of intellectual sophistication was seen until the seventeenth and eighteenth centuries, and even then only fitfully. What happened between the fall of Hellenistic Greece and the eighteenth-century Enlightenment in Europe, was of course the domination of quotidian life by religion, backed by military force and the apparatus of state.

Though one of the most important sources of Catholic theology, the *Summa Theologiae* of St Thomas Aquinas, incorporates Aristotle's famous notion of a *final cause* (the final cause of a thing is, roughly, the end

[52] 'Video meliora proboque, deteriora sequor'. *Metamorphoses*.

for which its nature has fitted it), there is a conceptual chasm between Aristotle's notion of *mankind's* final cause and Aquinas's. According to Aristotle, mankind is by nature a social species endowed with reason, whose end is to employ that reason to achieve a sort of contemplative fulfilment (*eudaimonia*) within an orderly civic society.[53] Aquinas retains Aristotle's idea of *natures* determining appropriate ends, but he takes the natures to be ordained by God, the theological analogue of Aristotle's Prime Mover,[54] and erects the usual authoritarian morality on them. According to Aquinas, acting contrary to those natures is acting in defiance of God's will, with the familiar litany of divine punishments meted out for such sins as adultery, masturbation, homosexuality, suicide and a failure to worship God. It is shocking to reflect that Aquinas lived over a thousand years after Aristotle. Though he admired Aristotle to the point of referring to him as 'the Philosopher' and appropriating much of his work, Aquinas marshalled it to an end of which Aristotle would certainly have disapproved.

Even if later traduced by Catholic theology, Aristotle's *Ethics*[55] signifies a momentous event in the history of thought. In it, for the first time as far as anyone knows, virtue was regarded not as doing moral work-outs to propitiate a divine tyrant, but the means to achieving an ideal of purely human virtue. It is true that references to the gods are liberally scattered throughout Aristotle's writings, but this was a conventional conceit and in any case these gods' characters and activities were nearer to those of a TV soap than to the lonely monomania of The One True God. It is also true that the word '*eudaimonia*' signifies a god-like state, but Aristotle used the term metaphorically to mean merely living well: his theory of virtue, and the reasons he believed that virtue should be pursued, owe absolutely nothing to theology. According to the classical scholar Jonathan Barnes, Aristotle's worship of the divine seems to have been no more than a reverence for the world and the order and beauty immanent in it,[56] and to that extent very much like that of Einstein 2,000 years later who was also prone to frequent mentions of God but disclaimed any belief in religion as it is normally understood.

[53] Virtuous action for Aristotle consists in using reason to ensure a sustainable, which meant *moderate*, way of satisfying one's natural appetites. Aristotle is very modern in feeling and in his appeal to reason to determine optimal ways of satisfying those desires has a claim to be called the father of modern decision theory (in which the rational agent calculates optimal decisions by weighing the desirability of the various possible outcomes of each contemplated act against their probabilities).

[54] Aristotle's Prime Mover is entirely unconcerned with anything human, or indeed with anything except the nature of its own thought.

[55] In fact Aristotle wrote two books of Ethics, the *Nicomachean Ethics* and the *Eudemian Ethics*, but the *Nicomachean Ethics* is usually considered the more fundamental.

[56] Jonathan Barnes, *Aristotle* (London: Oxford University Press, 1982), pp. 64–5.

The third President of the United States, Thomas Jefferson, had a very Aristotelian attitude to the pursuit of virtue. In a letter Jefferson wrote to his nephew, he encouraged him not to fear an enquiry into the foundation of his religious belief since

> [i]f it ends in a belief that there is no God, you will find incitements to virtue in the comfort and pleasantness you feel in this exercise, and the love of others which it will procure you.[57]

Quite so. Jefferson was the author of the American Declaration of Independence, that ringing endorsement of an 'inalienable' human right 'to life, liberty and the pursuit of happiness'. Whether the right to the pursuit of happiness was a conscious echo of Aristotle I do not know, but it is highly probable: Jefferson was an enthusiastic classical scholar with a keen interest in political and moral philosophy, both classical and contemporary (he took his account of inalienable rights in general from Locke), and would certainly have been aware that Aristotle had laid it down as a fundamental principle in the *Ethics* that the end, or *telos*, of man is happiness, and that of the state is to promote it.[58]

Aristotle's concept of *eudaimonia* is, I believe, of the greatest importance in moral/social philosophy, and crucial to forging a stable and rewarding social and political climate in which human beings can achieve such potential as they have for happiness. It speaks to the best in human nature rather than the worst, to which speaks the religious concept-cluster of sin, punishment, atonement, expiation, repentance, forgiveness and a salvation not of this world (the Anglican hymn tries, unsuccessfully, to put an optimistic gloss on this basic crime-and-punishment package:

> New perils past, new sins forgiven
> New thoughts of God, new hopes of Heaven).

In the eighteenth century that other great philosopher, David Hume, adopted this key element of Aristotle's moral theory and mixed it with seminal ideas of his own. In Chapter 6 I will argue that the result provides a basis for a secular morality in which human beings become, in Kant's arresting phrase, 'self-legislating members of the kingdom of ends', taking

[57] Quoted in Christopher Hitchens, *Thomas Jefferson: Author of America* (New York: Atlas Books/Harper Collins, 2005). Jefferson founded the University of Virginia, the first American institute of higher learning in which education was totally separated from religion (the university had no chapel or church).

[58] Aristotle, *Nicomachean Ethics*, Christopher Rowe (trans.) (Oxford University Press, 2002), Book VII.

ultimate authority for their own standards of right and wrong and of good and bad.

15. 'SAY NOT, THE STRUGGLE NAUGHT AVAILETH . . .'

Repatriating our moral constitution, like most attempts to gain independence, is easier said than done, however. The struggle is not so much against the Great Governor himself, who has seldom personally intervened, especially recently, but against the large number of those who claim and believe themselves to be his followers on earth. Sometimes, as we know, they can respond with the utmost savagery, but these days usually more insidiously through the institutions of education and the enactment of protective laws and regulations like UN Resolution 62/154. The main battle is intellectual: people in their billions are still not prepared to admit that they can or should be independent of the will of God. The best way to remove that obstacle is to show them that the person to whom they believe themselves subject is in all probability nothing but a figment of their own imaginations. Although, like George Orwell's Big Brother, he is never seen, believers nevertheless think that he has given more than enough evidence of his existence to remove any reasonable doubt on that score. In the remainder of this book I will explain why that opinion is very far from the truth.

EXERCISE

'Evil acts committed in the name of religion in no way impugn the truth of the faith; they instead impugn the nature of human beings, those rusty containers into which the pure water of that truth has been placed.' Comment.

MAIN POINTS OF CHAPTER 1

- The Abrahamic religions are totalitarian belief-systems. They have been responsible for large-scale persecution and oppression, and still constitute a serious threat to individual freedom and autonomy.
- Even today the equality of the sexes and what should be reasonable freedoms, like that of sexual orientation, and in particular the freedom to arrange a dignified and peaceful end to one's life, are still opposed by some or all these religions.
- According to all these religions we are created and owned by God, and thereby obliged to obey his commands.

- Apologists use a pick'n'mix policy with the scriptures to avoid both internal inconsistency and also conflict with our intuitions. This policy leaves it open, and in any case reveals that one is using one's own moral faculty to discriminate between the acceptable and the unacceptable parts of scripture. But that implies that one's own moral intuition is primary, in which case still insisting on finding scriptural backing is a form of moral cowardice.
- By elevating obedience and a-rational faith into cardinal virtues these command-religions discourage critical thought and threaten thereby the single most important safeguard of civil liberty. The argument is an old one, going back to John Stuart Mill and before, but such is the continuing power of religious propaganda that it is in constant need of restating.
- A more enlightened, secular ethics based on the principle of *eudaimonia* was proposed two millennia ago by Aristotle – and almost forgotten. A religiously based ethics was subsequently imposed, and has been dominant since. It is time to return to an Aristotelian view.

CHAPTER 2

God unlimited

'Blessed are they who have not seen, and yet have believed.'[1]

1. ROCK(S) OF AGES

One of Richard Dawkins's most illuminating insights was to identify what he called *memes* as a key explanatory variable in the evolution of ideas, giving them the same sort of role in cultural evolution as genes play in the evolution of biological traits: we are vectors of memes just as we are vectors of genes. From that it is a quick inference, unsurprisingly made in a characteristically trenchant way by Dawkins himself,[2] and then developed at length by Susan Blackmore,[3] to see religion as a sort of memetic *virus*. Not only do the Abrahamic religions enjoin breeding and the inculcation of the same faith in their offspring, but as Blackmore emphasised, they also embody a very efficient self-protective mechanism in elevating *faith* above evidence, and the possession of faith into a prime virtue. Faith, as St Paul reminded the Hebrews, is 'the substance of things hoped for, the evidence of things not seen'. '*The evidence of things not seen.*' This arresting phrase is approvingly quoted time and again, as if its beauty excuses what in fact is simply oxymoronic sophistry.[4] Should you believe in fairies *because* you don't see them? But now comes the real *coup*. The corollary of elevating faith into a supreme virtue is that the desire for what ordinary people might think of as evidence to justify religious belief – reliable eye-witnesses and so forth – becomes a corresponding *vice*. And so we have the scene set for

[1] John 20:26.

[2] '[F]aith is one of the world's great evils, comparable to the smallpox virus but harder to eradicate.' Richard Dawkins, 'Is Science a Religion?', *The Humanist* 57 (1989), 26–9.

[3] Susan Blackmore, *The Meme Machine* (Oxford University Press, 1999).

[4] Believers themselves appear to sense its absurdity, preferentially citing as evidence *seen* things: things such as the Turin shroud, angels in clouds, Jesus crucified on a telegraph pole in Louisiana (a climbing shrub when viewed close to), countless sightings of the Virgin Mary (once in a loaf of bread) and so on.

a nice Catch 22: a request for evidence is to display doubt, which is to lack faith, which is, as St Paul was at pains to make clearly understood, to be *sinful*. 'Whatsoever is not of faith, is sin', he told the Romans.[5]

Christ himself reserved blessedness for those who need no observational evidence to ground their belief. His were the words in the epigraph to this chapter (according to John's gospel, though remember that the gospels were written *after* the Pauline epistles), uttered in the course of a rebuke to poor 'doubting' Thomas, the disciple who famously had the presumption to ask for empirical evidence for the claim that the man to whom he was speaking had risen from the dead. Thomas's doubt was of course entirely reasonable. He was being asked to swallow a fantastic story, for which there was no evidence at that point other than a mere claim, and a claim is in itself no evidence for anything. But for the canonical doctrines of Judaism, Islam and Christianity, doubt is something to be suppressed, however reasonable it might be. In both Judaeo-Christian eschatology and that of Islam, doubters are often lumped in with disbelievers to have literally a Hell of a time after they die. And for much of the history of the monotheisms, to doubt publicly the truth of the scriptures would ensure a quicker death than normal, and usually not a pleasant one.

There is a profound *moral* issue in the elevation of faith over evidence. Impartial evidence is the defence of honest people against imposters and frauds. To devalue it is – I do not want to sound melodramatic but it is difficult not to – to *subvert reason*. Once it is taught that there are knowledge-claims for which evidence can be dispensed with in favour of personal conviction and the word of authority then the dark night of unreason is upon us – as, of course, were the Dark Ages following what Matthew Arnold famously described as the 'sweetness and light' of Hellenistic civilisation with its attitude of critical enquiry for which nothing was off-limits – an attitude so foreign to the Catholic Church that it retains 'for moral guidance' its obnoxious *Index Librorum Prohibitorum*. Evidence is literally the foundation on which our scientific understanding of the world rests. For that reason alone, it is all the more surprising to find the distinguished late scientist (biologist) Stephen Jay Gould contending that Thomas actually *deserved* his rebuke, and that evidence is all very well, indeed mandatory, in what Gould calls the 'magisterium' of science, but not in that of religion.[6]

[5] Romans 14:23.

[6] Stephen Jay Gould, *Rocks of Ages: Science and Religion in the Fullness of Life* (New York: Ballantine Books, 1999), p. 16. I am guessing that Gould's nomenclature was inspired by the fact that the Catholic Church calls its teaching authority the 'Magisterium'.

Coming from a scientist that verdict comes, in my opinion, very close to intellectual treason. I say that with genuine regret because Gould was not only a very distinguished biologist, but from the pages of his partly autobiographical book, *Rocks of Ages*, published shortly before his death, emerges the picture of a very decent, generous and humane person. But in mitigation, I think that Gould's thesis results more from intellectual confusion than any deliberate betrayal of his own high standards. Saying, as he does, that evidence is not needed for a claim under the 'magisterium' of faith but is required, *for the same claim*, under the 'magisterium' of science, seems to me simple nonsense.

Gould's NOMA ('non-overlapping magisteria') thesis, that science and religion are incommensurable domains of belief and enquiry, is scarcely more tenable. Their respective jurisdictions, he tells us, are on the one hand morality, value and meaning, and on the other factuality. Thus, he concludes, there is no conflict between the two. But this thesis itself fails a simple factuality test. In the first place, the idea that religion makes no factual claims will come as news to all those Muslims and evangelical Christians who reject the theory of evolution because it contradicts the Koran and the Bible. And what of the fundamental claim of the Abrahamic religions that God is the creator of the universe, that he is omniscient, omnipotent and all-loving and that he accords humanity a central if at times uncomfortable place in his creation? Specific claims are made by nearly all religions about the origin of the universe, when it occurred, why it occurred, and the manner of the arrival of mankind in it. On a somewhat lighter note, the Pope, in the course of inveighing against the use of body-scanners in airports, informed us that there is nothing that man does 'which does not escape the eyes of God, who sees all of Man's works, even those that are hidden'.[7] His Holiness also reported that various benign social practices threaten the fabric of civilisation. Factual statements do not cease to be factual because they are absurd.

Secondly, and even more off the mark, is Gould's claim that science cannot investigate the ultimate origins of matter (which he includes under the heading of 'meaning'). Why, one wonders, did he think particle-accelerators are built? It really doesn't need saying that exactly the contrary view is at the heart of the current research programme of fundamental particle physics. Why otherwise search for the elusive particle which according to the Standard Model is responsible for creating mass? Nor is it true that moral issues themselves lie beyond the remit of science. Any moral system worth its

[7] Reported in the *Daily Telegraph*, 21 February 2010.

name will have to be sensitive to some relevant empirical facts, particularly biological facts. But latterly science, equipped with new explanatory tools, is encroaching further and further on the domains of ethics and social behaviour. As we shall see in Chapter 6, developments in modern science, in particular in neuroscience and evolutionary theory, are revolutionising the way we view moral norms, their origin and function.

Gould seems to have fallen victim to the Church's propaganda disseminating the claim that morality is the sole preserve of God, a claim which, as we have seen, would have been rejected out of hand by Aristotle. In fact it is precisely here that Gould's claims rebound badly on him, since the moral codes enjoined by the three monotheisms arise more or less directly from their *factual* claims about the relation of God to man and God to the cosmos. That God made the cosmos, and man in it, so that man might obey and worship him is a fundamental claim elaborated in various ways by the theologians. For example, according to Thomas Aquinas, the author of the doctrine of Natural Law on which the Catholic Church bases much of its theology, man was created to fulfil certain ends, and wilfully impeding or frustrating any of these is an act of direct disobedience, meriting condign punishment at God's hands.

Gould appears to sense that something is wrong with his thesis early on in his book where he poses an obvious, if rather convoluted, question:

> As a first implication for potential suspicion, I have stated that, while every person must formulate a moral theory under the magisterium of ethics and meaning, and while religion anchors this magisterium in most cultural traditions, the chosen pathway need not invoke religion at all, but may ground moral discourse in other disciplines, philosophy for example. If we all must develop a moral code, but may choose to do so without a formal appeal to religion, then how can this subject claim equal importance and dignity with science . . . ?[8]

How indeed? Gould's answer is so weak that it is difficult to credit his sincerity in offering it: it is to appeal to etymology! Quoting T. H. Huxley's remark that science cannot disprove the immortality of the soul, Gould continues:

> I will accept both Huxley's view and the etymology of the word itself – and construe as fundamentally religious (literally, binding us together) all moral discourse on principles that might activate the ideal of universal fellowship among people.[9]

What, you might well ask, is 'fundamentally religious' in that? I will answer for you: nothing whatever. In a final paroxysm of logic Gould even goes so

[8] Gould, *Rocks of Ages*, pp. 59–60. [9] *Ibid.*, p. 62.

far as to claim that a recent rather obvious violation of his thesis actually *supports* it:

> Modern Creationism, alas, has provoked a real battle, thus supporting NOMA with a positive example of the principle that all apparent struggles between science and religion really arise from violations of NOMA.[10]

Undo that if you can.

The fact is, appeals to NOMA notwithstanding, that science and religion are dissonant world-views that for most of their joint history have been in conflict and – for fundamentalists – still conflict. In 2008 almost half of Americans still rejected evolutionary theory because they believed that it conflicts with the Bible. Similarly mainstream Islam insists that the theory of evolution and Big Bang cosmology *must be* incorrect since they conflict with the Koran. To the extent that conflict has ceased it is because religion has been forced to accept the scientific account: usually reluctantly, as the century's lapse before the Vatican could bring itself to acknowledge the Darwinian theory as likely truth bears eloquent witness (even then the concession was limited: souls remain excluded from the evolutionary process). Gould himself tells us that the ancient Greek theory of atomism – that all matter is composed of particles so minute that they are invisible to the unaided eye – was declared heretical by the early Christian Church, though today its descendant, the Standard Model of particle theory, is the foundation of modern physics. Galileo was forced by the Roman Inquisition to 'abjure, curse and detest' his scientific work in 1633, and Gould observes in his book how at various times members of the Catholic Church hierarchy advised strongly against pressing any factual claim in which there might be a potential conflict with science, aware that the result would always be a foregone conclusion. But this is not, as he seemed to think it is, evidence for his view. Far from springing from any recognition by their practitioners that religion and science are non-overlapping magisteria, the concessions are *forced*.

There is a powerful case that religion simply *cannot* relinquish its claim to provide ultimate explanations of the cosmos: if it adopted the Gould programme of resolutely abstaining from factual claims it would no longer be revealed truth *about the world*, and consequently would probably die out within a few years. It is precisely because it makes such claims that it exercises a hold on people's hearts and minds, as the mawkish cliché has it. I pointed out in Chapter 1 that one can invent any number of

[10] *Ibid.*, p. 125.

Gothic horror stories and people the imagination with all sorts of terrifying monsters, but if no-one believes the stories to be true and the characters correspondingly real then they will at worst only give us nightmares, from which we can of course awake. Persuade people that they are true – though some people do already believe in such fairy-tales – and they will do everything in their power to placate the demons, worship the monsters, and in general behave as those behave who still have faith in the God of our Fathers.

Claims to factuality are of course attended by the risk that they might one day be shown to be false, or probably false, by the facts. But there is really no choice: religion has to retain some factual content to survive, but in so doing it will offer a hostage to fortune, especially where there is a formidable rival in the form of science, that epistemological juggernaut that once set in motion cannot be stopped and which acknowledges no limits to its remit. Indeed, to claim, as many theologians do, that there are factual questions that *in principle* science cannot address is something on which it would be extremely unwise to place money. We shall be looking at some of these claims later in this book, in Chapters 6 and 7, where we shall see that they fail to be underwritten by any convincing arguments. True, we are witnessing an evolving religion, stressing increasingly its sacramental and numinous aspects and moving further and further away from what might be even remotely testable claims about reality, and it is difficult and probably foolish to hazard sociological/theological guesses about where exactly this process will end, if it will. But what we do know is that for its own sake it must stop short of vacuity.

But where? Well, it must at least contain some core principles, and it is not difficult to write out a minimal list if religion is not to degenerate into an empty shell. All we have to do is identify those functions God is required to fulfil. Putting aside the purely sacramental and ritualistic, these functions are *explanatory*: to explain the existence and purpose of the cosmos; to explain our sense that we are subject to an implanted moral law that frequently seems to be in conflict with our own personal interests; and to explain the apparent *injustice* of things, both in the frequent rewarding of evil and the brevity and harshness of lives, our own and others'.

2. LET THERE BE GOD!

The individual we arrive at is, not surprisingly, the common core of the monotheisms, a unique Creator of heaven and earth possessing the famous three properties of omnipotence, omniscience and pure goodness[11] (good through and through, one might say): a true trinity, whose purpose in creating the universe was to create a world in which the creatures made in his image would come to understand his love and goodness. That he is the Creator and that he loves us follow immediately from the explanatory wish-list above. Omnipotence and omniscience are complementary features that allow this God to do everything needed to construct the universe and its governing laws in a way sufficient for human life to emerge and be maintained, to keep a check on the inner feelings and motives of every one of his people to see how genuinely virtuous they are, to see whether doubt and scepticism are being secretly harboured and to compile an exhaustive list of the external circumstances, actual and possible, which might exonerate or further inculpate sinful acts or thoughts. Monitoring any tendency to Doubt, as we have seen, is of particular importance.

That religion discharges such an explanatory function might seem so obvious as not to need pointing out. All the more surprising then that it has been explicitly denied by the anthropologist Pascal Boyer.[12] Boyer's objections are broadly twofold: (i) that religion is not a response to a felt need for explanation because people by and large do not feel the need to explain things even when no explanation seems at hand (he cites as an example the way thoughts and intentions result in bodily movement), and (ii) the accounts provided by religion increase complexity by raising more questions than they answer, whereas the function of explanation is to reduce it.[13] Boyer cites in support of this second claim the fact that religious accounts typically invoke a troupe of supernatural entities together with a substantial amount of theory concerning them.

I find these objections not at all convincing. Objection (ii) is based on a model of explanation as *scientific* explanation, but Boyer's own model is inaccurate. He seems not to realise that an analogous role to peopling the world with invisible ghosts is played in physics by the invocation of unseen entities, like the whole menagerie of elementary particles including virtual particles which pop in and out of existence, together with a great deal of highly sophisticated theory regulating their behaviour. If one has a false picture of science, one will have a false picture of scientific explanation. The fact is that answering questions by raising deeper questions that

[11] The Koran lists them succinctly: all-knowing, all-mighty, most-forgiving, merciful and wise (4:24, 4:25, 4:158). These admirable qualities are also enumerated in Jewish and Christian scripture.

[12] Pascal Boyer, *Religion Explained: The Evolutionary Origins of Religious Thought* (New York: Basic Books, 2001).

[13] *Ibid.*, p. 15.

probe beneath surface phenomena is common to practically all scientific explanations, and it is responsible for science continually, if not uniformly rapidly, advancing the frontiers of knowledge.

The putatively scientific explanations that Boyer himself provides are rather less impressive. Lumping together with primitive religions the sophisticated belief-systems of Judaism, Christianity and Islam as a potential subject for explanation seems hardly scientific, and like all attempts at averaging over very inhomogeneous data its conclusions are unlikely to be very informative. The Abrahamic religions, with their attendant body of theologians and scholars who have been refining, systematising and often changing doctrine for close on two millennia, are much more like the systematic theories of science or philosophy than the relatively inchoate jumble of practices and oral tradition that constitute much of primitive religion.[14] Boyer himself regards systematic theology with its categorical assertions about the cosmos and man's place in it as anomalous, not part of authentic religion which according to him is a by-product of largely unconscious, innate inferential templates with which evolution has equipped us for more straightforwardly predictive tasks. But this is the sort of selective use of evidence that scientists are adjured to avoid like the plague. Boyer likes to invoke evolutionary mechanisms to explain the roots and tenacity of religion,[15] but his own account largely ignores the fact that in the pool of world religions some are vastly more evolved from primitive beginnings than others, to the extent that the former bear practically no resemblance to, say, that of the Fang, the African tribe who make frequent exemplary appearances in Boyer's book.

Objection (i) also overlooks some rather obvious facts. Firstly, people have for more than two millennia found the way mind operates on matter extremely puzzling and have proposed, and are still proposing, a variety of explanations of it. Secondly, the main religions tend to commence by describing the formation of heaven and earth and the arrival of life on it, a narrative implicitly explanatory in purpose, together with an explicit explanation of the rather less-than-perfect state that mankind finds itself in through the transgressions of Adam and Eve. Hesiod's *Theogony* (ninth century BCE) is an account of the creation of the world out of the void

[14] 'Torah', the name of Judaism's sacred scripture, can be translated as 'theory'.

[15] Part of his explanation appeals to a 'modular' theory of cognitive processes which many cognitive scientists, I think for good reason, do not accept. According to them the mind is a much more general-purpose theorising machine than his account credits; see, for example, Richard Samuels, 'Evolutionary Psychology and the Massive Modularity Hypothesis', *British Journal for the Philosophy of Science* 49 (1998), 575–603.

by Kronos, the ancestor of all the gods in the Greek pantheon. Creation myths, many of them variations on a single early model, are ubiquitous. We now call most of them myths, although they were once part of live religions, but mythology is merely the terminal, ossified stage of religion. In due course the God of Abraham will probably be stripped of his divinity to swell the ranks of the gods of mythology: 'There is a supreme God in the ethnological section.'[16]

3. A NOTE ON RELIGIOUS EXPLANATION

We shall be looking in some depth at religious explanations later in this book, but an immediately striking difference between them and the typical sorts of explanation provided by science is that the former are usually rather easily accomplished by contrast with those of science, which employs on the whole a much greater expenditure of intellectual labour combined with a much greater degree of rigour in testing its conjectures (in the next chapter we shall see some examples of the rigour with which the Vatican evaluates miracle-claims). This difference is symptomatic of an interesting pathological character of typical theological explanations – of the origins of the universe, of life, of what Francis Collins calls the Moral Law and so on: they are *bespoke*, tailor-made, essentially ad hoc – after the fact. As the editor of a series of volumes on science and religion reminds us, 'where nature is studied through scientific methods, scientific knowledge is unavoidably incorporated into religious thought'.[17]

Francis Collins's so-called *Biologos* explanation of the evolution of the cosmos[18] is typical in this respect. According to it, God employs the laws of physics and the evolutionary process to bring about intelligent life. But no such evolutionary account was mentioned by churchmen before Darwin and the theory of evolution was anathematised by the Church for almost a century after it was first published. Eventually, as it was forced to do with the Copernican theory, Rome bowed to the inevitable. The claim often made by theologians that science and theology are providing *convergent* explanations reveals no deep fact that should cause anyone to celebrate a remarkable consilience achieved by two independent research programmes. On the contrary: one has simply shanghaied the other.

[16] First line of William Empson's poem 'Homage to the British Museum', in *Collected Poems* (London: Chatto and Windus, 1977).

[17] Geoffrey Redmond, *Science and Asian Spiritual Traditions* (Westport, CT: Greenwood Press, 2008), p. ix.

[18] Francis Collins, *The Language of God* (New York: Free Press, 2006), p. 203.

But that does not stop theologians and theologically minded philosophers from insisting that theology can nevertheless reach parts that science cannot, and for these it can provide what science cannot: *ultimate explanations* – of where the universe came from, why it came into being, and even – a favourite preoccupation of theologically minded metaphysicians – *why there is something rather than nothing*. Why is there a universe at all, for that matter? With God as the only conceivable *ultimate* explanation many theologians feel they have an ace in their hand. Of course, playing it implicitly raises the question of the provenance of God himself, but those who do play it feel they have the answer to that too: *God is self-caused*, and not only self-caused but possessing a *necessity* flowing, they claim, from his definition as 'the supremely perfect being' (this is the celebrated *Ontological Argument*, which we shall review in Chapter 5).

Some, I suspect most, physicists and cosmologists nevertheless refuse to see in the invocation of God as the explanation of the universe, let alone an ultimate explanation, anything but a form of wordplay, a spurious explanation in which God is merely the postulated x such that 'x made the universe' is true. The fact remains, however, that writing such explanations off as scientifically valueless doesn't prove that they are false, or even probably false. In their weakness, it seems, lies their strength. How after all can you disprove an x?[19] Notoriously not one to flinch from such a challenge, Richard Dawkins has recently attempted to do just that, arguing that it follows from the hypothesis that God made the universe that He must be so extremely improbable that his existence can be safely discounted.[20] Dawkins thinks that an improbability proof is actually the best negative result that can be achieved, claiming that it is impossible to give a deductive demonstration that God does not exist.[21] But he overlooks something of which mathematicians are well aware, that deductive proofs of non-existence are far from impossible or even that infrequent (Euclid produced a famous one over 2,000 years ago[22]).

That is all very well, it might be said, but how can you prove that God is impossible just from the hypothesis that he made the universe? It may be a big hypothesis, but it is not an obviously inconsistent one. Well, of course you can't prove the impossibility of God just from that

[19] St Paul rebuked the Athenians for an altar he had seen with the dedication 'TO THE UNKNOWN GOD' (Acts 17:23). I suspect the sophisticated Athenians knew better than Paul not to offer hostages to fortune.

[20] Richard Dawkins, *The God Delusion* (London: Bantam Books, 2006), chapter 4. I will review Dawkins's argument in Chapter 8 and argue that it doesn't work.

[21] *Ibid.*, p. 77.

[22] He proved that there is no upper bound to the sequence of prime numbers.

hypothesis. But the objection fails to take into account the fact that God has to be endowed with some fairly substantial properties in order to carry out all his explanatory duties, and it is these properties that do the trick. A logical analogy will give the essential idea. Suppose you want a compact set of postulates that implies every true proposition in some field of enquiry. A truly remarkable theorem, proved in the 1930s by the Austrian mathematician and logician Kurt Gödel (who will make periodic reappearances in the following chapters), shows that subject to some very general conditions *the only way this can be done is by making that set of postulates inconsistent.* It will certainly then imply every true proposition, but unfortunately it will also imply every false one as well. As we shall see later, this is exactly what happens in endowing God with the unlimited power to explain and do everything he is alleged to explain and do. Without it, there is no guarantee that he can do everything and know everything he is supposed to; with it, he becomes so top-heavy with explanatory power that he topples over into logical inconsistency.

4. TOO MUCH OF A GOOD THING

The logical problem was glimpsed, if only through a glass darkly so to speak, long ago in antiquity and, perhaps surprisingly, by theologians themselves. I refer to the discovery and subsequent discussion of the so-called 'paradoxes' associated with the nature of God, and in particular to the 'paradoxes of omnipotence'. The most famous is implicit in the question: 'Can God create a stone that he cannot lift?', and was pondered by such venerable thinkers as Anselm and Augustine. The problem is obvious: if God can create such a stone, then it follows immediately that there is something he cannot do and so he is not omnipotent. If on the other hand he can't create such a stone then he is not omnipotent, period.

Much theological and philosophical ink has been spilt over this paradox, but it has never been uncontroversially resolved. C. S. Lewis, one-time Oxford academic and Christian apologist, best-known now for his fantasies like *The Chronicles of Narnia*, characteristically tried to settle the issue with bluster: God can't do what is asked 'not because His power meets an obstacle, but because nonsense remains nonsense even when we talk about God'.[23] Lewis was wrong. People don't persist in talking about a problem over the centuries, right up to the present, in sentences that make sense

[23] C. S. Lewis, *The Problem of Pain* (New York: Macmillan, 1962), p. 18.

to them and others, if they are simply talking nonsense. The Oxford philosopher J. L. Mackie summarily sets Lewis right:

> It cannot be replied that the question which sets this paradox is not a proper question. It would make perfectly good sense to say that a human mechanic has made a machine which he cannot control: if there is any difficulty about the question it lies in the notion of omnipotence itself.[24]

One attempt to resolve the paradox, which goes back to St Augustine, is to claim that since God is being asked to perform an inconsistent action then it is no limitation on God that he can't do it, any more than it is a limitation on the weather that it both cannot rain and not rain here, now. But as many have since pointed out, this is not a good defence because 'making a stone God can't lift' is not *in itself* an inconsistent action-description, even when predicated of God himself (I can make a heap of bricks that I can't lift); it is inconsistent only together with the additional claim that God is omnipotent. *That* is the problem. It is a very real problem if one wishes to follow established theological tradition in regarding it as an *essential* property of God that he has absolutely unlimited power. To quote Mackie again:

> It is clear that this is a paradox: the question cannot be answered satisfactorily either in the affirmative or in the negative. If the answer is 'Yes', it follows that if God actually makes things which he cannot control, or makes rules which bind himself, he is not omnipotent once he has made them: there are *then* things which he cannot do. But if the answer is 'No', we are immediately asserting that there are things which he cannot do, that is to say that he is already not omnipotent.[25]

No way out there, then.

5. AN ECHO DOWN THE AGES

Those early theologians who were perplexed by the paradox can be forgiven for failing to foresee what only became evident well over a thousand years later: that in postulating an entity the scope of whose power includes literally everything, *including himself*, they were on the threshold of a deep problem that was to arise in – of all things – mathematics. Towards the end of the nineteenth century mathematics became plagued with paradoxes which on examination turn out to share important features with that of omnipotence. Here is a famous example, due to the philosopher, mathematician and general *savant* Bertrand Russell. Ask yourself the admittedly

[24] J. L. Mackie, 'Evil and Omnipotence', *Mind* 64 (1955), p. 212. [25] *Ibid.*

rather peculiar question whether the set of all sets which are not members of themselves is a member of itself. However you answer it, yes or no, you will quickly arrive at a contradiction. 'Russell's Paradox', as it is now called, initiated a crisis in contemporary foundational work in mathematics, and caused one of the foremost of those involved, the German mathematician Gottlob Frege, despair since it struck at the heart of his own system (aware of this, Russell initially communicated the paradox to Frege).

A word about words. These quirky puzzles are called 'paradoxes' because they start from something seemingly innocuous and move quickly to an outright contradiction. If you look closely at Russell's paradox and the paradox of omnipotence you will discover a shared feature that seems to be causing the problem. Both define an entity in terms of a property that explicitly or implicitly makes reference to the entity itself. In the case of the set of all sets which are not members of themselves, that set itself falls under the scope of what logicians call a universal quantifier, 'all sets'. In the case of omnipotence, since *all* possible actions fall under its scope, they include those of God himself. Russell's suggestion, which he called 'the vicious circle principle', was to exclude such apparently circular definitions entirely. That is easier said than done, however, because although the circularity causes trouble in certain cases, in others it does not and in mathematics itself there are completely benign examples which are almost indispensable (for example, the set of real numbers is defined in terms of a property which makes reference to that set itself: every subset must have a least upper bound in the set).

But where such a definition does generate inconsistency it clearly has to be either eschewed completely or appropriately restricted to preserve consistency. A suggestion of Mackie himself is that the scope of God's powers should be so restricted by explicitly excluding God himself from it.[26] But as theologians have unhappily pointed out, this implies a limitation on God and so conflicts with a central theological and philosophical tradition that God is a being who *by definition* cannot be limited in his power.[27] I will postpone further discussion of this interesting problem to Chapter 8, where we shall see the other omni-property, omniscience, turn out to be at least as logically problematic as omnipotence.

God's characteristic omni-properties are a source of concern not just because of their intrinsic properties, problematic enough though these are,

[26] *Ibid.*

[27] Cf. Spinoza, *The Ethics*, Edwin Curley (ed. and trans.) (London: Penguin, 1996), Proposition XV, Part I.

but also because of an extrinsic fact about the world expressed in the simple observation that it is often not a very nice place even for the virtuous. A cynic might add: especially for the virtuous. This dissonance with the declared nature of God is, not altogether surprisingly, a perennial problem for believers. It is the *Problem of Evil.*

6. 'FAR BE IT FROM GOD, THAT HE SHOULD DO WICKEDNESS'[28]

I suggested earlier that God is an entirely human *invention*, and that one of the reasons why he was invented was to take the strain of an uncaring universe. But can he? There are logical limits to wishful thinking and no less so to wishful inventing. And there is one area of activity in which this all too human Superhuman has always found it very difficult to perform his task. The human condition itself is notoriously not always a happy one: it rains on the just and the unjust, with if anything more delivered on the former. Approaching the inevitable end of one's personal existence is also often seen as anything but an enjoyable experience. There are even worse things. There are dreadful diseases which pay no respect to the character or age of the afflicted; there are natural calamities, like earthquakes, tidal waves and so on, which also bring disease in their train; and there are humanly wrought calamities too, like war (including those many wars in which religion itself played a significant role), massacres and in our own age the Holocaust, from which many Jews not unreasonably concluded that God's covenant with them was broken.

How, it might well be asked, can God permit the suffering – which includes innocent suffering – that is such a perennial and ubiquitous feature of the world he created? The God of Abraham did so, of course, because he thought we all deserved it because of the horrifically sinful actions of our remote ancestors Adam and Eve in eating the forbidden fruit, but thoughtful theists rightly repudiate that story of semi-insane vengeance. But that does bring them face to face with the problem of evil. Even worse for them, since God is the cause of everything that happens it would seem to follow that *God must be the cause of that suffering.* How could a supposedly all-knowing, all-powerful and all-good God be a cause of evil?

On the usual understanding of the words in that question the answer might seem obvious: he can't. Unsurprisingly, the problem has haunted theologians though the ages and, to quote the ever-quotable Dawkins,

[28] Job 34:10.

still keeps some of them awake at night.[29] The mystery is why it doesn't keep them all awake, every night. Maybe it does. It certainly should. J. L. Mackie, whom we encountered earlier, makes the point with characteristic clarity:

> In its simplest form the problem is this: God is omnipotent; God is wholly good; and yet evil exists. There seems to be some contradiction between these three propositions, so that if any two of them were true the third would be false. But at the same time all three are essential parts of most theological positions: the theologian, it seems, *must* adhere and *cannot consistently* adhere to all three.[30]

Mackie points out that to make this a logician's *formal* contradiction one needs a few supplementary premises, namely that good is opposed to evil in such a way that it eliminates evil so far as it can, that there are no limits to omnipotence, that what we regard as evil really is evil, and so on. But these are merely what philosophers call *analytic principles*: they just render explicit what is implicit in the relevant words. Most inferences we take in ordinary informal deductive reasoning employ such principles, usually suppressed because thought to be too obvious to need stating explicitly, as when one might report the throw of a die 'it was a two; hence it wasn't an odd number'. People would think it very strange if one pedantically added 'because two is an even number and no even number is odd'.

7. I'VE ONLY GOT A FINITE MIND!

The only way to resist the conclusion that the existence of evil is inconsistent with the hypothesis of an omniscient, omnipotent and omnibenevolent God is by attacking one or more of those premises, and this theists have duly done across the passage of the centuries. One of the more radical suggestions periodically rolled out is that God's notion of goodness is almost certainly not ours since by assumption God knows vastly more than we do: God is infinite in knowledge and wisdom, and the workings of the divine mind are not to be penetrated by merely human reason. God's standards are not ours. They are not only not ours: they are infinitely *higher* than ours. Moreover, they just can't be ours because God is infinitely good whereas we see a problem in what he does. At its most extreme, this doctrine has it that God is essentially unknowable by us. How that claim, a popular

[29] Dawkins, *The God Delusion*, p. 135.
[30] Mackie, 'Evil and Omnipotence', p. 200 (italics in the original).

one, can be reconciled with our knowing that it is true is a question I have never seen asked, let alone answered (I once read a newspaper article by a well-known theologian making the claim, and ending with the usual list of God's properties: omniscient, omnipotent, loving, etc.). At any rate, despite its popularity and the important endorsement of St Thomas Aquinas, it is not difficult to see that this response is a losing strategy. Since by the universal consent of theologians our very notion of good and evil is implanted in us by God, to enable us to recognise each for what it is and employ our free will to move toward the one and away from the other, it is little more than a piece of audacious *trompe l'œil.* Moreover, it is accepted theological wisdom that God is not a deceiver (otherwise he would not be perfectly good), so he cannot have implanted in us *false* ideas of good and evil. It might be argued that we are unjustifiably identifying moral goodness with a different *type* of goodness. For example (Leibniz at various times held this view), it might be the goodness of a beautifully-designed machine that is the standard, and the cosmos is arguably just that. But the obvious reply to that move is that we do not usually feel we should worship Dr Guillotine because he designed a highly efficient means of execution.

Another popular reply is to observe that much of the evil in the world is due to humanity's endowment with free will: only if their choices are free can agents be judged at fault, i.e. *sinful.* This exculpatory strategy is no better than the first. Firstly, innocent victims of other people's wickedness should arguably not have to suffer, and in indirectly causing them to do so God has therefore not exercised his benevolence to the full: which, because he is omnipotent, he must. A standard theological answer to this objection is that in order for people to be free to sin others must unfortunately be free to bear the brunt: if there is no possibility of causing harm to others then there is no free will. It not difficult to rebut this either: let people have the intention of acting in a way that is harmful to others, but let God prevent them from performing those actions. Having the intention is enough to convict, so God can discharge his function of judgment in a no-harm world in which actors have free will. God is quite capable of constructing such a world since it is logically possible and he is, we can remind ourselves, bounded only by logical possibility.

Secondly, and more importantly, only a small proportion of the misfortunes of suffering humanity is due to the exercise of (supposedly) free will. Most are the result of natural calamities and chance. It is sometime suggested that these offer convenient opportunities for the display of tokens of compassion and succour to the afflicted, and also the opportunity for exercising the Christian capacity for forgiveness.[31] Francis Collins mixes this response with the we've-only-got-finite-minds one:

We may never fully understand the reasons for these painful experiences, but we can *begin to* accept the idea that *there may be* such reasons. In my case I can see, *albeit dimly*, that my daughter's rape was a challenge for me to try to learn the real meaning of forgiveness in a terribly wrenching circumstance. *In complete honesty, I am still working on that.*[32]

As many people have pointed out, this type of response has an unpleasant air to it, implying as it does that some people are to suffer for the benefit of others. Be that as it may, it is difficult if not impossible to understand why an all-powerful, all-good God should arrange things thus. According to James P. Carse, Emeritus Professor of Religion at New York University, it *is* impossible:

It is the problem known as theodicy – the attempt to reconcile an omnipotent God's goodness with the ubiquity of evil. Any number of books have been written on the subject of theodicy attempting to untangle the contradiction within God – unsuccessfully; the problem simply does not go away.[33]

But people keep on trying. Some in desperation fall back on the Original Sin excuse, still orthodox Catholic theology. While there may still be a sizable constituency worldwide sympathetic to it, it depends on accepting a story that is contradicted by the scientific evidence about the origin of life on earth, and a notion of inherited culpability which is, literally, incredible. In any event it conflicts with the hypothesis of an omnibenevolent, omniscient and omnipotent God. So does that other, equally incredible, response much favoured by fundamentalists, that the periodic visitations of indiscriminate suffering are the exhibition of God's anger with a *still-sinning* humanity. Let us move on to saner territory.

Those familiar with the history of modern (i.e. post sixteenth-century) philosophy will know that some distinguished philosophers have tried to resolve the apparent inconsistency by claiming that the evil inflicted on innocents is the necessary condition for a greater good (which, being

[31] E.g. by Richard Swinburne, *The Existence of God*, rev. edn (Oxford: Clarendon Press, 1991), p. 259.

[32] Collins, *The Language of God*, p. 46 (my emphasis). The phrases I have put in italics make it clear how difficult it has been even for this devout man to reconcile a dreadful experience with his professed faith.

[33] James P. Carse, *The Religious Case Against Belief* (London: Penguin, 2008), p. 179. I strongly recommend Carse's excellent book. It is an attempt to extricate what he sees as authentic religion, a frank confession of ignorance in the face of unfathomable mystery, from the divisive, implicitly totalitarian belief-systems which are what the world's religions are to the masses of people who count themselves believers.

omniscient, God can see but we can't). For logical reasons, it is claimed, an optimal world must possess some positive degree of suffering and unpleasantness, since removing it here will simply reproduce something worse there, rather like trying to remove a wrinkle from a badly made suit. At any rate, we can be certain, this argument continues, that God selected the world which contains the least evil: it may not be ideal, but it is the best of all possible worlds. The originator of this argument was Leibniz, co-inventor with Newton of the differential and integral calculus and famously satirised by Voltaire in his novel *Candide* as the hapless Dr Pangloss. As several commentators have remarked, this solution is most plausibly seen as the result of working backwards. For Leibniz, as for many of his contemporaries, the existence of the theistic God was simply taken as a *fact*, since otherwise the universe would have been – for them – totally inexplicable. Given that presumption, it follows that this *must be* the best of all possible worlds.

Working backwards or not, those adopting that solution face the problem that logical consistency does not demand that suffering is the price which has to be paid for some desirable state of affairs to be realised. That good cannot consistently exist in the absence of some contrastive experience of suffering is just not true, and in fact a world of nothing but delight is so far from being thought to be impossible within the creeds of the world's most subscribed-to religions, that they describe the afterlife of the virtuous in precisely those terms.

Which brings us to Heaven . . .

8. THE NEW WORLD

By far the most striking attempt to get round the existence of evil has been *to add an extra dimension*, as physicists are apt to do in similarly pressing circumstances. In this case the extra dimension is *another world* – the next world, in fact. The dolorous history of the Jews between the destruction of the First Temple and the Second raised the question found in early rabbinical literature of why the righteous seemed to suffer as much as the wicked. The Biblical scholar G. A. Wells tells us that at the start of the Common Era some Jews were drawing from the ubiquitous suffering in the world the not-unreasonable inference that God really was *not* omnipotent, and that he divided his rule over creation with powerful demons and devils.[34] This of course contradicted a, if not the, fundamental

[34] G. A. Wells, *The Historical Evidence for Jesus* (Buffalo, NY: Prometheus Books, 1992), p. 34.

tenet of Judaism that God was all-powerful. The reconciliation is recorded in Leviticus Rabah, a series of commentaries and sermons on Leviticus dating from the fifth century CE or before, in which it is stated that there is another world beyond this in which the righteous, and only the righteous, receive their reward. The Christian philosopher Richard Swinburne is also explicit in maintaining that the promise of a heavenly afterlife can be held to reconcile God's love with the seemingly arbitrary and cruel way his creation deals with some of its recipients.[35]

Not only will entry into heaven end all suffering, but in a daring *coup* the tables are deftly turned and suffering, far from being the negative experience it is naively believed to be, becomes a wholly *positive* one. Christian, and especially Catholic, theology now pronounces suffering to be *good*, indeed *very good*. It has a priceless value all its own, for it deepens the sufferer's relationship with God, who in the person of his son also suffered, on the cross. 'In bringing about the Redemption through suffering, Christ raised human suffering to the level of the Redemption', wrote John Paul II, continuing 'Thus each man, in his sufferings, can also become a sharer in the redemptive suffering of Christ.'[36] St Paul, the true fount of Christian theology, was a notorious promoter of suffering, to be fair including his own, extolling its virtues time and again in his Epistles. '[I] now rejoice in my sufferings for you', he told the Colossians.[37]

Nevertheless, it would have been difficult to sell this depressing and unlikely package of the joys of suffering were it not for the promise of the suffering ceasing immediately with the entry (of the virtuous) into heaven and into everlasting joy. Even then, though, there is a rather obvious problem: it is one thing to promise a heavenly afterlife for the righteous, and quite another to provide any tangible evidence for it. After all, people don't seem to come back from the dead to report on the bliss they have been experiencing. But the problem received a dramatic resolution, one familiar to all those with any knowledge of Christianity . . .

9. JESUS CHRIST SUPERSTAR

Suppose there is (i) a representative or avatar of God involved in miraculous events linking him with God, and (ii) a promise supposedly conveyed by God, through that person, of an eternal afterlife in heaven for the virtuous. It is easy to see that (i) enhances the credibility of the promise made in (ii).[38]

[35] Swinburne, *The Existence of God*, pp. 262, 265.

[36] Apostolic Letter, *Salvifici Doloris*, 11 February 1984.

[37] Colossians 1:24.

[38] In Mark 1:24 the unclean spirit driven from the man recognises Jesus: 'I know thee who thou art, the Holy One of God.'

Though there were Old Testament miracles, like the parting of the Red Sea to allow the Israelites to cross in safety, they happened long before they were recorded, and the recording was confined to a mere assertion of fact – and improbable fact at that. With the gospels all that changed, containing as they did what appeared to be detailed historical accounts of a gifted teacher possessing the personal charisma of a Hollywood star, whose claim to be the son of God was strikingly confirmed by the concordance between the Old Testament prophecies and the miraculous events attending his birth and subsequent life, culminating in the most crushingly convincing of all proofs of his divinity, the resurrection and his subsequent reappearance to his disciples.[39] This act of atonement for the collective sin of the human race, this transcendent, redemptive self-sacrifice, was followed by the dramatic affirmation that the sacrificial victim was none other than a persona of the godhead itself.

It's a story made for Hollywood – as, indeed, it turned out to be: *The Greatest Story Ever Told*, in fact. Jesus Christ Superstar was born between three quarters of the way into the first, and the end of the fourth centuries CE. The Christ story has the dramatic and emotional impact of a great novel, as it was intended to: generations of committed writers added, subtracted and generally refined earlier versions of the narrative with that end in mind. The first recorded Christian literature that remains part of the canon are the letters of St Paul, who in the following tortuous sequence of syllogisms (in which familiarity with the deductive rule of contraposition is displayed in a virtuoso, if tiresomely repetitive, performance) links Christ's resurrection directly to the promise of an afterlife with God:

> But if there be no resurrection of the dead, then is Christ not risen. And if Christ be not risen, then is our preaching vain, and your faith is also vain. Yea, and we are found false witnesses of God; because we have testified of God that he raised up Christ; whom he raised not up, if so be that the dead rise not. For if the dead rise not, then is not Christ raised: And if Christ be not raised, your faith is vain.[40]

This lengthy exordium is followed by more in the same vein until we reach the pertinent observation:

> If in this life only we have hope in Christ, we are of all men most miserable.

[39] The Prophet Mohammed was of course also involved in miraculous events. He was an illiterate to whom God, via the Archangel Gabriel, dictated the Koran, by whom he was also taken up into Heaven. Via Mohammed, God promises, in graphic detail, an afterlife in Paradise to the pious. Conditions (i) and (ii) are therefore fulfilled, which helps explain why Islam, like Christianity, became one of the great world religions.

[40] It may have read better in the original Greek.

The miracle of the resurrection of Christ thus assumes crucial importance. It is the promise – in the translation in the King James Bible, 'the first-fruits' – of all our resurrections when, if we obey God, we shall enjoy life everlasting. But when Paul wrote this letter to the Corinthians there was no direct evidence of the resurrection of Christ and his ascent into heaven. Paul himself heard about it from others. Paul did claim that he, among others, had 'seen' Christ, but it is not clear that he meant this literally, or merely that he had had a vision. At any rate the defect was noted and quickly remedied. In the gospels, the first of which (Mark) was written a score of years after this letter, Christ not only rises but makes sure everyone is aware of the fact by returning on a short visit to show himself to his disciples (much the same also had happened of course to his illustrious forebear Moses when the latter returned from Sinai with the Law, except that Moses did not have to die first). Here occurs the famous exchange with Thomas, the doubter. Thomas, a sort of Everyman, needs to be convinced in the way that Everyman does, by empirical evidence – and he is given it by witnessing the spear-wound in Christ's side. Convinced now? You bet, says Thomas. And who wouldn't be?

According to the gospels, the miracle of Christ's resurrection and reappearance on earth was the triumphant culmination of an already highly successful career as a miracle-worker. Significantly, that career is not once mentioned by Paul. It is not even clear, for that matter, and scholars remain divided on the question, whether Jesus as a real historical character ever existed. There seems to be little or no reputable independent evidence to support the claim that he did. There is a passage in Tacitus that mentions his crucifixion, but this was written after the gospels and textual evidence suggests that Tacitus is reporting what he had been told by evangelical Christians. The first-century Jewish historian Josephus mentions him in two passages in *The Antiquities of the Jews* but these appear to be later interpolations. Be that as it may, the *coup de théatre* provided by the resurrection-and-return narrative appeared to give the ultimate patent of celestial authority to the promise of an afterlife in heaven.

And of course many people believed it: it was, as Paul realised it would be, the foundation-stone of Christian belief. Unfortunately or fortunately, depending on how you look at these things, the later gospel accounts of the resurrection and subsequent reappearance are known to be the result of sometimes arbitrary inclusions in and exclusions from the canon, 'harmonisations', many imperfect, shot through with inconsistencies even in the central story of the death and resurrection, copying errors, and all originating in hearsay or simply made up. None of the gospels' authors, whoever they were, were eye-witnesses.[41] The gospels were written anonymously forty years or so after Christ's death, in Greek, not Aramaic which was the language he spoke. The synoptic gospels are widely thought to have their origin in Mark's, and Mark's account of the resurrection was added later by another hand. Many Christian commentators cite the degree of unanimity in the gospels that something truly miraculous happened to someone called Christ at the end of the first third of the first century CE. If there is such agreement, must there not be something to have caused it which was broadly as described? That claim displays only an extraordinary naivety. The gospels which emerged from all the siftings *aimed* to tell that story, so it is hardly surprising that they did.[42] The only thing that is surprising is that they still manage to contradict each other to the great extent that they do.

Miracle-working also seems to have been something of a stock-in-trade of itinerant shamans, and it has been argued that Jesus's were fairly typical of the sort of magic peddled in the region at the time.[43] Some seem to have been contrived to be similar to familiar scriptural stories, like the feeding of the five thousand with five loaves and two fishes, with some left over after the meal, evoking the memory of Elijah feeding a hundred men with twenty loaves. For added effect Mark at a later point in his gospel increased the number of people fed and decreased the amount of food. Two-and-a-half centuries ago David Hume enunciated what in retrospect is the fairly obvious principle that 'no testimony is sufficient to establish a miracle, unless the testimony be of such a kind, that its falsehood would be more miraculous, than the fact, which it endeavours to establish'.[44] Given everything that is known about the provenance of the texts relating the life and doings of Jesus, and the fact that they were written precisely with a view to gaining followers, they are not evidence to hang a dog. The Biblical scholar Geza Vermes makes the following comment:

[41] Robin Lane Fox argues that the author of the fourth gospel, St John, was none other than the 'beloved disciple' John himself (*The Unauthorized Version: Truth and Fiction in the Bible* (London: Viking, 1991), chapter 21). This is disputed by other scholars, however, among them Geza Vermes, *The Authentic Gospel of Jesus* (London: Penguin, 2004), pp. xii–xiii.

[42] For a much more detailed account see Matt McCormick, *The Case Against Christ: Why Believing is No Longer Reasonable* (Buffalo, NY: Prometheus Books, forthcoming).

[43] Nicholas Humphrey, *Leaps of Faith: Science, Miracles and the Search for the Supernatural* (New York: Copernicus, 1999), p. 96.

[44] David Hume, 'Of Miracles', in *An Enquiry Concerning Human Understanding* (Lasalle, IL: Open Court, 1988). Hume's observation is just the easily provable assertion that the miracle is more likely than not, given the testimony, just in case the probability that the testimony is false is smaller than the prior probability of the miracle occurring.

The [Christian] church, in the footsteps of St Paul, its true founder, succeeded in removing the major obstacle impeding the dissemination of Jesus' message. Jesus considered his mission to be restricted to Jews and explicitly ordered his envoys not to preach the gospel to Gentiles. The apostles, who were delivering a freshly-tailored message to Jews about the Messiahship of Jesus, on witnessing the progressive fiasco of the evangelization at home gave in to Paul's insistent pressure, and opened the church to all the nations. The pagans entered in droves, first diluting and soon entirely transforming the Jewish heritage of Jesus. They justified the change by the belief, arising from the late Gospel of John, that the Holy Spirit was sent by Jesus to hand out new revelation and dispense afresh 'all the truth' (John 14:16–17; 16:13).[45]

Before we leave the genuinely fascinating story of Jesus we might reflect on a curious feature of it, namely his atonement to God for the sins of mankind. One might object that he has not really atoned for the sins I personally might, and almost certainly will, commit as an essentially sin-ridden human being, since according to received theological doctrine these will still cause me to be judged adversely. The orthodox resolution of the problem is that Jesus's crucifixion gave mankind the *possibility* of redemption, a redemption that can be achieved by *choosing* to be saved, i.e. by following Christ's precepts. Even if you are disposed to accept that, however, you are still not out of the logical wood, because of the fact, or fact according to Christian theology, that it is *God himself* who is atoning in the person of his son who, as Bishop Arius had to be reminded, is consubstantial with his father. St Anselm, keenly aware of the magnitude of the problem, made a valiant attempt to resolve it by arguing that since the payment owed by mankind to God, to annul the terrible sin of Adam and Eve, was of such magnitude that only God could pay it, but did not of course owe it, it was necessary to create a God-Man to redeem the debt.

James Carse remarks that Anselm's argument was 'certainly ingenious',[46] but to a rational person not already desensitized to theological squarings of the circle it fails in any way to lessen the muddle (Carse agrees). The following lines of Shakespeare's allegorical poem 'The Phoenix and the Turtle[dove]' might well have been written with the mysterious joint personage of God the father and God the son in mind:

> Property was thus appalled,
> That the self was not the same;
> Single nature's double name
> Neither two nor one was called.

[45] Vermes, *The Authentic Gospel of Jesus*, p. 417.
[46] Carse, *The Religious Case Against Belief*, p. 122.

Reason, in itself confounded,
Saw division grow together,
To themselves yet either neither,
Simple were so well compounded,

That it cried, How true a twain
Seemeth this concordant one!
Love hath reason, reason none,
If what parts can so remain.

The mystery of God the father and God the son being one is only deepened by the addition of one more component, God the Holy Ghost, to make up the Threefold God. 'All good things are three', says the German proverb.[47]

The historical anthropologist's explanation of the puzzlingly discordant features of Christianity is that they are the result of mixing various ancient myths and religious traditions into a sort of theological *tutti frutti*. The Trinity might be, for example, the merging of a prior polytheism into a (sort of) monotheism with a multi-part God. There are certainly strong echoes of older religions and cults: of the sacrifice of the king to propitiate the gods and ensure the harvest; of the Greek myths in which demigods and even gods are born to mortal women impregnated by a god (compare the Virgin birth); of the different powers and responsibilities of lesser divinities becoming assumed by the Christian saints, Mary and the multi-charactered God himself; of solstitial and equinoctial rites (Christmas was deliberately dated to coincide with the pagan celebration of the rebirth of the unconquered sun); and so on. As punishment for his enormous bequest to men (fire stolen from Olympus), the Titan-god Prometheus is sacrificed by being tied to a stake and having his liver consumed by an eagle; as further punishment – of men this time – Zeus created woman in the form of Pandora, who out of curiosity released all the evils on humanity.

Sir James Frazer was one of the first anthropologists to comment on the appropriation of older myths and rituals by the Christian Church. This characteristic passage from *The Golden Bough* imaginatively associates the death and resurrection of Christ with that of Adonis, and Michelangelo's famous *Pietá* with pagan Greek art:

When we reflect how often the Church has skilfully contrived to plant the seeds of the new faith on the old stock of paganism, we may surmise that the Easter celebration of the dead and risen Christ was grafted upon a similar celebration of the dead and risen Adonis, which, as we have seen reason to believe, was celebrated

[47] *Alle guten Dinge sind drei.*

in Syria at the same season. The type, created by Greek artists, of the sorrowful goddess with her dying lover in her arms, resembles and may have been the model of the *Pietá* of Christian art, the Virgin with the dead body of her divine Son in her lap, of which the most celebrated example is the one by Michael Angelo in St Peter's.[48]

Of even more ancient lineage, Frazer might have added, is the cult of the Virgin Mary herself, to whom the Synod of Ephesus in 431 CE gave the title 'Mother of God', and whom modern Catholicism, without any scriptural foundation whatever, has on her death being taken 'body and soul' into heaven (the Assumption). The absorption of what is most likely the cult of the ancient goddess of fertility and motherhood, the Magna Mater,[49] into Christianity was one of history's great merger deals, transforming the masculine abstraction of the Trinitarian God into a more down-to-earth, mixed-sex *family team.* Coincidentally or not, St Peter's in Rome is built on the site of a temple dedicated to the Magna Mater. It might also be added that the virgin goddess Diana, also a patroness of motherhood and frequently referred to as the Queen of Heaven, had a vigorous cult at Ephesus, especially powerful at the time St Paul was making his whistle-stop tour of southern Europe and Asia Minor. Her feast day was around the date of the Assumption . . .

10. COPING WITH LOGICAL DISASTERS

The theological counters to the problem of evil have more than an air of desperation about them, like someone doing their best to square the circle while knowing full well that it cannot be done. From the time of Tertullian onwards (he was the author of the famous remark 'It is certain because it is impossible'[50]), some people have invested a great deal of time and effort in following the White Queen in *Through the Looking Glass* in believing as many as six impossible things before breakfast. The odds, a priori and a posteriori, against the existence of an omniscient, omnipotent and omnibenevolent God certainly seem too long to be comfortable. This is not to say that those who deny that pessimism on that score is justified

48 Sir James Frazer, *The Golden Bough* (New York: Macmillan, 1922), p. 345.

49 Astarte and Isis were other incarnations (so to speak). Frazer comments on the fact that a typical picture of Isis with the infant Horus at her breast was actually worshipped by 'ignorant Christians' as an image of Mary with the infant Jesus.

50 'Certum est, quia impossibile.' Tertullian was a third-century CE Roman convert to Christianity and one of its earliest theologians. Among his other distinctive doctrinal contributions was the claim that contraception is a form of murder, a claim still maintained today, with disastrous consequences for an overpopulated world, by the Catholic Church.

are all necessarily ignorant of logic or science. How people respond to conflicts with the facts and with other parts of officially approved doctrine is usually a complex matter, depending on a number of factors most of which have little to do with a sensitivity to logic. Emotional and practical considerations are typically pre-eminent. If someone holds a gun to my head and tells me to declare publicly that $2 + 2 = 5$, I will do so promptly, as would any rational person. You would certainly be naive to think that what you might feel to be compelling evidence against or for a position should necessarily influence your policy. The leaders of the Soviet bloc up to 1989 were confronted daily with evidence that the socio-economic system they imposed on a mostly very unwilling population was failing badly to deliver the goods, literally and figuratively. It is unlikely that very many believed in the genuine merits of the system they were defending, and much more likely that they were determined to maintain the power and privileges which their position within it bestowed on them. The parallels with religious leaders today are too obvious to need underlining.

But not everyone who persists in believing what all the evidence declares extremely unlikely is a cynical crook. The sorts of desperate measures to avoid inconsistency that we have witnessed are very often made by people who are what contemporary jargon calls 'deeply conflicted', incapable of abandoning a very strongly held belief despite an obvious disagreement with the facts. There is also, of course, that distressing feature of human psychology much exploited by the unscrupulous: gullibility and a desire to believe what one wishes were true even when the facts unequivocally declare otherwise. There are stories of many ordinary people in the Soviet Union of the 1930s and 1940s who, even when given the most detailed evidence of the horrors of Stalin's regime, still managed to find ways to exonerate him (and still do: something like a rehabilitation of this human monster seems to be under way in Russia), even though Stalin certainly knew what was going on ('omniscient'[51]), had absolute power ('omnipotent') and, most importantly, was the loving Father of his People, Papa Stalin.[52]

11. DEAD BUT HE WON'T LIE DOWN!

'God is dead', famously proclaimed the German classical philologist/philosopher/guru, Friedrich Nietzsche, in the late nineteenth century.

[51] 'Genghis Khan with a telephone', to quote Trotsky's arresting – and sadly prescient – phrase.

[52] Apparently he would roar with laughter on being told that some poor victim had been dragged off to execution declaiming that when Stalin heard about it the executioners would be shot.

Though the obituary notice was, as it turned out, premature, there seemed nonetheless a fairly clear indication that God's days were numbered and that the number was not large. Always in more or less desperate trouble with the increasing successes of secular science, He was subjected to brutal punishment at the hands, if not of Darwin, then Darwin's less delicate followers, and came close to being counted out when it was finally demonstrated that the Biblical story of the Creation could not be literally true.

It is not only science that seems to have put a large question mark over God's future. So has humanity's moral conscience. Where man was at one time content to fear, he has increasingly demanded of his God that He work a little harder to earn His keep. To some extent God was able to respond to public opinion by undergoing the great theological revolution whose issue was Christianity and the partial replacement of the old tribal God of Abraham with a new God of Love whose son preached the Sermon on the Mount. Liberal theological wisdom now dispenses the idea of something like a People's God, a pleasant, considerate individual, superhuman indeed, but in a Nice sort of way, constantly worrying about His people and their problems, sorrowing where they sorrow and rejoicing where they rejoice. Old sins are steadily giving way to new quasi-medical pathologies, like the 'objective disorder' which the Roman Catholic Church now deems homosexuality, and the Devil could be reasonably excused for considering a severance-payment.

But in retrospect that revolution looks as if it might have contained the seeds of its own destruction. Earthquake, tempest, disease, to say nothing of the periodic infliction of terror and suffering by one part of human creation on another, might have posed no logical threat to the vindictive warlords of the ancient religions, but they seem barely consistent with this new super-social-worker. Woody Allen's suggestion[53] that God is simply an underachiever might exonerate a less capable individual but hardly an omnipotent, omniscient, omnipresent and all-caring Demiurge. Does God simply doze off from time to time? Unthinkable, surely. And a promised afterlife of pure felicity for the deserving might offset the problem somewhat if it came with a copper-bottomed guarantee, but even the most devout have been known to harbour doubts that they are actually devout enough to evade the all-seeing eye of God, and worse, that the promise might after all be false.

[53] As Count Boris Grushenko in the film *Love and Death*, a hilarious burlesque of *War and Peace*.

But in what is looking like one of the greatest reversals of fortune ever witnessed, God in His darkest hours seems to have gathered new strength from the very quarter from which he looked most threatened: science itself. The reversal is quite remarkable. In book after book and article after article, with arguments ranging from the very simple to the highly recondite and technical, a number of physicists, biologists, geneticists and even mathematicians are now pronouncing that the world which science is uncovering is pointing more and more unequivocally to the existence of a Cosmic Designer, of a Supreme Intelligence which shaped it, and shaped it specifically for human purposes.

To some extent this had happened before. The natural theology of the eighteenth and early nineteenth centuries held up nature and its workings, in particular the miraculous complexity of living things, as the work of an intelligent designer. Darwin put paid to that, but now it seems that the check may have been only temporary: new calculations of the immense improbability of an orderly, life-supporting cosmos are being cited by people of established scientific reputation as evidence of intelligent design by a super-intelligent Someone who assigns us central importance in His scheme.

The old prizefighter, on the point of being counted out, seems to have been suddenly pulled to his feet and handed the title – by his opponent! Can this really be true? The short answer is no. The long answer will start in the next chapter, with a little excursion into logic and methodology, and carry through to the end of the book.

EXERCISE

'But support for the existence of God moves far beyond the realm of science. Within the Christian faith, there is also the powerful evidence that God revealed himself to mankind through Jesus Christ two millennia ago. This is well-documented not just in the scriptures and other testimony but also in a wealth of archaeological findings.' Comment.

MAIN POINTS OF CHAPTER 2

- The claim of Stephen Jay Gould that science and religion are overlapping 'magisteria', with science governing the domain of factuality, and religion that of morality and 'meaning', is rejected. The Abrahamic religions, like nearly all major religions, are based on fundamental *factual* claims without which they would merely be unexplained lists of prohibitions and injunctions.

- Pascal Boyer's claim that religions do not aim to explain is rejected, at any rate as far as the Abrahamic religions are concerned. These all purport to explain, in terms of God's will, the existence of the universe, of the distinctive character of mankind and mankind's obligation to keep the moral law.
- A core explanatory principle of all three of those religions is that God is all-powerful, all-knowing and all-good. This leads to problems of consistency, sometimes purely internal, like the omnipotence paradox, and sometimes conflict with accepted fact, as with the so-called Problem of Evil.
- The promise of a joyous afterlife for the virtuous attempts to bring religious theory and the Problem of Evil into harmony.
- The credibility of that promise is supposed to be enhanced by the appearance of an individual who shows himself in close contact with God by being the subject of suitably miraculous events.
- In Christianity that individual, who may or may not have been a real person, is Jesus. He was credited after his death not only with being a charismatic leader, but most importantly the guarantor of the promise that those who lived sufficiently good lives would achieve eternal bliss in heaven.

CHAPTER 3

How to reason if you must

'There are lies, damned lies, and statistics.'[1]

1. INFINITY-NOTHING

In this chapter we shall be developing the logical tools – very minimal tools which require no special expertise to use – for evaluating a type of argument – *probabilistic* – which has always been a feature of the discussion of the evidence for, or against, God's existence. We shall start by looking at one of the most famous, and still widely employed, due to one of the great pioneers of the modern theory of probability, the mathematician and Christian mystic Blaise Pascal. His argument is actually a prudential argument less for belief as such than for acting as if you believed, but as he pointed out, a long enough period of habituation to a life of apparent devotion will very likely lead to the devotion becoming more than just apparent. 'Appetite comes with eating', says the French proverb.

Pascal's argument turns on the infinite bliss rewarding the devout in the afterlife. In the preceding chapter we observed that belief in such an afterlife gave anyone beset by misfortune in this life a compensatory hope of something better to come. Like John Bunyan's Pilgrim:

> Hobgoblin nor foul fiend
> Can daunt his spirit.
> He knows he at the end
> Shall life inherit.[2]

And a very nice life indeed. Heavenly, in fact. Together with the other part of the deal, eternal damnation in Hell being prodded by demons, it gives one a good reason for living a less exciting and possibly less convenient life

[1] Benjamin Disraeli.

[2] There is a poignancy to these lines. They were written in Bedford jail where Bunyan was serving a twelve-year sentence for unauthorised preaching. *Twelve years.*

of Christian virtue. The heaven and hell of Islam are presented in more graphic terms: the damned in hell 'will taste no coolness or drink, except one that is scalding and dark', while in heaven there are 'private gardens, vineyards, nubile, well-matched companions, and an overflowing cup'.[3] It is very much a male paradise. Martyrdom is worth it, as indeed many of the current wave of (male) terrorists believe it to be. But there is the small matter of how *likely* you think the package, Christian or Muslim, is. If you entertain any doubts on the matter – you may not be entirely convinced by the Resurrection story, since you know no eye-witnesses and the Gospels contain grave inconsistencies – you may not feel it so worth your while to resist sinful temptations in this life. It all seems to depend on the probability you should attach to God. How are you supposed to evaluate that?

Pascal's ingenious argument is that in fact you don't have to: *once you have correctly specified the decision-model* (to use today's jargon), *it becomes evident that you should believe in God.* This argument, now known as Pascal's Wager, was discovered after Pascal's death in a collection of handwritten notes intended to be an extended argument for Christian belief. Later collected and published, in 1670, under the title *Pensées*, those notes have passed beyond the confines of Christian theology into the treasury of world literature. The Wager occurs in a section of the *Pensées* entitled '*Infini-rien*' ('Infinity-nothing'; we will see in a moment why this is an appropriate title). In fact there is more than one argument in this section, but there is one in particular that people generally have in mind when they refer to Pascal's Wager, and it is the one I will now describe.

The argument, often called the *dominating expectations* argument, is very simple, based on a rule for choosing among different courses of action which is still regarded, subject to some mathematical qualifications, as no less valid now than it was when Pascal wrote. The rule is that when choosing among different courses of action the rational agent selects that act – if there is just one – having the greatest *expected utility*, where the expected utility of an act is the probability-weighted average of the utilities (i.e. *values*) attaching to its various possible outcomes. Applied to the act of believing, or to be more accurate behaving as if you believed, the rule computes the expected value of believing as the probability of God's existing multiplied by the reward accruing to believing if he actually does exist, *plus* the probability of God's not existing multiplied by the penalty of believing when in fact he doesn't exist. The 'infini-rien' are those rewards and penalties respectively. But because infinity multiplied by any nonzero

[3] Koran 78:24–35.

number, however tiny, is still infinity, then as long as the probability of God's existing is nonzero, the expected value of believing is infinite. So you should act as if you believed: 'Wager then, that He exists.'

Ingenious though it may sound, the argument is fallacious. There is actually nothing wrong with the purely probabilistic part of it: it barely plays a role. What does the real work are two add-ons to the underlying probability theory: (i) the rule that the criterion for choice between alternative courses of action is the expected utility rule, and (ii) the assignments of utilities themselves. (i) is still widely touted today and claims rigorous justifications from first principles, but some of those principles (mainly, a type of independence principle) have been questioned in the light of rather compelling intuitive counterexamples.[4]

But (ii), with its infinite value attached to believing, is a complete non-starter. The basic axioms of utility theory, adopted to avoid the inconsistencies known to arise from postulating infinite utilities, have as a consequence that all utility functions, i.e. functions which assign goods a value on a so-called utility scale, are bounded above by a finite value (it immediately follows that utilities cannot be arbitrarily *finitely* large either). But if only a finite utility is attached to heaven then that cannot always be guaranteed to outweigh a sufficiently small nonzero probability of God's existence. So Pascal's argument collapses. Don't by the way think that you can rescue it by refraining from putting the 'number' infinity to the reward for belief, reasoning that an eternity in heaven is its own reward without having to be quantified. Unfortunately for Pascal's argument, the infinity is essential to it since in being greater than any finite number it is the only quantity that can multiply an arbitrarily small but finite probability and still yield a quantity greater than any finite number.[5]

It is not only in assigning infinite utility to the reward for belief in God if God exists that dooms Pascal's argument. People have pointed out that it fails also if you are allowed so-called 'mixed strategies' (an example of a mixed strategy is tossing a fair coin and believing if it lands heads and disbelieving if it lands tails), but there is a much more obvious

[4] The so-called Allais paradox is the best known and most persuasive. See L. J. Savage, *The Foundations of Statistics* (New York: Dover Publications, 1954), pp. 101–3 for a discussion.

[5] From the late nineteenth century to the second half of the twentieth, it was almost universally assumed by mathematicians that talk of infinitely large and infinitely small numbers was inconsistent nonsense. Using a result in mathematical logic the logician and mathematician Abraham Robinson proved that it is consistent to assume that such numbers exist *and that they obey the same arithmetical rules* as the real numbers themselves.

objection. God is just a bundle of properties, the salient one for Pascal's argument being a propensity to reward belief with heaven and disbelief with hell. Once you assign a positive probability to this bundle existing, the argument speeds through. But here is another bundle of properties, gathered into the person of Dog: Dog is thoroughly bad, but also has the capacity to reward belief with infinite pleasure and disbelief with infinite pain. Dog is certainly a possible existent if God is. Assign the existence of Dog a positive probability and you have a Pascal's Wager for Dog. But, you might say, Dog merits *zero* probability, while for the great majority of Pascal's audience the Christian God didn't. That is far from clear, however: publicly avowed atheism was very dangerous while not a few, with memories fresh of war, disease and death, might well have opted for equality.[6]

2. THE PROSECUTOR'S FALLACY

Pascal's Wager is the only decision-theoretic argument I know of to be enlisted in a theological cause – and though fallacious, it isn't incorrect *probabilistic* reasoning as such that is the cause. That is not the case with the great majority of the probabilistic arguments for God, and it is these that will occupy a good deal of the remainder of this book. To evaluate these some exposure to the basic rules of probability is usually desirable, and sometimes more than just desirable. It is a frequently documented fact that people in general are vulnerable to being seduced by certain patterns of fallacious probabilistic reasoning. Unfortunately, these patterns of reasoning are rather strongly represented in the recent literature on God and the evidence for and against his existence.

A highly topical example is the so-called *fine-tuning problem.* In the last half-century or so it has been observed that some fundamental physical constants – never mind which for now; we shall be going into that later – seem to have been fine-tuned to permit a life-friendly universe, with a tolerance for some of these constants so small it is widely agreed to be vastly too improbable to be due simply to chance: indeed, people have worked out the magnitude of the improbability and it is billions to one against:

[6] The playwright Christopher Marlowe, the contemporary of Shakespeare to whom we owe the much-quoted question 'Was this the face that launched a thousand ships?', was once accused of, among other things, spelling 'God' backwards, for which he might have been executed. In fact he was acquitted, only to be later murdered in a brawl in Deptford (now thought to have been an assassination ordered by the Secretary of State Sir Robert Cecil).

> [t]he chance that all those constants would take on the values necessary to result in a stable universe capable of sustaining complex life-forms is almost infinitesimal. And yet, those are the parameters that we observe. In sum, our universe is wildly improbable.[7]

Certainly improbable enough, Collins implies, that it should be dismissed as a serious possibility. But if it is rejected then it seems we are left with only one possible explanation: the universe was *deliberately* fine-tuned for life (and we all know by Whom).

There are two questionable, indeed more than questionable, moves in reaching that conclusion. One, fairly easily spotted, is the assumption that some sort of purposeful agency is the only alternative to chance. In fact, as we shall see later, there is rather a large number of possible alternatives (to put it mildly). Possibly less obviously fallacious – it has beguiled many and continues to do so – is the inference that if the truth of a hypothesis would make some phenomenon extremely unlikely to be observed, then the observation of that phenomenon makes the hypothesis correspondingly unlikely to be true. This inference is known as *the Prosecutor's Fallacy*. That it is certainly a fallacy is evident when we consider all the possible sequences of heads and tails that could result from flipping what looks like a fair coin enough times: say, 20. Each one of the possible resulting sequences has a probability smaller than one divided by a million (actually it's a half to the power 20) given the assumption that the coin is fair. That is a very small number, far below a common standard set by statistical tests for rejection (I shall come back to that topic later: its own rationale is also questionable). But one of those sequences must occur, so it seems that whatever happens, even if we get a sequence with roughly 50% heads and 50% tails, we have to infer that the hypothesis of fairness is exceptionally unlikely, come what may. That can't be correct on purely logical grounds.

Despite the existence of easily manufactured counterexamples like that, the Prosecutor's Fallacy continues to exercise a peculiar allure. Nearly all the recent probabilistic arguments for God, like Collins's above, rest on it. Even highly numerate non-theistic scientists commit it. Having argued that a random shuffling of amino acids would have a chance of only $10^{-40,000}$ of producing the 2,000 or so enzymes, Hoyle and Wickramasinghe continue:

7 Francis Collins, *The Language of God* (New York: Free Press, 2006), p. 74. Collins's observation is not quite accurate. What was shown (by Steven Weinberg and others) is that those constants need to take values within what appears to be a remarkably small region of their possible values if the universe is to be a stable enough platform for life to evolve on it.

any theory with a probability of being correct that is larger than one part in $10^{40,000}$ must be judged superior to random shuffling. The theory that life was assembled by an intelligence has, we believe, a probability vastly higher than one part in $10^{40,000}$ of being the correct explanation.[8]

Notice how Hoyle and Wickramasinghe simply transfer *unchanged* the very small probability of the data – in this case the construction of the enzymes – given by the random-shuffling hypothesis to the probability of the hypothesis itself, given the data. But that is just the Prosecutor's Fallacy.

The Prosecutor's Fallacy is so-called because it first came to widespread attention in courts of law, where it has been known to be partly or wholly responsible for several unsafe convictions. It supports, if that is the right word, a common misapprehension about DNA matching. Suppose that there is a match between your DNA and a good sample taken from a crime scene. The chance of the match if you are not the perpetrator is usually very, very small, but it is of course much larger if you are the perpetrator. Hence, many people conclude, in the absence of any further information it is much more likely than not that you are the perpetrator. Unfortunately for that inference, if there were only two people whose DNA matched the sample, it would incriminate them equally! If, moreover, there is ample documentary evidence that at the time of the crime you were addressing the local antiquarian society on the subject of Assyrian pottery then it is of course practically certain that you're not guilty.

There have been some recent chilling judicial examples of the fallacy. It was involved in the conviction for murder several years ago in the UK of a young mother whose two children died in what are called 'cot-deaths', and also in the conviction in 2003 of a Dutch hospital nurse, Lucia de Berk, who was sentenced to life imprisonment for seven murders and three attempted murders allegedly carried out in a children's hospital in The Hague. Both women were subsequently acquitted, though the British woman later committed suicide and the Dutch woman spent seven years in jail, subject to 'coerced psychological treatment', before being released. There was little or nothing to incriminate either woman directly, and the prosecution relied largely on an estimate of the improbability of the deaths on the presumption that the accused were innocent of murdering the victims. In both cases the calculations of the improbability were shown to be incorrect and revised downwards: in the Dutch case from 1 in 342,000 to 1 in a million – still very small.

[8] Fred Hoyle and Chandra Wickramasinghe, *Evolution from Space* (London: J. M. Dent & Sons, 1981), p. 141.

3. THE HARVARD MEDICAL SCHOOL TEST

A less tragic, indeed positively entertaining and certainly instructive, example of the Prosecutor's Fallacy has become celebrated in the literature on pathologies of reasoning. The efficiency of a diagnostic test is often characterised in terms of two known or estimated statistical parameters, the so-called *false negative* and *false positive* rates of the test. These are respectively the chance of the test giving the outcome 'negative' when the subject does in fact have the disease, and the chance of the test giving the outcome 'positive' when the subject doesn't have the disease. A simple fictitious test-question involving the interpretation of these parameters was given to faculty and students at the prestigious Harvard Medical School, and – because most of the replies were wrong – it has become a famous cautionary lesson for aspiring medical practitioners.

The question asked was this. Suppose that a diagnostic test for a disease has just the two outcomes, positive and negative, and that the false negative rate is 0 and the false positive rate is 5%. Suppose also that the incidence of that disease in the population is 1 in 1,000, i.e. 0.1%. A subject, assumed to be randomly selected from the population, is given the test and the result is 'positive'. What is the probability, given that evidence, that they have the disease? Most of the respondents gave the answer of 95% or thereabouts, inferring from there being a 5% chance of testing positive when the disease is not present to a 5% chance of the disease not being present when the test shows positive. In other words, just as we saw Hoyle and Wickramasinghe do earlier, those respondents straightforwardly equate a small probability of testing positive without the disease being present to the same small probability of the disease not being present in a test with a positive outcome. And it is fallacious. Indeed, it isn't difficult to see that the answer of 95% is actually *wildly* wrong, and what the correct answer is. Think of 1,000 balls in an urn, with one of them labelled D (the 1 in 1,000 having the disease). Suppose that all the balls are also numbered 1 or 0: 1 means testing positive, 0 testing negative. Given the false-negative rate of 0%, the D-ball must be numbered 1. We have to approximate the false-positive rate of 5%, but of the 999 non-D balls it is close enough to think of 50 of them carrying the number 1. That means that of the 51 balls carrying the number 1, only one carries the D label. Assuming random selection from the urn, that gives a 1 in 51 chance of a selected 1-ball being the D-ball. In other words, the probability that a subject who tests positive has the disease is about 1 in 51, i.e. *slightly under 2%* – a bit different from

95%![9] Note the crucial role played by the 1 in 1,000 incidence of the disease in the population. We shall shortly discover the role that it plays in the general formula for calculating odds in the light of evidence, and how to calculate *exactly* the correct answer.

4. AND SO TO GOD

There is a common variant of the Prosecutor's Fallacy which we will come across time and again in the following chapters. The Fallacy, recall, is the inference that if the occurrence of an event A is assigned a very small probability by a hypothesis H, then the occurrence of A implies a correspondingly small probability of H. This variant is the inference that if H assigns an event E a much smaller probability than does H′, then the probability of H given the occurrence of E must be correspondingly smaller than that of H′. Here is a straightforwardly God-related example, due to Keith Ward, Regius Professor of Divinity at the University of Oxford. Discussing the origins of the chemistry necessary for life, Ward states that

> [t]he hypothesis of God makes the existence of [molecular] replicators much more likely than the materialistic hypothesis, and it is *therefore* to be preferred[10] (my emphasis).

Even if the premise is granted that the hypothesis of God makes the existence of those replicators much more likely than the materialistic hypothesis – and as we shall see later, that is far from obviously true – the 'therefore' is quite fallacious. Consider the flipped coin again (coins are always good examples). This time I flip the coin not 20 but 100 times and observe 52 heads. Let E describe the sample-sequence. One might well think that E supports the claim that the coin is approximately fair (a fair coin is defined to be one that has a half chance of landing heads). But the fair-coin hypothesis gives the outcomes, in the order of heads and tails in which we observed them, an absolutely minuscule probability ($^1/_2$ multiplied by itself 100 times). Now consider the alternative hypothesis 'Santa Claus willed that exact sequence of 52 heads and 48 tails, and whatever Santa wills, happens.' It gives E the maximum probability of 1. So it 'is therefore to be preferred', according to Ward's logic (perhaps it is

[9] You might now like to think twice before immediately having follow-up treatment after a positive result from a diagnostic test – which will also usually have much worse false-positive and false-negative statistics.

[10] Keith Ward, *God, Chance and Necessity* (Oxford: Oneworld, 1996), p. 118.

*theo*logic). But of course the Santa Claus hypothesis is *not* to be preferred. We all know why not, and that is because we have a very good prior reason to suppose that it is false, indeed we are (assuming no otherwise-abnormal circumstances have occurred) certain that it is false.

The Prosecutor's Fallacy and its variants are endemic. The classical reversing-the-improbabilities version is probably so beguiling because it mimics a deductive rule, known as the *Rule of Contraposition*, which we use very often and in a variety of circumstances, even if we don't know its name or even that we are using a rule at all. This says that if the truth of H entails the falsity of E, then the truth of E entails the falsity of H. There is a probabilistic counterpart to this which is valid: if the probability of E is zero given H, then the probability of H is zero given E (assuming that the so-called 'prior probabilities' of H and E are themselves nonzero). The Prosecutor's Fallacy, that if it is *very unlikely* that E would be true given H, then it is very unlikely that H would be true given E, may seem only a small perturbation of this probabilistic counterpart. Even so, where that is valid, the perturbation is not: move away from zero, *by however small an amount*, and the implication fails. Why? Well, we can guess the answer from the examples we have looked at: *it can be overridden by a sufficiently large antecedent probability of H being true.*[11] There was a very large antecedent probability of the subject in the Harvard Medical School Test *not* having the disease (999/1000); there is a much larger antecedent probability that the sample of coin-tosses was produced by a random mechanism (the fair coin) than that it was the work of Santa Claus.

It would be nice, however, to have a clear set of universally agreed rules that will transform that conjecture into a rigorous formal argument. Well, we do. The rules are called *the laws of probability*, and it is time to inspect them – or some of them. No recondite technical material is about to be thrust on anyone in what follows: the discussion will proceed at a very informal level.

5. THE LAWS OF PROBABILITY . . .

Historically, the first way that people expressed their uncertainties using numbers was in terms of *odds*. Probabilities as such, which are just odds

[11] There are other ways. For example, E might entail the truth of H, so that H would certainly be true if E were, and yet be very improbable if H is true. For example, suppose a number from 1 to 1,000 is selected randomly, and let H state that the number is not 1,000, and E state that it is 1. E is very unlikely if H is true but H is certainly true if E is.

on a finite, symmetrical scale, arrived much later. Shakespeare gives us a typical example of odds-speak:

> *Speed:* Sir, Proteus, save you! Saw you my Master?
> *Proteus:* But now he parted hence, to embark for Milan.
> *Speed:* Twenty to one, then he is shipp'd already.

To quote another distinguished source, the venerable British Horseracing Authority: 'In the world of betting, the odds . . . are a way of expressing the probability of a horse winning a race.'

For those who have not spent much time at the racetrack, or in casinos, odds are the ratio in which the total stake in a bet is divided between the bettors, where the total stake is just the sum of what each person risks losing – their own stake – if they lose the bet. For example, suppose A is some factual prediction being bet on, with two individuals Esther and Lester doing the betting, where the terms of the bet are that Esther gets 10 dollars from Lester if A turns out to be true, and Lester gets 20 dollars from Esther if A is false. Esther's stake is 20 dollars and Lester's is 10, and the total stake is thus $10 + 20 = 30$ dollars. The odds at which Esther is betting on A are then said to be the ratio 20:10, i.e. 2:1 (Lester is betting *against* A at the reciprocal odds 1:2). Obviously, in risking 20 dollars to receive just 10 if A is true Esther must think A quite likely to be true, and certainly more likely than not. If those odds also happen to be her *fair odds*, in the sense that she thinks they don't actually differentially advantage her over Lester, then as we shall see in a moment, she's putting a probability of $^2/_3$ on A's being true.[12]

As any ratio x:y is equal to x/y: 1 we can make the odds scale a simple linear scale going from 0 to infinity. That scale is however obviously very asymmetrical, since the point 1 on it representing even-money odds is much closer to 0 than infinity. The probability scale, of real numbers between 0 and 1 inclusive, was invented to 'symmetrise' and put an upper number bound on the odds scale. It does this by transforming odds (od) into probabilities (p) by the rule $p = od/(1 + od)$. This is how we get the probability of $^2/_3$, $2/(1 + 2)$, from odds of 2:1. Under this transformation even-money odds become the probability $^1/_2$, lying nicely in the middle of the finite probability scale bounded below by 0 and above by 1. For

[12] Referring back to the discussion of Pascal's Wager and the notion of expected value, the condition of fairness is that Esther's *expectation* from the bet is the same as Lester's, zero dollars.

this reason, and because it has a nice property of additivity over exclusive alternatives,[13] the probability scale is usually the numerical scale adopted for most scientific work, though as we shall see it is sometimes more informative to use odds.

We have already linked probabilities to strength of belief. Since they are numbers we can think of them as *degrees of belief*. What we shall now do is extend the link to *changes* in strength of belief. I think we can all agree that rational beliefs can and occasionally will change in response to appropriate evidence. That much is obvious. Less obvious is the answer to the question: according to what criteria? Once we know that answer, we can start to evaluate more confidently the maze of argument and counterargument that characterises the recent debate about how new scientific evidence does – or does not – point to the handiwork of a cosmic Master-Builder. The answer is implicit in the formal rules that assignments of probability have to obey. These are nothing but rules of consistency, and they are very simple to state. One is that logically equivalent propositions have the same probability. Another is that the probability of a necessary truth, for example 'if it is raining then it is raining', is 1, and the probability of a necessary falsehood is 0. Another rule is the additivity rule mentioned above, and the final one is that the probability of the conjunction 'A&B' of two propositions A and B is equal to the probability of A given the truth of B times the probability of B. This is a sort of probabilistic analogue of the deductive rule that the conjunction of B and the conditional 'if B then A' is equivalent to the conjunction simply of A and B.

It is really just that last rule that tells us how uncertainty about a hypothesis is consistently changed by new evidence. Let $\mathrm{Prob}(H|E)$ be the probability of H given E, where we can think of H as a hypothesis and E as evidence. Let $\mathrm{Prob}(H\&E)$ be the probability of the conjunction of H and E, and let $\mathrm{Prob}(H)$ and $\mathrm{Prob}(E)$ respectively be the probabilities of H and E. The rule says that $\mathrm{Prob}(H\&E) = \mathrm{Prob}(H|E)\mathrm{Prob}(E)$. Using it again we have $\mathrm{Prob}(E\&H) = \mathrm{Prob}(E|H)\mathrm{Prob}(H)$. H&E is obviously equivalent to E&H, so by the first rule their probabilities are the same. Equating the right-hand sides of the two equations and doing some rearranging, we find that if $\mathrm{Prob}(E)$ is nonzero then

$$\mathrm{Prob}(H|E) = \mathrm{Prob}(H)[\mathrm{Prob}(E|H)/\mathrm{Prob}(E)] \qquad (1)$$

[13] This means that if A and B are two propositions which cannot logically both be true together, then the probability that either A is true or B is true is the sum of their individual probabilities.

Prob(H) is called the *prior probability* of H,[14] and Prob(H|E) the *posterior probability* of H in the light of E. (1) tells us that the posterior probability of H is the prior probability boosted by the factor Prob(E|H)/Prob(E). The boost will be upwards or downwards depending on whether Prob(E|H) is greater or smaller than Prob(E). In other words: *if a hypothesis makes the evidence more likely than it would otherwise have been, then the evidence increases the probability of the hypothesis.* It will do so to a greater or lesser extent depending on how *much* more probable the hypothesis makes the evidence.

This seems eminently commonsensical. The great French mathematician and physicist Laplace said just that, and he proceeded to write the first popular textbook of probability as the logic of uncertain inference.[15] (1) itself is called *Bayes's Theorem*, or more simply *Bayes's Rule*, in honour of the English mathematician and Nonconformist clergyman Thomas Bayes who first derived it; his Memoir containing it, together with the first rigorous development from first principles of what is often called the probability calculus was published posthumously by the Royal Society in 1763. Thus was born what has become the flourishing theory of so-called *Bayesian probability*. It is that probability which furnishes the logic, a *logic with numbers*, of inductive inference, that is to say the logic of evaluating hypotheses in the light of data. It will be the logic we will be invoking for the remainder of this book.

6. . . . AND WHAT FOLLOWS FROM THEM

An interesting new perspective on (1), but in fact an equivalent form of it, is gained by seeing what happens to the corresponding odds. Intuition tells us that an important criterion in evaluating H's probability in the light of E should be the extent to which the event described by E would be more likely to occur if H were true than if H were false. Intuition is, happily, borne out. The inverse transformation from probabilities (p) to odds (od) is od = p/(1–p). Where A is any proposition, if p = Prob(A) and –A is the negation of A (read –A not as minus A, which is obviously nonsense, but as 'A is false'), then 1–p = Prob(–A), by the additivity property of probabilities

[14] *Warning*: do not interpret 'prior probability' as 'probability in the light of no evidence at all', whatever that may mean, if it has any meaning at all. 'Prior' and 'posterior' are always relative to a specified E. In fact, the prior probability of H with respect to E may well be its posterior probability with respect to some anterior evidence E.

[15] Laplace said that probability theory was 'commonsense reduced to a calculus' ('*le bon sens réduit au calcul*'). His book, which appeared in 1815, is titled *A Philosophical Essay on Probabilities* (*Essai philosophique sur les probabilités*). It is published in an English translation by Frederick Wilson Truscott and Frederick Lincoln Emory (ed. and trans.) (New York: Dover Publications, 1951).

I have mentioned. Hence the odds on A are equal to Prob(A)/Prob(–A). Dividing Prob(H|E) by Prob(–H|E) we see that Prob(E) cancels and we get

$$\text{Posterior odds} = [\text{Prob}(E|H)/\text{Prob}(E|{-H})]\text{Prior odds} \qquad (2)$$

i.e. the boost factor which changes the prior *probability* into the posterior *probability* has become transformed into the boost factor Prob(E|H)/Prob(E|–H) which changes the prior *odds* into the posterior *odds*. But that factor depends on Prob(E|–H) and it is therefore *just the sort of factor that intuition told us should play that role*. This rescaled boost factor is often represented by the Greek letter λ, and is called the *likelihood ratio*. So we can simplify the equation above to

$$\text{Posterior odds} = \lambda \cdot \text{Prior odds}.$$

(This equation is often called the *odds form of Bayes's theorem*.) The statistician I. J. Good, who worked with the great logician, mathematician and 'father of computing' Alan Turing on the Enigma Project during the Second World War, tells us that Turing, who used Bayesian calculations in that work, called λ the 'factor in favour of the hypothesis H in virtue of the result of the observation E'.[16] It is now also often called the *Bayes factor* in favour of H.

The denominator Prob(E|–H) of λ is a significant quantity in its own right, since it is a weighted average of E's probability given each possible alternative to H, where the weights are the prior probabilities of those alternatives (a proof of this statement, not difficult, is in my book with Peter Urbach on Bayesian inference[17]). In other words, Prob(E|–H) is a sum of factors of the form Prob(E|H′)Prob(H′), where the sum is over all those alternatives H′ such that Prob(H′) is positive (in principle, there may be infinitely many of them). This is important, indeed very important, because it implies that the posterior probability of any hypothesis H will depend not only on the extent to which the phenomenon described in E is well-explained by H, *but also by how well it can be explained by plausible alternative hypotheses*. The more of these there are, the smaller in general will be the evidential boost to the prior probability of H. In fact, depending on the numbers it may well be that E does not raise the prior probability of H at all. If in a trial designed to test the effect of a drug the

[16] I. J. Good, *Probability and the Weighing of Evidence* (London: Griffin, 1950), p. 63.

[17] Colin Howson and Peter Urbach, *Scientific Reasoning: The Bayesian Approach*, 3rd edn (Lasalle, IL: Open Court, 2006).

design is so flawed that a number of possible known factors might have been responsible for a 'successful' outcome, that trial shouldn't do much if anything to increase your confidence in the effectiveness of the drug. Of course, everyone knows this; what may not be so widely known is that there is a rigorous demonstration of this commonsense principle within formal probability theory.

A possibly more surprising feature of the logic of probability is that it subsumes the logic of conjecture and refutation. It tells us that if evidence is inconsistent with a hypothesis under test, i.e. if it is *refuting* evidence, then *that evidence reduces the probability of the hypothesis to zero*. The formal theory of probability implies that if H entails that E is not true then $Prob(E|H) = 0$ so long as Prob(H) is nonzero, as in all applications it will be. Looking at Bayes's Theorem, we see that if Prob(H) is nonzero and $Prob(E|H) = 0$ then $Prob(H|E) = 0$. *Thus the logic of probability subsumes the deductive logic of refutation as a special case*. What is more interesting is the vastly more extensive territory outside the relatively small and safe domain where deductive logic can play its protective role. It is that potentially dangerous territory where, among other perils, the Prosecutor's Fallacy lies in wait to ambush the unwary traveller.

7. THE FALLACY EXPOSED

To commit the Prosecutor's Fallacy is in essence to equate the probability of H given E with the probability of E given H. An immediate consequence of Bayes's rule is that *only in exceptional circumstances* are these two equal. We have just seen that it follows immediately from (1) that if $Prob(E|H) = 0$ then $Prob(H|E) = 0$ (assuming that Prob(H) is nonzero). But those *are* very exceptional circumstances where the logic of deduction itself takes over. In general, when Prob(E|H) is nonzero, we can easily see from the odds form of Bayes's rule that *the value of Prob(E|H) by itself tells us nothing whatever about the value of Prob(H|E)*. For the posterior odds, and hence Prob(H|E), depends on Prob(E|–H) and Prob(E) as well as on Prob(E|H). If Prob(E|–H) is sufficiently smaller than Prob(E|H) then λ will take an arbitrarily *large* value, and so will the posterior odds and hence also Prob(H|E). Secondly, however small λ might be as a result of being driven down by a very small value of Prob(E|H) (as long as it is not 0) its smallness is compatible with an arbitrarily *large* value of the posterior odds if the prior odds on H are large enough. This confirms the guess we made from our informal analysis of the earlier examples, that even if Prob(E|H) is very small, a sufficiently large value of the prior odds can yield a large value of the posterior odds.

We are now in a position to revisit the examples of the Prosecutor's Fallacy we looked at earlier. First, the Harvard Medical School Test, which is a simple exercise in using equation (2), since the data given to the respondents in the test question allows us to put values to all the terms in it. We shall now see that when we do, the result confirms the value of the probability-value we arrived at earlier by approximate methods. Let H be the hypothesis that the subject has the disease, and let E be the report that they tested positive. The false positive rate of 5% translates into $\text{Prob}(E|{-H}) = 0.05$, and the false negative rate of 0% translates into $\text{Prob}({-E}|H) = 0$, which implies that $\text{Prob}(E|H) = 1$. Hence in the odds form of Bayes's rule we have $\lambda = 20$. The prior odds on H are implicit in the information that the subject was randomly selected for test from a population in which the incidence of the disease is 1 in 1,000, which translates into prior odds of 1:999. Plugging these values into the odds equation, we see that the posterior odds on the subject having the disease after testing positive are 20:999, or almost 50 to 1 *against*, i.e. a probability of only 2.02% (remember that earlier we calculated the answer to be just under 2%).

The wrong answer of 95% given by most respondents is an example of what Kahneman and Tversky in their own influential analysis of fallacies of reasoning[18] call the *base-rate fallacy*, because the information about the incidence of the disease in the population that the respondents who gave that answer didn't take into account is often called the base-rate. The fallacy is however just a very nice example of the Prosecutor's Fallacy. But never mind what it is called: a rose by any other name would smell as sweet. Or not.

Now look at Ward's comparative version of the Fallacy. Let H be Ward's hypothesis of a human-oriented God, H′ what he called the materialistic hypothesis, and E state the existence of molecular replicators. From the probability form of Bayes's Theorem we infer

$$\frac{\text{Prob}(H|E)}{\text{Prob}(H'|E)} = \frac{\text{Prob}(E|H)\text{Prob}(H)}{\text{Prob}(E|H')\text{Prob}(H')} \tag{3}$$

We can see clearly that it does not follow that if $\text{Prob}(E|H)$ is larger than $\text{Prob}(E|H')$ then $\text{Prob}(H|E)$ is larger than $\text{Prob}(H'|E)$. In fact, it is obvious

[18] Daniel Kahneman and Amos Tversky, 'Judgement Under Uncertainty: Heuristics and Biases', *Science* 185 (1974), 1124–31.

that if Prob(H′) is sufficiently greater than Prob(H) the *reverse* inequality can hold between Prob(H|E) and Prob(H′|E). Indeed, the Problem of Evil would arguably justify any but the most committed to assign an extremely small prior probability to H.

Finally, consider the case of Santa versus the fair coin. Where E reports an outcome-sequence containing roughly 50% heads, and H and H′ are now respectively the Santa Claus hypothesis ('Santa willed that outcome and Santa is all-powerful') and the hypothesis that E was randomly generated by a fair coin, then even though Prob(E|H) = 1 and Prob(E|H′) is 2^{-20}, most normal people would set Prob(H) practically equal to 0, making the ratio of posterior probabilities for all practical purposes infinite. This does not imply that I think, or that anyone should think, that the hypothesis of God is quite as preposterous as that of Santa. It was the *inference* that Ward was making that is wrong, and it is wrong because, as Bayes's Theorem makes clear, we can't decide whether one proposed explanation is the best among a group of potentially competing alternatives just by looking at how probable it makes the evidence relative to how probable the others make it: we also have to consider how probable it is *independently* of that evidence. And it may well be, as it is in the coin example, that the prior probability of the one hypothesis trumps the greater likelihood which the other gives the data.

8. MIRACLES AGAIN

As far as most people are concerned, miracles are among the most persuasive arguments for God in the Vatican's arsenal (now that torture is out of fashion). Perhaps they shouldn't be. An amusing miracle, or series of miracles, is reported in Norman Douglas's literary masterpiece, *Old Calabria*. During his peregrinations around Calabria shortly before the First World War, Douglas was told about a certain seventeenth-century Franciscan monk, later canonised as St Joseph of Copertino, who was credited with being able to fly unassisted. That he did so several times, without apparent effort, was testified to many times and by many witnesses. As Douglas notes, these included some very notable people: the Lord High Admiral of Castile (Ambassador of Spain at the Vatican), the Duke of Brunswick and none other than Pope Urban VII himself. This account of St Joseph's various flights is taken from the website Catholic Online:

> The mere mention of God or a spiritual matter was enough to take him out of his senses; at Mass he frequently floated in the air in rapture. Once as Christmas carols were being sung, he soared to the high altar and knelt in the air, rapt in

prayer. On another occasion he ferried a cross thirty-six feet high through the air to the top of a Calvary group as easily as one might carry a straw.

Douglas reports that St Joseph even managed to take a short flight the day before his death. Like some other legendary figures thought to possess a curious spiritual grace, St Joseph was very simple (Parsifal is another example). *Sancta simplicitas.* He was also born in a stable . . . Joseph was canonised in 1767: he is the patron saint of pilots and air travellers.

Nowadays the criteria which have to be satisfied before the Vatican admits that a miracle has been performed by a candidate for canonisation are somewhat stricter – or so it is alleged. The miracle usually has to be that of healing a person of a condition, where the healing cannot be explained by any natural cause, but was preceded by praying to the candidate to intercede with God. The Vatican has a panel of medical experts, drawn from a larger available group, who are required to pronounce that the healing is lasting and that it has no known medical explanation. If the panel agrees by a majority then a panel of cardinals and priests determines whether the effect was due to praying to the candidate for sainthood. But how could a panel of theologians, or anyone at all, determine that? It is simply not the case that if there is no currently available medical explanation then the observed effect *must* be due to appropriate solicitations of the Almighty. There may well be a whole spectrum of natural causes for the remission that are as yet unknown. That medical science advances, and that one generation's miracle cure is a later one's ingestion of antibiotics, or whatever, is a rather obvious fact the Vatican seems to be in denial about. But one can understand why: were the Church to acknowledge it there would be no miracles, and a public hungry for proofs of God's intercession might well seek another spiritual medium more ready to feed its appetite.

Francis Collins, a non-Catholic Christian, investigates the conditions under which we might determine *merely to the extent of its being more probable than not*, that a medically inexplicable recovery, say from cancer, is an authentic miracle. We are now in the territory of probabilistic reasoning, and Collins does in fact perform a Bayes's Theorem calculation, from which he concludes that a miracle is more probable than not supposing only that 'no such cure should have occurred by any known natural process', and that the prior probability assigned to it is nonzero.[19] The fact that the

[19] Collins, *The Language of God*, p. 51. Collins describes Thomas Bayes as a Scottish theologian.

last condition is so weak, being in effect simply the condition that you acknowledge the *mere possibility* of a miraculous cure, should arouse a suspicion that something is wrong with Collins's calculation. As indeed it is. Let H be the hypothesis that the cure was a miracle, and E be the evidence of spontaneous recovery. The condition that H is more probable than not given E is the condition that the posterior odds on H are greater than 1. Let x be the prior odds on H. These are nonzero just in case the prior probability is nonzero. The odds form of Bayes's Theorem tells us that the posterior odds are greater than 1 just in case λx is greater than 1, i.e. λ is greater than $1/x$, where λ is the likelihood ratio $Prob(E|H)/Prob(E|-H)$. But the only way that λ can be greater than $1/x$, *for all nonzero x*, is by λ being infinite, which will be true (assuming that $Prob(E|H)$ is nonzero) only if $Prob(E|-H)$ is exactly 0. But $Prob(E|-H)$ being 0 means that it is *certain* that no non-divine cause could have been responsible for the remission, and that obviously doesn't follow from Collins's condition that no *known* natural cause is responsible. In implicitly identifying the condition that no known natural cause is responsible, with the condition that no known *or still-unknown* natural cause is responsible, Collins is of course making the same mistake as the Vatican. But Collins's is all the more remarkable since in his book he tells us that we must always 'leave the door open', as he puts it, to the possibility that science will eventually supply an explanation where one is currently lacking.[20]

As one might expect from the fact that its reasoning is radically unsound, the Vatican continues to 'verify' miracles at a steady rate. It credited the remission of a serious illness to St Marie-Marguerite d'Youville (beatified in 1959 following a highly successful first miracle), after it emerged that the patient had been praying to her. It did not apparently bother to investigate, among other things, how often prayers to Marie-Marguerite *failed* to be followed by miraculous results. The miraculous vision at Fátima was accepted as such by the Vatican without any serious attempt to consider alternative explanations. A lay brother, Brother André Bessette, who founded St Joseph's Oratory in Montreal, has recently been canonised for being responsible for the miraculous healing of a boy. The evidence which the Vatican's Congregation for the Causes of Saints was reported to have used to arrive at this conclusion was that the boy's parents had been praying to Brother André at the Oratory and rubbed Brother André medals against the boy's skin. It is time to move on.

[20] *Ibid.*, p. 78.

9. FOR CRYING OUT LOUD

Bayes's name is taken in vain not only by Francis Collins. The Canadian philosopher John Leslie does so too. Leslie asked the question why we hear some events 'crying out' for explanation – like fine-tuning, the example we saw Collins earlier deem too improbable to be explained by chance. Leslie agrees in that assessment, and enunciates a general principle that we only regard events as demanding explanation when we can glimpse what he calls a 'tidy' explanation of them.[21] As Collins himself did, Leslie finds the tidiest explanation of fine-tuning in God, or to be more precise in a God-surrogate which Leslie calls 'the Creative Ethical Requirement'.[22] According to Leslie, 'chance' is not a tidy explanation if it confers only a small probability on the data, citing the example of being dealt thirteen spades in a hand of bridge, and observing in language reminiscent of Ward's:

> *in all such cases you prefer the hypothesis that more than Chance was involved.* Why? Well, because this hypothesis [that the hand was fixed] gives so dramatic a boost to the probability that you would be seeing what you do. (That is to say, it gives the boost even if its own probability is rather low . . .)[23]

Glimpsing the tidy explanation(s) of what is very poorly explained by chance is glimpsing what Leslie calls a 'feedback loop'.

In the italicised sentence in the quote we have the comparative version of the Prosecutor's Fallacy which earlier we saw Ward commit. We know that Bayesian probability certainly doesn't sanction the fallacy – it is a fallacy, after all! – so it is all the more surprising to be told by Leslie that it does:

> This is just one aspect of the point – fundamental to all science and formalized in Bayes's rule of the calculus of probabilities – that observations improve your reasons for accepting some hypothesis when its truth would have made those observations more likely.

It is certainly true that Bayes's Theorem implies that observations may 'improve your reasons' for accepting some hypothesis, but it does not follow that that should lead you to *prefer* H to any of the other possibilities being considered, like that of chance for example. It all depends on the

[21] John Leslie, *Universes* (New York: Routledge, 1989), p. 121. Emphasis in the original.

[22] According to Leslie a less tidy, but still tidy, explanation is the hypothesis that there are very many universes with all sorts of values for those constants. Why Leslie thinks that the many-universes ('*multiverse*') hypothesis should make fine-tuning in this one more likely is a question I will return to in the next chapter.

[23] Leslie, *Universes*, p. 121 (my emphasis).

prior probabilities, as equation (3) above tells us: if H and H′ are any two alternative hypotheses then

$$\frac{\mathrm{Prob(H|E)}}{\mathrm{Prob(H'|E)}} = \frac{\mathrm{Prob(E|H)Prob(H)}}{\mathrm{Prob(E|H')Prob(H')}}$$

Leslie may claim that his feedback loop provided him with a 'glimpse of a tidy explanation' in his 'Creative Ethical Requirement'. But depending on the prior probabilities it might have given him a glimpse of pure chance – or even of Santa.

10. A SIMPLE SYLLOGISM

The Prosecutor's Fallacy tends to be compounded with another fallacy in the classic argument for God from improbability which Collins implicitly appealed to in section 2. We'll see a lot more examples in the next chapter. Here's the logical form of the argument:

Premise 1: A phenomenon E is to be expected if a hypothesis H is true.
Premise 2: If H isn't true, and no other explanation is visible, the occurrence of E must be due to chance.
Premise 3: The probability of E is vanishingly small on the chance hypothesis.
Premise 4: Science correctly rejects explanations in terms of improbable coincidences.
Conclusion: H should be accepted.

Premise 4 is a barely-disguised Prosecutor's Fallacy. To reject an explanation in the light of data is just another way of saying that you think the explanation is simply too improbable to be considered seriously. Premise 2 is the other fallacy. It is a fallacy because as we know from Collins's 'Bayesian' argument for miracles, we are never in a position *in principle* to rule out a possible infinity of alternative possible explanations other than chance and H.

So the argument is doubly fallacious. Nevertheless it has become entrenched in certain parts of science, particularly in statistics, where an inessentially different version of it trades under the name of *significance testing*, and where the chance hypothesis is known as the *null hypothesis*, or just the *null*. The famous terminology is due to the statistician and geneticist R. A. Fisher. Fisher argued that where the null H implies that the values of an observable random variable X have a specified statistical distribution, for example the familiar bell-shaped Normal distribution, then values of X sufficiently far out under one of the 'tails' of the curve would suffice to reject H were they to be observed. Such values, according to Fisher, effectively 'contradict' the hypothesis, which should be regarded as 'definitely disproved' by them.[24] Typically, the results of a randomised controlled trial are stated in terms of what are called (following Fisher) *p-values*, where the p-value of an observed outcome is the probability given H of getting that or a more extreme result, i.e. one further out under a tail of the distribution-curve, and the outcome is said to be 'significant' at that value ($p = 0.05$ was a value often regarded by Fisher as sufficiently small to justify the verdict of experimental disproof). The intelligent-design advocate William Dembski also informs us that a p-value below a certain magnitude (in Dembski's reckoning 10^{-150}) corresponds in effect to a physical impossibility.[25] To see why this is wrong consider a screen which randomly displays an integer between 0 and 9 inclusive, and let it do so 151 times. It will produce a physical impossibility according to Dembski's reckoning.

The obvious problem with Fisher's talk of disproof is that statistical hypotheses are not disproved by any among the possible outcomes of an observation since they are not *inconsistent* with any. Those hypotheses merely ascribe to each a definite probability of occurrence. Suppose for example a hypothesis predicts that a recovery rate at least as good as the one observed would be seen on the average five per cent of the time in indefinitely continued trials. Even if you repeat the observation, say twenty times, and find you are getting the same result in eight of them, this new result is itself predicted to occur with a definite frequency in indefinitely repeated trials consisting of twenty-fold repetitions of the first trial. And so on: at no point will you ever observe a result that is inconsistent with the hypothesis. As we have already noted, events with vanishingly small probabilities occur all the time without our thinking that they falsify some 'null hypothesis': on the contrary, Bayes's Theorem tells us that Prob(E|H) can be as small as you like so long as it is not zero, and it is still possible for Prob(H|E) to be close to 1.

II. FALSIFICATION AND TESTING

I pointed out earlier that the probabilistic logic contains that of falsification as a sub-logic. What is even more important is that it is a strict sub-logic, i.e. the probabilistic logic has strictly more content. This is important

[24] R. A. Fisher, *Statistical Methods for Research Workers* (Edinburgh: Oliver and Boyd, 1932), pp. 83. To be precise, the bell-shaped curve of the Normal distribution is that of a probability-*density*. This means that the probability that X lies in a subinterval (x_1,x_2) of its range is equal to the area under the curve between x_1 and x_2.

[25] Dembski calls it an improbability too small to be physically achieved. *The Design Revolution: Answering the Toughest Questions about Intelligent Design* (Downer's Grove, IL: Intervarsity Press, 2004), p. 118.

because outright falsification almost never occurs in practice (despite the significance attached to it in the well-known methodological writings of the philosopher Karl Popper), and typically one needs exactly the sort of guidance provided by the probability-rules. In the first place, any inspection of experimental reports will show that quantitative evidence displays more or less scatter, or *dispersion*, due to errors and uncertainties of various kinds and from various sources. Thus the textbook example 'Let H be "All crows are black". I have observed a white crow. Hence H is false' is a parody of an actual experimental test, where experimental scientists have to employ a variety of statistical models with parameters supplied by the theory, call it T, under test, to generate probability distributions for the observed data conditional on T. Secondly, statistical hypotheses are the foundation of chemistry and microphysics, since quantum mechanics is a statistical theory. And as we know, statistical hypotheses are unfalsifiable in principle: any attempt to force them into the Procrustean bed of deductive falsification fails.

Another quite different reason to downplay the significance of falsification is that not only is there an unavoidable presence of statistical hypotheses in most test processes, but there are also other assumptions besides – about the theory of the equipment used, about the 'right' statistical model of the data, etc. What is actually tested, in other words, is a bigger or smaller, but always nonempty, *conjunction* of the theory in question together with all these auxiliaries. In the event of an adverse test-result all you can infer deductively is that at least one of this usually very large conjunction is false. To make any finer discrimination, and in particular to say whether the main theory is counter-indicated, one needs an appropriate prior probability weighting in order to generate a posterior probability ranking (I mean this only in a more or less rough, qualitative sense: in practice people don't assign numbers in this way and diligently work through Bayes's Theorem calculations).

Hence if the principal theory is duly rejected, it will not be because it is strictly falsified. The most that can be said is that it is deemed *likely* to be false, or possibly *almost certainly* false. But those qualifications are indispensable to understanding the true logic of the situation, and any attempt to pretend them away will fail. A distinguished scientist, the geophysicist and statistician (Sir) Harold Jeffreys, made the point with characteristic pithiness:

> the tendency to claim that scientific method can be reduced in some way to deductive logic . . . is the most fundamental fallacy of all: it can be done only by rejecting its chief feature, induction.[26]

[26] Sir Harold Jeffreys, *Theory of Probability*, 3rd edn (Oxford: Clarendon Press, 1961), p. 2.

What Jeffreys described as 'the tendency' when he wrote this passage was less directed at Popper than Fisher, whose theory of significance tests was then dominant and who, as we saw, dressed it up in the language of deductive logic (as a matter of historical interest Fisher and Popper made startlingly similar manifesto-like pronouncements on the subject, roughly contemporaneously[27]).

12. SUBJECTIVISM

Dawkins repudiates Bayesian probability citing a supposed subjectivism as the reason[28] and – as we shall see in Chapter 8 – goes badly astray as a result. The charge is based on the fact that the prior odds in Bayes's Theorem appear as essentially undetermined parameters which one is apparently free to choose as one likes, unlike the likelihood terms Prob(E|H) which are typically computed according to an assumed statistical model. But the objection is based on a confusion: in fact, two confusions. Firstly, probabilistic logic, of which Bayes's Theorem is of course a part, determines completely *objective criteria* of valid inference from premises consisting of assignments of real numbers in the unit interval. Secondly, as with deductive logic, the truth or accuracy of those premises themselves is not for logic to decide. But in neither case, deductive or probabilistic, does that make these logics 'subjective'. In any responsible investigation the initial assignments of probability are typically anything but: usually scientists will give closely reasoned arguments why, taking account of the scientific milieu in which they are inducted, they regard some possibilities as more plausible in the light of that background information than others.

No less a person than Einstein himself is a very good example. When his theory of general relativity was dramatically corroborated by experimental evidence that light was bent when passing close to the sun, he famously remarked that it was just as well because his theory was correct anyway! Here he is, comparing the prior probabilities of the constancy of the speed of light and the Galilean relativity principle:

> I knew that the constancy of the velocity of light was something quite independent of the relativity postulate and I weighted which was the more probable.[29]

'Weighted' here should be taken very seriously. To think of Einstein's account as merely 'subjective' in anything like the usual sense of the word

[27] I list some of them in my book *Hume's Problem: Induction and the Justification of Belief* (Oxford University Press, 2000), pp. 100–1.

[28] Richard Dawkins, *The God Delusion* (London: Bantam Books, 2006), p. 133.

[29] From a letter quoted in Don Howard and John Stachel (eds.), *Einstein: The Formative Years, 1879–1909* (Boston: Birkhauser, 1998).

is simply false to the facts. He was making a delicate comparison, which turned out to be fully vindicated by later experiments, of how fundamental each of these principles was, and it was because the constancy of the speed of light was deeply embedded in Maxwell's equations for electromagnetism, which Einstein regarded as a truly fundamental theory, that he opted for it.

Like most working scientists, Einstein employs the language of probability to express his reasoning from data: it is the natural medium, and the rules of probability merely codify informal probabilistic reasoning into a formal logic. Einstein was far from alone in this. Laplace was one of the most distinguished physicists to have lived, and his short classic which I mentioned earlier, the *Philosophical Essay on Probabilities*, introduces the basic rules in a way that is still one of the best introductions. In the next chapter we shall see the Nobel physics laureate Steven Weinberg give an explicitly Bayesian argument for why we should expect the observed value of the cosmological constant to take the sort of value it does, while another Nobel physics laureate, Philip Anderson, summarises nicely the way in which the Bayesian logic applies to science:

> What Bayesianism does is to focus one's attention on the question one wants to ask of the data: It says, in effect, How do these data affect my previous knowledge of the situation? It's sometimes called 'maximum likelihood' thinking, but the essence of it is to clearly identify the possible answers, assign reasonable a priori probabilities to them and then ask which answers have been made more likely by the data.[30]

13. 'WHO IS THIS THAT DARKENETH COUNSEL . . . ?'[31]

I talked earlier, in Chapter 2, about Stephen Jay Gould and his NOMA theory. Gould was only one of a very large number of people who desire to see science and religion publicly reconciled. But it is not so many who, as was Gould, are qualified to speak with equal authority about both. In a recently published book[32] based on her Terry Lectures at Yale University, Barbara Herrnstein Smith, the Braxton Craven Professor of Comparative Literature at Duke University and Distinguished Professor at Brown University, illustrates the dangers of knowing presumably a good deal about one but possibly less about the other. Herrnstein Smith grinds

[30] Philip Anderson, 'The Reverend Thomas Bayes, Needles in Haystacks, and the Fifth Force', *Physics Today* 45:1 (January 1992), 9–11.

[31] Job 38:2.

[32] Portentously titled *Natural Reflections: Human Cognition at the Nexus of Science and Religion* (New Haven, CT: Yale University Press, 2009).

a contemptuously dismissive axe throughout her book about claims to objectivity for scientific research, its ability to reveal a truth lying behind appearances. Its methodology (which she calls 'methodological naturalism') she likens to a slimming regime:

> like using low-octane fuel or following a low-fat diet, the minimalisation and self-restraint that defines it can only be thought more or less appropriate for the purpose at hand.

'*Defines it*'? Since when has an attempt to obtain authentic knowledge about the world been *defined* as minimalisation and self-restraint? Herrnstein Smith's polished, epithet-laden prose, with its tone of high authority, encourages the reader to let its tendentious rhetoric through on the nod. In fact, when the rhetorical pushes and pulls are corrected for, what mostly remains is fashionable post-modernist dogma; for example:

> whatever else it is, 'nature' is a notion – an idea, an abstraction, a human construct. We (Westerners, scientists) keep constructing nature (*natura*, *die Natur*, and so forth) collectively out of our intersubjectively communicated experiences of publicly available phenomena.[33]

The rhetorical decoration in this passage is extreme even by Herrnstein Smith's high standards. Note the scare-quotes around the first occurrence of 'nature'. 'Nature' is a linguistic item, a *word*; and whatever else it is (to echo Herrnstein Smith), nature is not a word. Here and elsewhere in her book, the proliferating scare-quotes are a device to let Herrnstein Smith off the hook of actually arguing for a position where success is very far from guaranteed (on the contrary). The idea that nature is an *idea* harks back to the seventeenth- and eighteenth-century empiricists' view, reinforced by Kant, that we have no direct experience of things as they are, and everything we know about them, or claim to know about them, is mediated by our own sensory impressions and our constructions out of these: in a word, our ideas. In its trendy modern version, the doctrine emphasises the social and the allegedly gender-based components in these constructions. In any event Herrnstein Smith's claim that nature is an idea amounts to no more than the tautology 'our idea of what nature is like, is an idea'. What she is claiming, at least on this topic, is therefore either vacuous or false.

Some of the other claims in her book which purport to speak authoritatively about science are equally tendentious: for example, '[m]ost contemporary philosophers of science' she tells us, 'reject the idea or claim that

[33] *Ibid.*, p. 127.

science is automatically, dependably, or even somewhat miraculously "self-correcting"'.[34] No numbers are cited to support the 'most', and I think, being of the tribe on whose behalf she speaks, that the claim is very probably false. Anyway, what if they do? Surely among the people to consult for an informed opinion are the producers of scientific knowledge themselves, a group conspicuously absent from the pages of Herrnstein Smith's book. Can it be that she, buttressed by supporting sociologists, science-studies' personnel and philosophers of science, is better informed on the subject? The quotations I have given suggest otherwise. Here is another specimen:

> A number of familiar ideals in science, such as the unity and perfectibility of knowledge, appear to be the fairly direct heritage of Christian doctrine, transmitted through the medieval universities and extended by the Enlightenment and later, 'evolutionary' narratives of human rationality, development, and, again, perfectibility.[35]

I suspect that most physicists would be puzzled by the claim that a Grand Unified Theory, if it ever emerges, is a 'fairly direct heritage of Christian doctrine'. Nor does Herrnstein Smith tell us what the 'evolutionary' narratives she mentions are, nor why 'evolutionary' has scare-quotes (I have never read a book with so many), or how perfectibility is involved at all in evolutionary, or even 'evolutionary', narratives.

But enough of this. It is time to turn our attention (at last) to the main subject of this book: God, and the evidence for his existence. Is it compelling? I will start the discussion off, in the next chapter, by considering the prima facie puzzling phenomenon, at any rate to those who do not find the Deity the answer to every question, of the fact that the universe appears to have been a much more finely tuned affair than anyone had previously supposed; finely-tuned, moreover, for *life* and – not to put too fine a point on it – for *us*. The universe 'knew we were coming', wrote the physicist Freeman Dyson.[36] We shall see.

EXERCISE

'When we see a few letters of the alphabet spelling our name in the sand, our immediate response is to recognise the work of an intelligent agent. How much more likely, then, is an intelligent creator behind the human

[34] *Ibid.*, pp. 134–5. [35] *Ibid.*

[36] Freeman Dyson, *Disturbing the Universe* (New York: Harper and Row, 1979), p. 250.

DNA, the colossal biological database that contains no fewer than 3.5 billion "letters"?' Comment.

MAIN POINTS OF CHAPTER 3

- Arguments have recently been put forward, based on puzzling discoveries in physics and biology, that suggest that God is after all needed to make sense of the universe. Many of these arguments have an explicitly probabilistic structure.
- People notoriously do not by and large have well-developed faculties for detecting faulty probabilistic inferences, and there are some classic types that people succumb to over and over again. One is the so-called 'Prosecutor's Fallacy', and many of the arguments we will be examining commit it.
- To expose these fallacies and explain why they are fallacies, some acquaintance with the basic rules of probability is needed. Mostly one such rule, Bayes's rule, is enough. It is very simple to state, and it is shown to explain exactly why the Prosecutor's Fallacy is a fallacy.
- Appeal to Bayes's rule exposes and explains the faults in some other classic but problematic arguments, like the argument from miracles.
- Bayesian probability is an authentic *logic* of uncertain inference, and is indispensable in the context of scientific inference from data. Alternative methodologies, like the falsificationist methodology associated with the names of R. A. Fisher and Karl Popper, are discussed and shown to be inadequate.
- Some objections to Bayesian probability are considered, in particular the charge that it incorporates subjectivism. Today many physicists and statisticians adopt explicitly Bayesian standards of reasoning about uncertainty.

CHAPTER 4

The well-tempered universe

'There are more things in heaven and earth, Horatio, than are dreamt of in your philosophy.'[1]

I. IN THE BEGINNING WAS THE BANG . . .

According to what is called the standard cosmological model, the universe exploded into existence over thirteen billion years ago and almost immediately expanded superluminally in a very brief inflationary period. As cooling continued, protons and neutrons fused into helium, deuterium and lithium nuclei, mixing with the electrons in a plasma too hot to allow the formation of stable atoms. The atoms themselves appeared after a few hundred thousand years, and after a billion years gravity acted on small variations in density to cause matter to clump together in stars and galaxies. Even before the inflationary epoch, cooling had broken the initial symmetry to give the four fundamental forces: gravity, the weak and strong nuclear forces and electromagnetism. After the very rapid initial inflationary period ended the rate of expansion of the universe fell under the predominating influence of gravity and dark matter, but after another five billion years the repulsive influence of dark energy preponderated and the rate of expansion again increased.

The inflationary Big Bang[2] model has been seen by some, including some scientists like the astronomer Robert Jastrow, as signalling an agreement with the Biblical account in Genesis (or accounts: Genesis gives differing accounts of the events in the Creation):

Now we see how the astronomical evidence leads to a biblical view of the origin of the world. The details differ, but the essential elements and the astronomical and biblical accounts of Genesis are the same; the chain of events leading to man

[1] *Hamlet.*

[2] The name 'Big Bang' was given pejoratively by Fred Hoyle, who didn't accept the model.

commenced suddenly and sharply at a definite moment in time, in a flash of light and energy.[3]

Nor is the agreement coincidental, according to a substantial constituency of religious apologists, who regard the inflationary Big Bang model as direct evidence for God. John Lennox, a mathematician at the University of Oxford, tells us that 'even if the non-believers don't like it, the Big Bang fits in exactly with the Christian narrative of creation'.[4] *Exactly*? Come now. In Genesis 1 and 2 there are two rather blatantly *contradictory* 'narratives' of the creation and, according to scholarly authority, by different hands, one of which has its origin in Babylonian mythology going back millennia before the time of the Old Testament. They do agree that heaven and earth were made in six days, but that agreed claim is not consistent with Big Bang cosmology. Obviously, consistency can be restored between any two sets of claims by suitably redefining terms, but if the redefinitions are sufficiently radical the practice is quite properly regarded as cheating. Jastrow only avoids the logical brick wall the impetuous Lennox runs straight into with the concession 'The details differ.' I'll say they do. Saying that 'the essential elements are the same' is committing the scientific sin of being (very) selective with the evidence, accepting the bits that you like and ignoring or discarding the rest. Lennox and Jastrow are scientists, no doubt very good ones, but this isn't good science. It isn't good anything.

William Lane Craig is another who claims that the Biblical account is corroborated by Big Bang cosmology. Lane Craig also claims that there is a priori *proof* that there is a God who created this universe. His argument, sometimes called the *Kalam Argument* and which is an updated version of the venerable Cosmological Argument, is as follows:

> The universe had a beginning in time
> What has a beginning is caused
> Therefore the universe is caused (by a cosmic Creator, i.e. God).

As several people have been quick to point out, however, neither of the Kalam premises is compelling. Lane Craig uses an argument that originates with Kant to 'establish' that time cannot be infinite in the past and still proceed into the future, on the ground that an actual infinite cannot exist because, among other reasons, if it did it would be impossible to add to it.[5]

[3] Robert Jastrow, *God and the Astronomers* (New York: Norton, 1978), p. 14.
[4] *Daily Telegraph*, 4 September 2010.
[5] W. L. Craig and Q. Smith, *Theism, Atheism, and Big Bang Cosmology* (Oxford: Clarendon Press, 1993).

But this claim is vitiated by the facts that (i) in contemporary set theory it is easy to show that there exists a sequence of infinite discrete ordered sets each with a greatest but no smallest member, each set extending its predecessor by an additional largest element; and (ii) the things in the domain of any consistent theory, as set theory is thought to be, are possible existents. Adducing similar observations, the distinguished philosopher of physics Michael Redhead concludes a review of Lane Craig's argument with the remark that it 'seems a total muddle'.[6]

Mathematics aside, the standard model of cosmology itself contradicts the Kalam's first premise. There is no beginning *in* time of the universe, since the universe itself is the initial time-boundary – if there is one at all. Stephen Hawking and Roger Penrose showed in the 1970s that general relativity predicted an initial singularity, a *point* in terms of spatial dimensions, at which density, temperature and spacetime curvature are infinite (i.e. the equations in effect become meaningless), but that was on the assumption that the relativistic equations held all the way down to that point. But those equations are deterministic and below the Planck length quantum indeterminism reigns, leaving instead a fuzzy region of indeterminacy.

One doesn't even have to go back to the beginning to challenge premise two. According to the foundational theory of microphysics, quantum theory, nature is simply replete with uncaused events. It is also not only consistent with quantum theory to suppose that the universe generated itself spontaneously out of nothing in a quantum fluctuation, but many physicists do believe that happened. To the question 'Where did the initial energy come from?', the answer is 'nowhere'. The bubble-universe emerging from the fluctuation is empty of matter and radiation but has enormous energy stored in its curvature, exactly balanced by the negative energy (pressure) of the vacuum, called a 'false' vacuum because it is not a state of lowest energy. Following a phase transition the false vacuum expands exponentially for a very brief period. The numbers involved are staggering: in the estimated 10^{-35} seconds of inflation the universe grew from the Planck length of 10^{-33} cm to $10^{10^{12}}$ cm (the distance between its 'poles'). When inflation ceases the (negative) potential energy of the vacuum is converted into (positive) kinetic energy of matter and radiation. In the process the negative energy cancels exactly with the positive. The net energy of the universe remains zero, and no violation of the law of conservation of energy occurs. This universe is 'the ultimate free lunch'.

[6] M. L. G. Redhead, 'Review: W. L. Craig and Q. Smith: Theism, Atheism, and Big Bang Cosmology', *British Journal for the Philosophy of Science* 47:1 (1996), 133–6.

2. . . . AND THE BANG WAS GOD – OR WAS IT?

Nevertheless many people seem to find great difficulty in accepting that something momentous might just have *happened*, and moreover happened without a cause that does not somehow involve intentional agency. 'Causa', the Latin root of the English word 'cause', can mean either 'cause' or 'reason' (or both), and an inability or unwillingness to separate intelligible reason from physical cause has bedevilled (if that is the right word) discussions of the origins of the universe from time immemorial, and it shows no sign of dying out. According to Francis Collins the Big Bang

> cries out for a divine explanation. It forces the conclusion that nature had a defined beginning. I cannot see how nature could have created itself. Only a supernatural force that is outside space and time could have done that.[7]

But we have been here before. If quantum effects characterise the earliest phase of the universe there was no 'defined beginning', nor was there a time before which it did not exist. And Collins may not 'see' how nature could have simply come into being in an uncaused way, but as we have noted above, not only is that a definite physical possibility, but it is one subscribed to by many physicists. The divine explanation of course also raises the question of what caused God. The traditional answer is that he is the cause of himself. But whereas the idea that the universe might cause itself, in a manner of speaking, is backed by highly tested physical theory, the argument that God can be the cause of himself rests on an altogether shakier foundation, as we shall see in the next chapter.

Any crying out for divine explanation by the Big Bang certainly seems to fall on deaf ears as far as most physicists and cosmologists are concerned, who appear to have no difficulty in suggesting entirely non-divine explanations. There is a whole market stall of them currently on offer, whose average lifetime the physicist Andrei Linde has estimated at about five years. Some would strain the outsider's credulity to breaking point were they not considered as serious possibilities by distinguished scientists. In one, *chaotic inflation*, inflating universes seed other inflating universes in a fractal pattern, ad infinitum, where each universe may contain different effective laws, have different dimensions and constants. In another, there is simply an unending sequence of Big Bangs eventually followed by Big Crunches followed by Big Bangs ad infinitum. A version of that idea, the

[7] Francis Collins, *The Language of God* (New York: Free Press, 2006), p. 67.

so-called Cyclic Model proposed by Paul Steinhardt and Neil Turok, contains a continuous time (in both directions), in which three-dimensional brane universes move in an additional dimension and occasionally collide, generating – as far as our own universe is concerned – what their eventual inhabitants reconstruct as a Big Bang, though which from the outside observer's point of view (if there were one) is merely the momentary loss of a dimension. Some proposals do not even contain Big Bangs or analogues of the Big Bang at all. Max Tegmark has seriously suggested the radical possibility that every consistent mathematical structure has a physical instantiation as a kind of universe (he calls it 'full mathematical democracy'),[8] in which case our own universe, whether it contains an absolute beginning in a Big Bang or not, simply exists in its own right, owing nothing to any creative act.

3. WORLDS ENOUGH – AND TIME

The cosmological models mentioned above are examples of *multiverse* models, postulating a very large, possibly infinite, class of universes of which ours is only one. The idea of different real universes is not a new one in physics. It was suggested a half-century ago as the solution of an interpretational problem in quantum mechanics. In orthodox quantum mechanics a quantum-mechanical system can be and usually is in states, so-called superpositions, in which observables do not have definite values. Left to themselves quantum systems evolve over time according to a deterministic law, the Schrödinger equation, but in general do not move from an indefinite state to a definite one. But it is a brute fact that whenever a quantum-mechanical system is actually observed the observable is always found to have a definite value. In earlier versions of quantum mechanics the problem is solved in the simplest possible way, by the adoption of a postulate, often known as the postulate of 'wave-packet collapse', which states that when the system is observed its quantum state is immediately pushed into a non-superposition state (an *eigenstate*). The 'collapse' postulate is not only rather obviously ad hoc, but it also raises a problem of consistency. The act of observing a quantum system combines a classical system (the observer) with the quantum system he or she is observing, and the combined system is itself a quantum system (this is the phenomenon of

[8] Max Tegmark, 'Is "The Theory of Everything" Merely the Ultimate Ensemble Theory?', *Annals of Physics* 270 (1998), 1–51. There is a technical problem with this idea: according to the current mainstream view of the foundations of mathematics, all mathematical structures are set-theoretical structures, but on pain of inconsistency there can be no set of all set-theoretical structures.

entanglement) whose combined observables only take definite values when the combined system is observed by a further observer. But that further observer is also combined with the observed system into a still bigger quantum system whose combined observables only take definite values when observed by a further observer, etc. There is in principle no end to the process, which implies that the whole universe is a quantum system which typically does not occupy any definite state. So the postulate fails to fulfil its task of fitting quantum theory to a fairly basic property of things, namely that they are definite – at any rate up to the bounds of observational error – when observed. The so-called 'many worlds' interpretation is one attempted solution to the problem.[9] According to it, instead of one possibility being realised at any stage they all are – along all the different possibility-branches into different parallel worlds.

The idea of a multiplicity of worlds has become an increasingly common feature of cosmological models. Though it may sound merely – so far – an interesting piece of speculative physics merging on metaphysics (some physicists think that it is *just* metaphysics), there is one otherwise puzzling set of empirical facts where, it has been claimed, a multiverse theory offers the only currently available alternative explanation to a theistic one.

4. FINE-TUNED – FOR LIFE?

The empirical facts in question concern some physical magnitudes whose values the standard model fails to determine: among them the masses of the elementary particles, the strengths of the corresponding forces governing their behaviour, the gravitational constant and the cosmological constant. Quantities whose values are not determined by a physical theory and have to be established by observation ('put in by hand', in physics-speak) are called *free*, or *adjustable*, parameters. In the standard model there are twenty-eight. To most physicists the existence of adjustable parameters signifies a serious incompleteness, indeed *inadequacy*, in the theory. What they have mostly found even more unsettling, however, is the problem we saw Francis Collins, among others, raise earlier: that to square with a 'universe fit for life', some of those parameters must take values within extremely small intervals of their possible values. In the contemporary jargon, they are 'fine-tuned', and what is more, apparently fine-tuned *for life*.

[9] There have been several others. One, which does not involve other worlds or other minds, appeals to an effect known as *decoherence*, in which interaction with the environment can very rapidly suppress the interference components of an interaction.

For example, inflation provides the key to understanding why matter and radiation are distributed so evenly across space (an earlier 'fine-tuning' problem), but for inflation itself to have occurred two parameters must have been selected to be within millionths of their range of theoretically possible values. The fact that the heavier elements, starting with carbon, could have been formed and from the helium and small amounts of beryllium that existed demanded an extraordinarily finely balanced set of conditions to allow the reactions to proceed in a stable way. The chemistry of life is carbon based, but for carbon-based life to be possible at all the universe has to be capable not only of producing carbon itself, but of being able to maintain itself for a sufficiently long time and in a stable enough way for life to form and evolve. If the ratio of proton to neutron mass or the strength of the weak force differed from their actual values by as little as one part in a billion in some cases that could not have happened. Taking all these 'coincidences' into account, Lee Smolin makes this comment:

> One can estimate the probability that the constants in our standard theories of the elementary particles and cosmology would, were they chosen randomly, lead to a world with carbon chemistry. That probability is less than one part in 10^{220}.[10]

Scientific opinion differs as to how fine the tolerances on some of these values really need to be for some sort of stable universe to emerge. Victor Stenger[11] and F. C. Adams[12] investigated the amount of allowed simultaneous variation in some of the constants and found tolerances substantially larger than had been thought possible. But there seems to be general agreement that one coincidence is a real mind-bender: the value of the so-called cosmological constant Λ, a magnitude proportional to the energy-density of the vacuum and presumed responsible for the rate of expansion of the universe. According to observation, Λ is very small but not quite zero, whereas its predicted value, the sum of all the vacuum energies, positive and negative, of all the particles in the universe is enormously larger, by a factor of 10^{120}. By a process that physicists currently have no explanation for, there has been a cancellation of these energies in that sum to the extent of giving the value 0 in the first 120 decimal places in the observed difference. I say no explanation has been forthcoming, but Steven Weinberg famously set himself to work out the range of values that would permit

10 Lee Smolin, *Three Roads to Quantum Gravity* (New York: Basic Books, 2001), p. 202.

11 Victor Stenger, *Has Science Found God? The Latest Results in the Search for Purpose in the Universe* (Amherst, NY: Prometheus Books, 2003).

12 F. C. Adams, 'Stars in Other Universes: Stellar Structure with Different Fundamental Constants of Nature', *Journal of Cosmology and Astroparticle Physics* 8 (2008), 010.

the universe to evolve as ours has, with stable galaxies, stars, planets and so forth, and found that – *coincidentally*, as it were – one less zero would have prevented it (so would a negative value): if it is smaller than 0 the universe collapses; bigger than 0 by one more than 119 orders of magnitude and the universe blows apart. Interesting.

5. THE PROSECUTOR'S RETURN

A simple calculation suggests that the coincidence may be more than just interesting; even that it may be – hold your breath – *more than just a coincidence*. The probability that those first 120 digits would all take the value 0 *by chance* is absolutely minuscule: 10^{-120}. 'How much chance can we buy in scientific explanation?' asks Paul Davies rhetorically (intended answer: nowhere near that much), continuing in a by-now familiar strain:

> One measure of what is involved can be given in terms of coin-flipping: odds of 10^{120} to one is like getting heads no fewer than 400 times in a row. If the existence of life in the universe is completely independent of the big fix mechanism – if it's just a coincidence – then those are the odds against us being here. That level of flukiness seems too much to swallow.[13]

If it's a 'fix', on the other hand, all those 0s are not all coincidental: they enable the conditions propitious for life. Implicit conclusion: more likely than not it's a fix.

And we are back again with the Prosecutor's Fallacy. Let E be the statement that the first 119 digits in the value of the cosmological constant are all 0. Let H be the hypothesis that E is due to chance, and H′ that it is due to a pro-life Designer. Also, suppose that the chance calculation is correct (it isn't, but we shall come to that in due course). Then we have $\text{Prob}(E|H) << \text{Prob}(E|H')$, where '$<<$' as usual signifies 'much less than' – in this case an absolutely enormous amount less than, if we take the ratio of the two. Indeed, so close to 0 is Prob(E|H) that Davies seems to be authorising us to put it, in effect, to 0. At any rate, to echo Keith Ward, H′ is to be (much) preferred. John Leslie used the same argument to the same conclusion. In a review of Leslie's argument Quentin Smith called it 'the most powerful "argument from design" of the twentieth century'.[14]

[13] Paul Davies, *The Goldilocks Enigma: Why is the Universe Just Right for Life?* (London: Allen Lane, 2006), p. 170.

[14] Quentin Smith, 'Review of *Universes*, by John Leslie', *Nous* 28 (1994), 262–9.

Well, we know from the previous chapter that despite Smith's encomium the conclusion does not follow at all. It all depends on the prior probabilities, for as we know these can cause the large inequality between the likelihoods Prob(E|H) and Prob(E|H′) to be reversed for the posterior probabilities Prob(H|E) and Prob(H′|E). And not only can, but given the Problem of Evil, very arguably should: Smith himself in his review observed that Leslie's favoured hypothesis, his so-called 'Creative Ethical Requirement', is 'encumbered with the Problem of Evil'.[15] I am not entirely sure how the Creative Ethical Requirement views human sorrows, but the Problem of Evil is certainly the Achilles's heel of the orthodox theistic account.

But without God, or a Lesliean God-surrogate, what plausible explanation could there be for a universe apparently fine-tuned for life? One other possibility is that there is a God who simply liked to set the whole thing off as an exercise in creativity. But physicists in general typically don't seem to warm to theistic or deistic explanations, preferring something they find recognisably a physical explanation. At this point we should remember that there is always the possibility that an explanation will one day be found: in the case of a physical explanation of fine-tuning, many physicists regard it as not merely a possibility but a near certainty that current particle physics is merely some effective, i.e. low-energy approximation to a much more symmetrical theory which will unify gravity and quantum mechanics and reduce the number of apparently independent parameters to very few, and possibly none at all. Physics grows, particularly under pressure from unsolved problems or unexplained 'significant' coincidences like fine-tuning, and the results expected from the Large Hadron Collider will not only generate further, possibly rapid, growth (they may also cause a fundamental rethink of the standard model if they don't soon reveal the Higgs particle), but in doing so resolve at least some of the fine-tuning questions:

For example the case for low energy supersymmetry, or other TeV scale dynamics to be uncovered at the Large Hadron Collider (LHC), is based almost entirely on the fine-tuning problem for the scale of electroweak symmetry breaking. If there is new physics at the TeV scale, then there need not be any fine tuning at all and the electroweak scale is natural. We are all greatly looking forward to the results of the LHC, which will tell us if there in fact is new physics at the TeV scale.[16]

[15] *Ibid.*, p. 263.
[16] John F. Donoghue, 'The Fine-tuning Problems of Particle Physics and Anthropic Mechanisms', arXiv:0710.4080v1 [hep-ph], 22 October 2007.

6. THE ANTHROPIC PRINCIPLE

Nevertheless, there seem to be severe difficulties in the way of reconciling, let alone explaining, the anomalous value of the cosmological constant within a theoretical framework consistent with the standard cosmological model. Much the same, according to Paul Steinhardt and Neil Turok, goes for the appearance 'at just the right time', of dark matter.[17] They report that in despair physicists reluctant to appeal to divine intervention began turning to an explanatory principle which to others has all the appearance of alchemy: the *anthropic principle*. There is a large and confusing literature on 'the' anthropic principle, confusing largely because 'the' principle seems to mean very different things in different contexts (this is why I put 'the' in quotes).[18] The one that Steinhardt and Turok are referring to is a type of observer selection effect which in conjunction with the hypothesis of a multiverse of a suitable sort is supposed to explain why we should observe the phenomenon of fine-tuning. To be more precise, suppose that a very large number, effectively an infinite number, of universes have been generated in such a way that their parameters, and even laws, vary randomly across the entire set. A law of large numbers argument is then invoked to predict that there is a large chance that there will be some universes, not many relative to the whole set but at least one, in which the parameters take values permitting the evolution of life. Indeed, though the chance of life getting started even in the hospitable universes may be extremely small, the same law of large numbers argument predicts its emergence somewhere with a high probability.

It is at this point that the anthropic principle enters, in the form of the claim that we are justified in transferring that high probability to us ourselves observing fine-tuning in our own universe. We are justified, the principle claims, because we selected it to be that way by our existence: if our universe were not finely tuned for life, we would not be around to observe it. I will call this final step (A), for 'anthropic', and because we shall revisit it shortly. That established, the charge made by many physicists that the multiverse hypothesis is a piece of pure metaphysics can be dismissed, because we can now employ the machinery of Bayes's Theorem to show that the evidence of fine-tuning confirms the hypothesis. Where H is that hypothesis and E the fine-tuning evidence, we simply note that the boost

[17] Paul Steinhardt and Neil Turok, *Endless Universe: Beyond the Big Bang – Rewriting Cosmic History* (New York: Doubleday, 2007).

[18] There is a 'weak' anthropic principle, and a 'strong' one, and others besides. The ones I will be referring to fall into the last category.

factor Prob(E|H)/Prob(E) is greater than 1, and so Prob(H|E) is greater than Prob(H). Metaphysics can't be confirmed by observational evidence, so H is not metaphysics. Or so it might seem.

In fact, the argument is fallacious, and the fallacious step is (A). One of the most surprising aspects of the very extensive literature on the anthropic principle is the extent to which it has been endorsed by some very distinguished people. Yet it is *obviously* fallacious. It is a simple tautology that we will witness fine-tuning only if we are in a universe possessing it, and *it is a theorem of the probability calculus that adding a tautology to any hypothesis – of a multiverse, or whatever – does not alter the probability that gets assigned to any specified event.* John Leslie tried to dodge the objection with an analogy: two dice are being rolled a very large number of times, and when a double-six occurs you are invited into the room to witness the result. If the allowed number of throws is large enough it is very probable that at some point a (6,6) will occur. But given the background conditions of the problem, a (6,6) will occur if and only if you witness it. Hence the probability, given that background information, is equally large that you will witness the double-six.[19] This is of course quite consistent with assuming that the probability of getting the double-six at any given throw remains the same and small, namely $^1/_{36}$. The reasoning in this example is certainly valid, but it is only valid because it contains the assumption that you are brought in to see the double-six when and only when it occurs. And no analogue of this can be justified in the cosmological context. There is no 'we' waiting in logical space until a finely tuned universe is produced and we are then summoned to witness it.

The fact that (A) is clearly invalid has not prevented several distinguished scientists from finding it compelling. Here is the physicist Max Tegmark:

> Suppose you check into a hotel, are assigned room 1967 and, surprised, note that that is the year you were born. After a moment of reflection, you conclude that this is not all that surprising and that you would not be having these thoughts in the first place if you'd been assigned another one.

Richard Dawkins is another advocate:

> Any probability estimate is made in the context of a certain level of ignorance. If we know nothing about a planet, we may postulate the odds on life's arising on it as, say, one in a billion. But if we import some new assumptions into our estimate, things change. . . . the beauty of the anthropic principle is that it tells us, against all intuition, that a chemical model need only predict that life would arise on one

[19] John Leslie, *Universes* (New York: Routledge, 1989), p. 143.

planet in a billion billion to give us a good and entirely satisfying explanation for the presence of life here.[20]

The 'new assumptions', however, are simply the tautology that if life didn't exist here we wouldn't be around to observe it. And as we noted, a tautology is incapable of explaining anything. Yet another distinguished advocate, the physicist Leonard Susskind, unwittingly unmasks the anthropic principle to reveal that that is indeed just what it is, a tautology:

The kind of answer *that this or that is true because if it were not true there would be nobody to ask the question* is called the anthropic principle. Most physicists hate the anthropic principle.[21]

With reason.

The step (A) above, the anthropic step, failed to transfer the large probability attaching to 'There is fine-tuning in some universe', conditional on the assumptions contained in the multiverse hypothesis (random generation, large number of universes, etc.), to the observation that *this* universe is fine-tuned. What is needed for that to succeed is for some way to be found of relating what an observer in this universe might expect to see and what is happening in other universes. It is just this lacuna that Steven Weinberg and his two co-authors Hugo Martel and Paul Shapiro sought to fill by asking – and answering[22] – the question what an observer would expect to see *who had been randomly drawn from a multiverse of universes*, each containing a number of such observers and characterised by a specific value of the most recalcitrant of the finely tuned parameters, the cosmological constant. Like almost everyone else, they were puzzled by the fact that its observed value is so near the current mass-density of the universe rather than the 120 orders of magnitude larger which theory seemed to predict. Their strategy was to derive the probability distribution for the randomly selected observer over the range of anthropically possible values of the vacuum energy density. They show, subject to some assumptions that I will mention presently, that values close to those suggested by observation are fairly probable, while those orders of magnitude larger or smaller are extremely improbable.

The probability model they use in their derivation is basically a very simple one. It is a continuous model, since the anthropically allowed values of the vacuum energy density form an interval, but the discrete form of it

[20] Richard Dawkins, *The God Delusion* (London: Bantam Books, 2006), p. 166.

[21] *Edge* video. www.edge.org/edge_video.html.

[22] Hugo Martel, Paul Shapiro and Steven Weinberg, 'Likely Values of the Cosmological Constant', *Astrophysics Journal* 492 (1998), 1–57.

is randomly sampling differently coloured balls from boxes each of which contain a certain number of balls of the same colour, where there may be different numbers of boxes for each colour. The colours correspond to a partition into subintervals of the range of possible values of the vacuum energy density, the boxes to universes each characterised by an energy density in one of the given subintervals, and the balls to the observers in each universe. For anyone used to doing discrete probability-sums it isn't difficult to get an expression for the probability of sampling a yellow ball, say, in terms of the average numbers of balls in each of the boxes with differently coloured balls. Weinberg *et al.* give the continuous form of this expression. But they have to invoke some very substantial assumptions to obtain actual probability-values. These include the following: a uniform prior probability distribution over the possible values of the vacuum energy density; the number of observers in each universe must be finite; and the average number of observers in any set of universes in the same interval of values of the vacuum-energy is proportional to the fraction of matter (baryons) condensing into galaxies.

Weinberg *et al.* may have bridged the explanatory gap from an observer in this universe to observers in others by assuming in their model that he or she is randomly selected from the set of all observers in all universes,[23] but at the cost of rendering the prior probability of the model itself arguably extremely small. The constant prior distribution over the values of the vacuum energy density is justified by the extreme narrowness of the interval of anthropically allowed values of the energy density, but at the end of this chapter we shall see that this narrowness is not an absolute quantity but relative to the scale on which it is measured. But the most questionable aspect of the model is their own version of the anthropic principle, the indispensable bridging assumption that I, or you, are random members of the super-universe of all observers in all universes. The cost of making the multiverse less metaphysical an assumption in one way has merely increased its metaphysicalness, so to speak, in another. I certainly have no evidence, and neither do you dear reader, that you and I are randomly drawn from such a bizarre urn of possibilities, or indeed that we are randomly drawn from anything. Who or what is doing the drawing? By what method? Judging by the less than overwhelmingly enthusiastic response from his fellow-physicists to Weinberg *et al.*'s anthropic exercise, scepticism as to the genuinely scientific value of anthropic reasoning remains undiminished.

[23] One has to allow of course for the possibility that the populations concerned might have no sex, two sexes or more than two.

Steinhardt and Turok claim that their Cyclic Model, with its periodically colliding branes, tames the problem of the anomalous value of the cosmological constant that the observations suggest.[24] It does so by appealing to quantum jumps which gradually diminish the value of the constant to 0 over successive cycles, with an exponentially increasing time between each jump. Thus their model, they claim, explains the observed small magnitude of the cosmological constant by the hypothesis that the universe is much older, cycle after cycle, than had been thought. So now we need to assess the prior probability not only of the Cyclic Model itself but that model conjoined with the hypothesis that the universe has already been through sufficiently many cycles, based on the evidence independent of the observed value of the cosmological constant. Steinhardt and Turok concede that many of the details of their own model are still far from complete, but they claim that the cyclic model is less arbitrary than the multiverse-plus-anthropic principle model. What seems clear, however, is that their explanation is so highly speculative that assigning it now any substantial prior probability seems unjustified. This also seems to be the collective judgment of the physics community.

7. THE HUBRISTIC PRINCIPLE

Doesn't that rather negative conclusion cede the field to God, by default, even if he does have trouble explaining his strangely negligent attitude to human sorrow? Not at all. Judging by the literature, many physicists and cosmologists still believe firmly that there will one day emerge, if not a total theory of everything emerging fully armed from the collective heads of the physics community, then at least the convergence to one, in which those parameters fixed at their observed values for no apparent reason (if you are not a theist, and most of them are not) will become fixed according to the requirements of some new symmetry principle. According to Paul Davies, the hypothesis that a purely scientific explanation of this sort exists is regarded as 'the main scientific alternative to the multiverse'.[25]

But Davies sees a difficulty in judging such a theory, were it to exist, a *solution* to the problem posed by fine-tuning. The difficulty, according to him, is that it merely puts the problem one stage further back. His argument is as follows. Think of the space of all logically possible explanations of the way things are. It is easy to show that this space is infinite, and a little

[24] Steinhardt and Turok, *Endless Universe*, pp. 247–52. [25] Davies, *The Goldilocks Enigma*, p. 3.

more reflection shows that it is so vast as to be not merely infinite but so big that no boundary can be put round it. Consider the following homely example. I lift my hand up. It is a logical possibility that I might not have done. When I lifted it up a bell chimed somewhere. It might not have done. When the bell chimed a sparrow fell. It might not have done. That is already eight distinct possibilities for the way things might have been. One can obviously continue this exponentially ramifying list of possibilities through the finite. Now add to all those all the logically possible specifications of physical laws, all the logically possible types of universe, and the gigantic scale of the possibility-space becomes awe-inspiringly apparent. We can even include the multiverse itself in this endless panorama of possibilities. After all, the multiverse is still one possible universe, even if more so. The number of different possible universes satisfying all those different possible universe-specifications is unimaginably, open-endedly enormous.

Now that we are made duly aware of the scale of the possibilities, Davies puts what he thinks is the killer-question. Suppose there is a purely physical explanation of the way things are in this universe, including specifications of all constants now or ever that need to be determined. The question is this. Why should *that* particular set of specifications have been the one selected? More pertinently, what is the chance of a life-friendly set of specifications being chosen from among the innumerably many other possibilities? Practically zero, Davies concludes:

> [w]ho, or what, promotes the 'merely possible' to the 'actually existing'? . . . We still have to accept as 'given', without explanation, one particular theory, one specific mathematical description, drawn from a limitless number of possibilities. . . . Perhaps there is no reason why 'the chosen one' is chosen. Perhaps it is arbitrary. If so, we are still left with the Goldilocks puzzle. What are the chances that a randomly-chosen theory of everything would describe a life-permitting universe? Negligible.[26]

Subtract the rhetoric, however, and there is nothing in those observations that does not beg the question. Any universe of whatever character it is must necessarily have some specific features. If Davies is correct, the chance of *any* of those features being captured by a random choice among all possible types of universe is also negligible. So what? Does that tell us any more than that if you flip a fair coin 100 times (yes, we're back to that again) you should think there was something problematic in each and every possible sequence of outcomes? Of course not. Davies has picked

[26] *Ibid.*, pp. 236–7.

out life as the significant feature and focused his question on that. But without any further justification one might just as well flip the coin 100 times and ask why that particular sequence should have been observed when its chance is so remotely small. But I suspect that standing behind Davies, only partially obscured, is none other than God. Remember Leslie's analysis, discussed in Chapter 3, of what 'cries out' for explanation (and there is a lot of crying out in Davies's book) and what does not. Life cries out for explanation for Davies because God, for Davies, completes a Leslie-type 'feedback loop' to a 'tidy' explanation because God makes a life-permitting universe more probable than a purely random selection among all possible universes would.

And we are back again with the Prosecutor's Fallacy. We know that it doesn't follow from Prob(E|H) < Prob(E|H′) that H′ (God) is the preferable hypothesis to H (chance) on the basis of the evidence E. Nothing at all like that could be concluded without a specification of the prior probabilities of H and H′. Assign God the very, very low prior probability that he arguably merits on the basis of all the other evidence at our disposal and we might reasonably conclude, as many physicists do seem to conclude, that the existence of life ceases to supply a reason why this universe and its laws should have been 'chosen'. There is no reason to conclude, in fact, that it was 'chosen' at all. In that case, of course, there is no reason to conclude that the emergence of human life is any more significant than the fact that this universe contains rocks, plankton and neutron stars. The universe is every bit as fit for them as it is for us.

Davies's barely concealed bias in assuming that life is a factor demanding a better explanation than chance is not the only piece of question-begging in his discussion. That short quotation is disproportionately rich in them. That there is some sort of random draw for the true theory of everything is another question begged. Who or what is doing the drawing? No answer. But without that assumption there is, to use current cosmologists' jargon, no probability-landscape relative to which chances can be computed, and certainly none which unambiguously generates the answer 'negligible'. That answer, as we shall see, arises from trying to impose a probability-landscape of a particular type, namely a *flat* one. The flatness is supposed to reflect a lack of any relevantly discriminating information, but as we shall also see, the condition tying 'informationlessness' to flat probability distributions is inconsistent, to the extent that there is a simple recipe for deriving contradictions from it. *And that applies equally to the common calculations of the allegedly very small probabilities of fine-tuning.*

8. NO CHANCE

All these negligible-chance calculations on which this new argument from design rests are made using a simple and well-known rule. Suppose you are throwing an ordinary six-sided cubic die twice. What is the chance that you will get an even number both times? The number of possible ordered pairs of 6 numbers is 36, and the number of pairs of even numbers between 1 and 6 is 9. The rule says that we should divide 36 by 9, giving the chance as $^1/_4$. Here's another example (does it ring a bell?). Suppose you are predicting the first n decimal places of some physical magnitude. The possible number of different sequences of n decimal digits is 10 times 10 times 10 times . . . n times over, i.e. 10^n. What is the chance that all these n digits will be 0? By the same reasoning, $1/10^n$, or 10^{-n}: pretty small if n is greater than a relatively small number, and absolutely minuscule if n is, say, 120.

Those examples involve finite sets of whole numbers. For problems involving the continuum, i.e. decimal numbers, there is a natural extension of the rule of dividing the number of favourable possibilities by the number of all possibilities. For example, suppose you know that the temperature, x degrees centigrade say, of a pan of water is between 10°C and 90°C. What is the chance that x is less than 50? In this sort of continuous case the extended rule tells us to divide the length of the interval from 10 to 50 (the *measure* of the favourable cases) by the length of the interval from 10 to 90 (the *measure* of the set of possible cases[27]), making the chance equal to $^1/_2$.

Though this type of a priori reckoning of chances was very prominent in the history of probability (the rule goes under the rather cryptic name of 'the classical definition of probability'), it eventually became evident that it raised serious questions of principle, and not only of principle but also of *consistency*. The statistical model from which the rule is derived is *random choice*, in which each possible basic outcome is selected with the same probability. The chance of two even numbers in the double throw of the die is obtained by assuming that each possible pairs of numbers, between 1 and 6, is equally likely; hence each such pair has a probability of $^1/_{36}$. The additivity property of probability then tells us that the probability of a pair of even numbers is the sum of the probabilities of each of the even pairs, hence $^1/_{36}$ times 9. Random choice is explicitly assumed in this quotation from Lee Smolin:

[27] Length, area and volume all go under the technical name of Lebesgue measure. Lebesgue measure is the continuous analogue of size measure for finite sets, called *cardinality* measure.

One can estimate the probability that the constants in our standard theories of the elementary particles and cosmology would, were they chosen randomly, lead to a world with carbon chemistry. That probability is less than one part in 10^{220}.[28]

But who or what is doing the random choosing? Practically nobody who talks about chances assumes an *actual* random choice, and I am reasonably confident Smolin doesn't. I suspect that he is basing his estimate on the rule described above for producing numbers, and in default of any actual randomiser that rule is a totally arbitrary one. It is (perhaps surprisingly) also easy to prove that it generates inconsistencies. Consider the pan of water again. Consider the inverse $y = x^{-1}$ of the temperature x°C of the water. y lies in the interval between $^1/_{90}$ and $^1/_{10}$, and x is less than 50 just in case y is greater than $^1/_{50}$. But the length of the interval $[^1/_{50}, ^1/_{10}]$ is not half of that of $[^1/_{90}, ^1/_{10}]$: it is 90% of it. So what is the chance that y is greater than $^1/_{50}$? Using the same rule for calculating chances, it is 90%. But this is also the chance that x is less than 50. So now it is very likely indeed that x is less than 50! No longer is it an even-money bet that the temperature is less than half its possible maximum, but very big odds on. This is not in any sense new and important information, however: *it is an outright contradiction*. The diagnosis of what has gone wrong is fairly obvious. A fundamental rule of probability is that *the same probability has to be assigned logically equivalent propositions*. Probabilities, in other words, have to be invariant under equivalent descriptions. Unfortunately, as the example shows, *relative* lengths, areas and volumes will in general vary under continuous transformations unless these are linearly related to each other. That is true whether the quantities are dimensionless, i.e. so-called pure numbers, or are measured in definite physical units, like temperature centigrade or centimetres.

It's not a valid objection to say that when we ask what the chance is that x lies between given limits we are not asking what the chance is that y lies between corresponding limits. It is true that we might not *think* we are, but any question about x is logically equivalent to one about y. Nor is it a valid objection that y is not a natural magnitude. Physics, and science in general, are full of what might appear to be very 'unnatural' magnitudes. In special relativity the *rapidity* of a body is the inverse hyperbolic tangent of the velocity. Here we have a quantity defined from a directly observable one, which has nothing apparently to do with trigonometry, using the inverse of a trigonometric function! Rapidity is neither more nor less natural than

[28] Smolin, *Three Roads to Quantum Gravity*, p. 202.

the quantity it replaces: it is just more convenient to use in calculations.[29] The idea of natural and unnatural kinds is a hangover from Aristotelian science, though it continues to beguile many contemporary philosophers who should have moved on by now but sadly have not. Physics contains a range of often bizarre-seeming transformations of familiar quantities, and we saw earlier that there is simply no way of predicting now which exotic quantity might not one day be seen to be of fundamental importance in the statement of physical law.

But the not-a-natural-kind objection is anyway beside the point. For every statement about some quantity t there is a logically equivalent statement about another quantity f(t) obtained from t by some functional transformation f, and in moving from one to the other we are merely moving to a logically equivalent representation: anything true of the one must be true of the other. The fact that the 'chance' of a given event can change under a simple redescription is acknowledged by Robin Collins in his discussion of fine-tuning. However, his only comment is that 'we simply note that when we talk about fine-tuning, we are always referring to the fine-tuning of the parameters that are actually considered in physics'.[30] But that completely fails to answer the objection, because as we know any two logico-mathematically equivalent ways of representing exactly the same information must have the same probability.

The brutal fact is that this type of calculation of 'chances' is arbitrary and inconsistent even where we are talking about well-behaved possibility-spaces. Only in the late nineteenth century did mathematicians become fully aware that it was a prolific generator of contradictions. According to the custom of the time these were called 'paradoxes'. The most famous is Bertrand's Paradox, after the eponymous nineteenth-century French mathematician who showed how to obtain three different answers to the question: 'What is the probability that a randomly selected chord in a circle is longer than the length of side of the inscribed equilateral triangle?' Bertrand showed that the chance could be $^1/_2$, $^1/_3$ and $^1/_4$, depending on which of three equivalent representations is adopted.[31]

When one starts trying to reckon chances of what may happen in the context of all possible universes, as Paul Davies and other intrepid explorers

[29] Unlike relativistic velocities, rapidities add (a simple property) with respect to inertial frames in relative motion.

[30] Robin Collins, 'Our Evidence for Fine-Tuning', in N. Manson (ed.), *God and Design: The Teleological Argument and Modern Science* (New York: Routledge, 2003), pp. 178–99.

[31] For an informal account of Bertrand's 'paradox' see Mark Kac and Stanislaw Ulam's excellent little book *Mathematics and Logic* (New York: Praeger, 1968), pp. 37–9.

of conceptual infinity do, then literally all bets are off. Such a possibility space is at best ill-defined and at worst simply cannot exist for mathematico-logical reasons, as I pointed out earlier. Max Tegmark, another physicist not averse to playing the numbers game with whole universes, implicitly concedes the arbitrary nature of such calculations:

> Vilenkin and others have published predictions for the probability distributions of various cosmological parameters by arguing that different parallel universes that have inflated by different amounts should be given statistical weights proportional to their volume.[32]

But assigning probabilities proportionally to volumes is just the sort of procedure which we know to be vulnerable to transformational inconsistencies: the relative volume occupied by a set of values of a parameter t need not be the same as the relative volume occupied by the corresponding values of a new parameter $t' = f(t)$, and if f is chosen appropriately, will not be. I shall leave the last word to Steinhardt and Turok:

> What parameters and properties can vary from region to region? What is the probability distribution? In models such as eternal inflation, the relative likelihood of our being in one region or another is ill-defined since there is no unique time slicing and, therefore, no unique way of assessing the number of regions or their volumes. Brave souls have begun to head down this path, but it seems likely to us to drag a beautiful science towards the darkest depths of metaphysics.[33]

9. FAREWELL TO THE FINE-TUNING PROBLEM

One of the richer ironies of the fine-tuning discussion is that the same spurious chance calculation which supposedly shows that the probability of fine-tuning on the assumption that God does not exist is negligible, is just as capable of showing that its probability if God does exist is just as negligible. It is true that life as we know it is due to the abundant existence of carbon in the universe, for carbon is the only element that can form stable bonds of the right energy to create biological molecules. But if, as theologians almost unanimously tell us, God is bounded only by *logical* possibility, then he can do anything short of causing a logical contradiction to be instantiated. In that case, why go through this tortuous rigmarole of

[32] Max Tegmark, 'Parallel Universes', in J. D. Barrow, P. C. W. Davies and C. L. Harper (eds.), *Science and Ultimate Reality: From Quantum to Cosmos* (Cambridge University Press, 2003), pp. 459–92.

[33] Paul Steinhardt and Neil Turok, 'The Cyclic Model Simplified', *New Astronomy Reviews* 49 (2005), 43–57.

creating laws which, even in fairly optimal conditions, only seem to give small windows of opportunity for life? Why not create a much more life-tolerant universe? Why not create one which doesn't depend in any way on the vagaries of the hardware in our own rather haphazard universe? There is nothing in the concept of an entity capable of internal representations of its environment and able to draw inferences from them which demands that it be constructed of biological molecules, or even inorganic ones for that matter. Roger Penrose has pointed out that if God had simply wanted to create human life he could have done so far more economically than via a Big Bang with its extremely demanding initial entropy conditions.[34] Surely such a God who can do anything that is logically consistent could think of less complicated and hazardous ways of creating intelligent life. Victor Stenger, in the course of his own typically lucid discussion of fine-tuning, quotes his friend Martin Wagner as observing that '[God] could have created us in hard vacuum if he wanted'.[35] In any event, by the same sort of reasoning that concludes that fine-tuning is evidence for God, the probability that he would have selected *this* particular method, with *this* particular fine-tuning, out of all possible ways, must be vanishingly small. You can't have it both ways (even God can't).

But the calculations are spurious. The eminent philosopher Karl Popper memorably called chance calculations based on the Principle of Indifference 'Probability Magic'.[36] He could have added 'black magic', given the ease with which they generate inconsistencies. People nevertheless still habitually use that principle, and nowhere more profligately than in discussions of the fine-tuning 'problem'. The temptation to produce numbers at any logical cost seems irresistible. Consider this recent claim, based, if that is the right word, on a comparison of the 'numbers' of possible simulated universes versus actual ones: 'There is a significant probability that you are living in [a] computer simulation. I mean this literally.' Note the 'literally'. This is probability magic indeed: *black* magic. It is *voodoo probability*. Voodoo probability is there too in Paul Davies's claim that

> carbon-copy universes *must* be out there somewhere, if the universe is truly infinite. And there will be infinitely many of them: infinitely many universes identical *in*

[34] Roger Penrose, *The Road to Reality: A Complete Guide to the Laws of the Universe* (London: Vintage, 2005), pp. 762–5.

[35] Victor Stenger, *God: The Failed Hypothesis: How Science Shows that God Does Not Exist* (Amherst, NY: Prometheus Books, 2007), p. 154.

[36] Karl Popper, 'Probability Magic, or Knowledge out of Ignorance', *Dialectica* 11 (1957), 354–72.

all respects to the observed universe. Weird though these conclusions may seem, they follow incontrovertibly from the logic of simple statistics and probability theory.[37]

'The logic of simple statistics and probability theory' most certainly does not imply that in an infinite space every possibility must be realised, and indeed that claim is simply not true.

Let us now bid farewell to the fine-tuning problem. Victor Stenger's comment on it is brief and to the point: it 'ultimately makes no sense'.[38] I noted earlier that he and other physicists, including Steven Weinberg and F. C. Adams, have argued that the degree of fine-tuning required for a stable universe is actually not so fine at all. But whether it is or it isn't does not now matter. Even if it were, it does not give an iota of support to any inference to a human-friendly Demiurge.

The Old Testament of course told a very different story, that God just created man in his own image in a universe fabricated for that purpose. It is a much more *coherent* story, but it is also one blown out of the water by Darwin. But without that story, the universe seems a cold and friendless place: *meaningless*, in human terms. Moreover, it seems that no purely physical explanation can ever be ultimate because the questions 'why *that* explanation?', '*why* should the universe be like that?' are meaningful and deserving an answer – crying out for one, some might say. If that is the case then it seems that the potential infinite regress can be stopped only be a self-necessitating principle, more usually referred to as God. And with him meaning floods back into the world. But not everyone agrees. We shall take up the story in the next chapter.

EXERCISE

'The basic constants of nature need to be exactly what they are to produce life. This "may have the flavour of a miracle" [the quote is from Peter Atkins]. Well, it is just what one would expect if an immensely wise God wished to produce a life-bearing universe, if the whole thing was purposive. Whereas it is not at all what one would expect, if it was a matter of chance. Every new scientific demonstration of the precision of the mathematical structure needed to produce conscious life is evidence of design. Just to go on saying "But it could all be chance" is to refuse to be swayed by evidence.' Comment.

[37] Davies, *The Goldilocks Enigma*, p. 201. [38] Stenger, *God: The Failed Hypothesis*, p. 154.

MAIN POINTS OF CHAPTER 4

- A new and powerful argument for design seems strongly suggested by the so-called fine-tuning problem. This is the fact that certain physical parameters need to be within a very small range of their observed values in order for life to be possible in principle. Some of these tolerances seem to be very tight indeed: to within one part in 10^{120} in one case, the value suggested by observations of the cosmological constant.
- A multiverse hypothesis in combination with the so-called Anthropic Principle is a currently favoured scientific alternative to a theistic explanation.
- But this explanatory strategy nevertheless fails to explain why this universe should be finely tuned.
- The calculations of the supposedly minute probability of fine-tuning arising by chance are based on a principle that is both arbitrary and generates inconsistencies.
- The conclusion is that not only anthropic arguments but also the probabilistic arguments for theism generated by the fine-tuning 'problem' are fallacious.

CHAPTER 5

What does it all mean?

'There's a reason for everything.'

1. FROM HERE TO INFINITY

We have probably all heard of feedback cycles, where a permissible operation can send a system into an unending sequence of cycles. Something rather like one haunts the philosophical literature on God. Its origin is the apparently unremarkable fact that every natural language contains a word or words equivalent to 'Why?' The fact may seem unremarkable, but combined with what looks like an equally unremarkable assumption it generates an explosive mixture. For if X is any meaningful contingent statement, the expression 'Why (is it the case that) X?' is a grammatically well-formed question, and given the plausible assumption that to any meaningful question there is in principle an answer, we have the loop: to any answer, say Z,[1] you simply stick 'Why' in front of it and place '?' after it, and off you go again. Forever, or so it seems.[2]

That 'plausible assumption' has done more intellectual damage than possibly any other in the history of thought. We have already encountered various dubious – and more than dubious – assumptions elevated into so-called 'principles' in the recent literature on God (think 'anthropic principle'). This one has been endowed with the most imposing name of all in the history of philosophy: *The Principle of Sufficient Reason.* Enunciated by the philosopher/mathematician/jurist and supreme polymath of his time, Leibniz, it states that nothing contingent happens without a reason, but that of course is exactly what the 'plausible assumption' says. One of its first fruits was the posing of the somewhat strange question 'Why

[1] Y rules itself out. Don't ask why.

[2] Assuming, of course, that there is an infinity of days, which according to current cosmology seems unlikely.

is there something (rather than nothing)?' by Leibniz himself, who also thoughtfully provided an answer (see below). Courtesy of the Principle, the rather unexceptional fact that there are things (in the broadest sense which includes electromagnetic fields and the vacuum as well as stones, trees, etc.) suddenly becomes problematic. Now there has to be an explanation of the fact that there are things, even one thing. Not only has there to be an explanation, but to prevent the cycle repeating itself to infinity there has to be an *ultimate* explanation, which is not contingent. That ultimate explanation, Leibniz tells us, is (of course) God, the necessary cause of everything contingent and whose own essence implies necessary existence.[3] In the idea of existence flowing necessarily from essence, or *definition*, we have a reference to the celebrated *Ontological Argument* (of which more shortly).

2. THE SELF-MADE MAN

Traditionally, ultimate explanations are ultimate *causal* explanations. One possible explanation of where the universe came from is nowhere, and by chance (in a quantum fluctuation). But no self-respecting divine would accept it as an *ultimate* explanation. He (or she, in these enlightened times) would and does accept God, and only God, in that role, as *causa sui* (the cause of himself); truly a self-made man. Postulating God as the terminus of explanation also affords the opportunity for some creative boot-strapping. If God is the cause of everything, including himself, then he is also the *reason* for everything. Latin was the medium of scholarly and theological communication, at any rate in the western Church, at the time these great issues were being aired, and I pointed out earlier that in Latin 'causa' means both 'cause' and 'reason'. The move from cause to reason, besides being etymologically authorised, also answers a deeply felt need. It seems to be an entrenched feature of the human psyche that people are generally not satisfied with explanations that do not supply a *reason* for whatever it is that they want explained, and 'reason' modulates quickly into '*purpose*', and then, if it is the universe itself to be explained, into *God*'s purpose.

The notion that teleological, i.e. purposive, explanations are superior to others has an ancient pedigree. In Aristotle's enormously influential theory of causation, *final causes* are the ends or purposes for which something exists or happens, and he gives final causes explanatory priority over what he called the efficient and material causes, i.e. the sorts of causes and

[3] G. W. Leibniz, 'On the Ultimate Origination of Things', in G. H. R. Parkinson (ed.), Mary Morris and G. H. R. Parkinson (trans.), *Philosophical Writings* (London: Dent, 1995), pp. 136–44.

laws empirical science attempts to discover, but which Aristotle deemed insufficient to count as full explanations in their own right. In claiming that final causes are needed for the explanation of the material and efficient causes, and also in placing God[4] as the final cause of everything, Aristotle bequeathed an invaluable legacy to his theological posterity.

Identifying God as the natural, and only possible, terminus of explanation, and also the final cause of the universe, offers a further opportunity for bootstrapping. For if the universe exists to fulfil God's *purpose*, then it follows that the universe is *pregnant with meaning*. Probably the most important factor in explaining why many people are drawn to religion is that it gives a meaning to things and events which it is felt science by itself cannot. If for everything that happens there is a (divine) *purpose* behind it, then what may appear simply very unpleasant or simply coldly indifferent becomes transformed into the working through of a plan in which all such experiences have a proper place. Pascal expressed what many felt and still feel when he wrote about what appears to be a vast, unfeeling universe: 'The eternal silence of these infinite spaces fills me with dread.'[5] He, like many people, sought solace in religion: in his case, a type of Christian mysticism. A similar thought-process probably motivated Stephen Jay Gould to assign 'meaning' to the 'magisterium' of religion.

But not everyone seeks or expects meaning in the universe. Though many and probably most scientists strongly desire *explanations*, and attempt to push the boundaries of the explicable back as far as they can, few even among the most distinguished seem particularly upset not to discern meaning in the universe as so far revealed, and certainly not a meaning which endows human lives with any particular significance. The nearest mainstream physics gets to putting any reference to mankind into its laws is the Anthropic Principle, and even that is usually regarded as merely a convenient point for arguing backwards rather than a law in its own right. In a well-known, to some notorious, passage the physics Nobel laureate Steven Weinberg, said that he thought that the more the universe seemed comprehensible the more it seemed pointless.[6]

Several other Nobel laureates agree with Weinberg in thinking that whatever fundamental laws the universe might obey, they have scant respect for human concerns. One of them, Richard Feynman, wrote that

[4] Aristotle's God is nothing like the God of theism, however, as I pointed out in Chapter 1.

[5] 'Le silence éternel de ces éspaces infinis m'effroye.' Blaise Pascal, *Pensées*, Roger Ariew (ed. and trans.) (Indianapolis, IN: Hackett, 2005).

[6] Steven Weinberg, *The First Three Minutes: A Modern View of the Origin of the Universe*, updated edn (New York: Basic Books, 1988), p. 149.

scientific views end in awe and mystery, lost at the edge of uncertainty, but they appear to be so deep and so impressive that the theory that it is all arranged as a stage for God to watch man's struggle for good and evil seems to be inadequate.[7]

Even Einstein, who occasionally talked about God in his more philosophical discussions of physics, seemed to regard 'God' as no more than a synonym for Nature, and an indifferent Nature at that:

I believe in Spinoza's God [for Spinoza, God = Nature] who reveals himself in the harmony of all that exists, but not a God who concerns himself with the fates and actions of human beings.[8]

The eminent biologist J. B. S. Haldane spiced the widespread agreement with his habitual sharp wit:

If one could conclude as to the nature of the Creator from a study of creation, it would appear that God has an inordinate fondness for stars and beetles.

Not everyone, then, where the 'not everyone' includes some of the most distinguished scientists, sees any need to encumber the universe with 'meaning', and Weinberg as we have seen thinks that the universe is pointless. Paul Davies opposes that point of view with an attempt at a *reductio ad absurdum*:

If [the universe] isn't 'about' anything, there would be no good reason to embark on the scientific quest in the first place, because we would have no rational basis for believing that we could thereby uncover additional coherent and meaningful facts about the world. So we might justifiably invert Weinberg's dictum and say that the more the universe seems pointless, the more it also seems incomprehensible. Of course, scientists might be deluded in their belief that they are finding systematic and coherent truth in the workings of nature. Ultimately, there may be no reason at all for why things are the way they are. But that would make the universe a fiendishly clever bit of trickery. Can a truly absurd universe so convincingly mime a meaningful one?[9]

But the question itself is absurd: absurdly prejudicial. As well as being mildly insulting to Weinberg whose rationality is impugned in the first sentence, the whole quotation is permeated with rhetorical question-begging. Why should a 'meaningful fact about the world' presuppose anything beyond itself? Why is it irrational to look for patterns in nature if you think that

[7] Richard Feynman, 'The Relation of Science to Religion', *Engineering and Science* (June 1956).

[8] 1929, telegram to a Jewish newspaper.

[9] Paul Davies, *The Goldilocks Enigma: Why is the Universe Just Right for Life?* (London: Allen Lane, 2006), p. 18.

nature is all that there is? Why is there no point to the scientific enterprise if the universe is not 'about' something? Why are scientists 'deluded in their belief that they are finding systematic and coherent truth in the workings of nature' if there is no more ultimate 'reason' for that than that there is such systematic and coherent truth? Why would that cause the universe to be a 'fiendishly clever bit of trickery'?

We are back with the Argument from Design. God, though not necessarily the God of theism, is of course the traditional candidate lined up for the role of Designer, the shadowy figure, the *éminence grise* to whom oblique reference is made in many of Davies's books. He even makes a dramatic entrance right at the end of Stephen Hawking's best-selling *A Brief History of Time*:

> However, if we do discover a complete theory, it should in time be understandable in broad principle by everyone, not just a few scientists. Then we shall all, philosophers, scientists, and just ordinary people, be able to take part in the discussion of why it is that we and the universe exist. If we find the answer to that, it would be the ultimate triumph of human reason – for then we should know the mind of God.[10]

One must beware of reading literally such God-talk by physicists when they wish to express a sense of wonder at the cosmos. Hawking's remark was a nicely dramatic way to end a popular book, and any suggestion that the universe uncovered by science reveals the stamp of a designer, or needed a divine shove to push it into existence has since been firmly repudiated.[11] Einstein talked about the mysterious workings of 'the old one', and remarked (about the apparently fundamental stochastic character of quantum mechanics) that 'God does not play dice', but 'God', as I pointed out above, was for him just a synonym for Nature. The physicist George Smoot said at the press conference following his discovery of the ripples in the cosmic background radiation (a discovery for which he won the Nobel prize) that 'if one is religious, it's like seeing God'. In nearly all the reports of Smoot's remark that I have read, the antecedent 'if one is religious' is omitted. In none of these cases is the author advocating a religious view of

[10] Stephen Hawking, *A Brief History of Time: From the Big Bang to Black Holes* (New York: Bantam Books, 1990), p. 175. The physicist Étienne Klein, Director of the Laboratory of Research in Material Science at the French Atomic Energy Commission, and also Professor of Philosophy of Science at the École Centrale in Paris, ironically comments 'Gosh' (bigre) (*Le Point*, 5 August 2010).

[11] In his recent book *The Grand Design*, written with Leonard Mlodinow (New York: Bantam Books, 2010). Two centuries before Hawking wrote, Laplace famously replied in similar fashion to Napoleon's remark that God didn't make an appearance in Laplace's work: 'I had no need of that hypothesis' ('Je n'ai pas eu besoin de cette hypothèse').

the world at all: it's merely what the French call a *façon de parler* – a way of speaking.

Most prominent scientists seem to have little or no need for God, or much time for him. In a survey for the leading UK science journal *Nature* in 1994 Larson and Witham compared figures for belief in a personal deity among leading scientists in the USA with those for 1914: in 1914 28% in whole number percentages admitted to such a belief, while in 1994 only 7% did, and in 1914 53% expressed disbelief while in 1994 72% did. 'Leading scientists' in 1994 were those classified as National Academy of Science members; no such body existed in 1914 and those polled under that heading were leading scientists according to the *American Men of Science* classification (*Men*, notice). Even taking account of a possible slight disparity between the classifications, the decay in belief, never over 30%, is striking. Broadly similar results have been obtained in the UK, where the equivalent of the National Academy of Science is the Royal Society.

Are all these distinguished people irrational in rejecting God? I think not if that God is the God of theism. Even non-scientists can recognise a large mismatch between the properties of complete goodness and mercy that God is supposed to possess on the one hand, and the everyday occurrences of not only man's inhumanity to man but nature's tendency to trump it on the other. Einstein, Weinberg and others also quite reasonably feel that as the universe gradually reveals itself in its majesty and subtlety it becomes increasingly difficult, almost *sacrilegious*, to believe that even if there were a Divine Creator, it could possibly concern itself in any positive way with the affairs of the teeming billions of people, their frequent and savage quarrels, their often quite gratuitous cruelty, their apparent indifference to their destruction of their own habitat by the pollution they create and their uncontrolled breeding, and their general lack of curiosity and wonder about the world the Creator had created for them (if you think this unfair to humanity at large you haven't watched reality TV). The God of Abraham penalised Adam and Eve for eating the fruit of the tree of knowledge – but that God was a jealous God who disliked the thought of any sort of competition: the sort of deity capable of creating the cosmos of whose majesty we are still only dimly aware would presumably be, to mix the metaphor slightly, a rather different kettle of fish.

3. CHANCES AGAIN

I observed earlier that a refusal to find 'meaning' in the physical universe does not prevent physicists from continually attempting to push back the boundaries of the explicable. And it is a well-known fact that many do seek some sort of *ultimate* explanation, and a necessary one in the sense that it is a unique solution to some appropriate symmetry constraints (the Standard Model is built on the principle of gauge symmetry), which also unifies currently disparate parts of physics, like quantum mechanics and general relativity, under a single explanatory principle. Needless to say, there would be no adjustable parameters in the account it provides. However, while there may exist a unique solution to the sorts of constraints physicists like to think Nature is imposing (even if Her intentions on this score remain at present rather inscrutable), those constraints will of course not be unique in the class of all logically possible sets. This logical fact provides Paul Davies with a further opportunity for promoting a thinly disguised design agenda. We saw him earlier (Chapter 4, section 9) claim that whatever candidate might be put up for such a uniquely-specified Theory of Everything, it will still represent just one contingent possibility among infinitely many others, with the corollary (no surprises here) that its a priori probability should be set at zero or effectively zero. I quote him again:

> Who, or what, promotes the 'merely possible' to the 'actually existing'?... We still have to accept as *'given', without explanation*, one particular theory, one specific mathematical description, drawn from a limitless number of possibilities... Perhaps there is no reason why 'the chosen one' is chosen. Perhaps it is arbitrary. If so, we are still left with the Goldilocks puzzle. What are the chances that a randomly-chosen theory of everything would describe a life-permitting universe? Negligible.[12]

If that were true, it would mean that there can be no posterior probability greater than zero for any candidate Final Theory, because an immediate consequence of Bayes's rule is that no amount of evidence raises a zero prior probability to a nonzero posterior probability. So even if there is such a true theory, no amount of evidence should make us think that it is any more likely to be true than a logical contradiction. This is the same conclusion that the philosopher Karl Popper arrived at by broadly similar reasoning.[13] Fortunately for science, and for that matter rationality, Popper's and Davies's claims on this score are not correct. Firstly, as I mentioned in Chapter 4, there are serious doubts about whether sensible calculations are possible in the context of a space encompassing all

[12] Davies, *The Goldilocks Enigma*, pp. 236–7 (my emphasis).

[13] This was, however, a rather spectacular own goal since it commits him to the notorious Gamblers' Fallacy, as I show in my paper 'Popper's Solution to the Problem of Induction', *Philosophical Quarterly* 34 (1984), 143–7.

possible theories. There are so many possibilities, most of which have not yet been articulated, infinitely many of which will *never* be articulated, that there is not even a well-defined *possibility*-space, let alone a well-defined probability function defined on it. Secondly, as I also noted, these sorts of a priori chance calculations are question-begging and potentially inconsistent.

This hasn't however stopped Peter van Inwagen from applying just that sort of reasoning to the vexed question 'Why is there something rather than nothing?' Van Inwagen claims, on similar grounds to Davies's, that the prior probability of 'Nothing exists' is zero, since there is only one empty world and infinitely many different non-empty ones.[14] But we should be aware by now that any a priori assignment of that sort begs the question. Why, for example, not assign the universe-types, *empty* and *non-empty*, equal probabilities of $^1/_2$? If you object that one must only assign the same prior probabilities to the cells of the finest partition we can conceive – and 'non-empty' contains infinitely many specific possible worlds, whereas 'empty' contains just one – that begs the question that the cells of that finest partition *are* equally likely a priori. There are, moreover, very good reasons for thinking that the concept of a finest partition of a possibility-space is not an absolute one. The finest partition of the possibility-space for a quantum system of paired bosons each of which can be in state A or state B should, one might think, have four members: (A,A), (A,B), (B,A), (B,B). But a peculiarity of quantum possibility-states is that the 'correct' space only has three members, 'both A', 'one A and one B', 'both B', with the quantum statistics assigning probability $^1/_3$ to each. It is simply not permitted by the theory to consider (A,B) and (B,A) as distinct possibilities. A more homely example is pounds sterling in a bank account: clearly, there are only three possible ways of distributing two pounds between two accounts.

The sort of probabilistic theorising that assigns any a priori probability to 'nothing exists' is pure metaphysics, and potentially inconsistent metaphysics at that. The probabilities that emerge from it are no more valid estimates than any set of numbers between 0 and 1 that anyone cares to dream up of an afternoon. In fact, the probabilistic logic I outlined in

[14] Peter van Inwagen, 'Why is There Anything At All?', *Proceedings of the Aristotelian Society Supplementary Volumes* 70 (1996), 95–120. Modern logic is actually divided on the question whether 'something exists' (rendered in standard notation as $\exists x(x=x)$) is a logical truth or not. If = is taken to be a logical constant then in classical logic that formula is a logical truth; if = is taken to be just a binary relation then it is contingent. There is no fact of the matter as to whether = is 'really' logical or not.

Chapter 3 has nothing to say on the matter of what probability should be assigned any contingent proposition. That is a matter for each individual to decide, according to their criteria of what makes a theory a promising candidate for being the truth. So let us see what the physicists' are. Weinberg echoes many other contemporary physicists in proposing the following:

> a simplicity and rigidity in our principles [i.e. no ability to make ad hoc adjustments without destroying the structure – hence no free parameters] before we are willing to take them seriously. Thus not only is our aesthetic judgment a means to the end of finding scientific explanations and judging their validity – it is part of what we mean by an explanation.[15]

Another great physicist, Paul Dirac, who gave the relativistically invariant formulation of the Schrödinger equation that now bears his own name and which led directly to the discovery of antiparticles, also stressed aesthetic criteria: indeed, just one, *beauty*. The equations of a physical theory had to be beautiful if they were to be candidates for the truth. 'My main objection to your work', he wrote to Heisenberg, 'is that I do not think your basic . . . equation has sufficient beauty to be a fundamental equation of physics'.[16] In two of his most memorable (and most quoted) lines the English Romantic poet John Keats wrote that '"Beauty is truth, truth beauty, – that is all/ Ye know on earth, and all ye need to know."' It is perhaps strange – and certainly would have surprised him – that it should have received a ringing endorsement from one of the most eminent among twentieth-century physicists.

Dirac might have been an extreme case, but many physicists seem to be appreciative of abstract structural beauty, and more and more prone to see in it what the ancients called a *sigillum veri* – a sign of truth. The high-energy physicist and Anglican priest John Polkinghorne is one:

> we seek theories which have about them that unmistakable character of mathematical beauty. It is our expectation that it is precisely those theories with that character of mathematical beauty which will prove to be the ones that describe the structure of the world in which we live.[17]

This appreciation is often linked to a feature that seems to be entrenched in all, or at any rate nearly all, of us: the appreciation of *symmetry*. In physics, the realisation that abstract symmetry groups underlie some of the most successful theories was regarded as a strikingly significant

[15] Steven Weinberg, *Dreams of a Final Theory* (New York: Pantheon Books, 1992), p. 149.

[16] Quoted in John Barrow, *The Constants of Nature: From Alpha to Omega* (London: Jonathan Cape, 2002), p. 110.

[17] 'Religion in an Age of Science', *McNair Lecture*, University of North Carolina, March 1993 (web).

discovery, and symmetry is now seen as a, if not *the*, key to uncovering the fundamental laws of nature. But if the universe is indeed governed by laws of an outstanding abstract beauty, as it seems as if it might be, given the remarkable success of not only Dirac's theory, what is the explanation of why we seem attuned to see in it the sign of truth? The word 'attuned' of course is deliberately chosen to ring the bell of the fine-tuning problem. Surely even the toughest-minded anti-theist would have to concede that it is as if some skilful benevolent magician, a sort of cosmic-scale Prospero, is providing delicate clues to the secrets of his domain having previously seen to it that we are equipped with the desire and ability to follow the way they lead. And so we are back with the Goldilocks enigma: surely all this cannot just be an accidental coincidence, just *chance*?

At this point one might be excused for feeling like the character played by Michael Douglas in the classic thriller movie *Fatal Attraction*, when the other protagonist (played by Glenn Close) whom he thought finally subdued, revives yet again with a scream of nightmarish menace. But laying the demon to rest is now not difficult. In the first place, even if we were equipped by some great designer to understand its creation, there is every reason not to suppose that it has our interests at heart, and therefore that the great designer, if there is one, is emphatically not the God of theism. Secondly, as I shall explain in Chapter 6, there is very good reason to suppose that evolution rather than a Great Designer has equipped us with brains able to do advanced mathematics and comprehend abstract mathematical structure.

4. SIMPLICITY AND SWINBURNE

It is time to say something about that other desideratum on Weinberg's list, *simplicity*, for centuries linked to truth by philosophers and scientists alike. Richard Swinburne, who besides being former Professor of the Christian Religion in the University of Oxford is also an adept Bayesian, is another who believes that simplicity is a sign of truth, and furthermore has an argument to support the belief which I will examine in a moment. Granted the truth–simplicity link, Swinburne feels that he can assign a substantial prior probability to the hypothesis that the God of theism exists on the ground that it is, Swinburne claims, a very simple one. That prior probability is, according to Swinburne, also sufficiently substantial to allow God to offset the adverse effect of the evidence supplied by the evil and suffering in the world and still emerge with a posterior probability in excess of one half: to be judged more probable than not, in other words.

It is notable that Swinburne resists – with good reason – the traditional theists' temptation to argue that God is self-necessitating, preferring to employ the methods of science itself to achieve his goal. Those methods are, he claims, (i) the canons of Bayesian inference and (ii) the strategy of assigning higher prior probabilities to simpler hypotheses, other things being equal, because the history of science provides strong evidence that simpler theories are more likely to be predictively successful:

> There must be a criterion to choose between the infinite number of theories that are equally successful in predicting the observations already made, if we are ever to be able to make any justified predictions for the future. The history of science reveals that, in the absence of background knowledge, that criterion is basically the criterion of simplicity.[18]

While I endorse (i), I am less happy about (ii), and I also believe that Swinburne lets God off the hook of the Problem of Evil far too easily. I have given my grounds for not letting God off the hook at all and I will not repeat them yet again. But I will say why I think (ii) is wrong. (ii) is a conjunction of two separate claims, (a) that scientists typically assign higher prior probabilities to simpler hypotheses when considering the possible explanations of some data, and (b) that the history of science supports the belief that simpler theories are more likely to be true. I believe that both (a) and (b) are false. There are purely logical reasons why (a) is not even a possible strategy. One of Swinburne's criteria for simplicity is that the simplicity of a hypothesis increases with the number of independent entities referred to in it (this is a form of the ancient principle of *Occam's Razor*, that 'entities should not be multiplied without necessity', named after the fourteenth-century Franciscan friar William of Ockham[19]). In the sort of mathematically expressed theories common in the natural sciences this criterion can be taken to state that the more independent adjustable parameters a theory contains, the less simple it is.[20] But it is easy to show that making prior probability depend on simplicity in this way leads quickly to inconsistency. I have put the short proof in an Appendix to this chapter.

One way of avoiding inconsistency is to restrict scope of the criterion in various ways, for example to those hypotheses actually considered, but this seems not only ad hoc but also arbitrary. Considered by whom? If

[18] Richard Swinburne, *The Existence of God*, rev. edn (Oxford: Clarendon Press, 1991), p. 59.

[19] 'Occamus' is the Latinised form of 'of Ockham'. Ockham is a small town in southern England near London.

[20] Both Popper and the statistician and geophysicist Harold Jeffreys adopted this as their sole criterion of simplicity (*The Logic of Scientific Discovery* (New York: Harper & Row, 1968), pp. 378–86 and *Theory of Probability*, 3rd edn (Oxford: Clarendon Press, 1961), pp. 46–50 respectively).

practising scientists, who are these? Must they have official university or research lab affiliations? Einstein didn't when he wrote a seminal paper (on the photoelectric effect) for which he was awarded a Nobel Prize. And what does 'considered' mean? One can consider almost anything.

Even if there were some acceptable and uncontroversial scope-restriction, which for the sorts of reasons I have just given I think unlikely, Swinburne's claim (b) is, perhaps surprisingly, self-defeating, for the claim that historical evidence supports the conclusion that simpler theories are more likely to be predictively successful falls victim to a type of inductive circularity first identified, in a celebrated argument, by David Hume. Hume's argument is as follows. Suppose you believe that some correlation which has been observed to hold in the past will continue to hold in the future. Hume pointed out that however you try to justify that belief, you are in trouble. If you say 'because the evidence shows that it will', he replies that you are begging the question that, as he put it, 'the course of nature will not change'.[21] If you appeal to the fact that the empirical method of basing predictions on past evidence has always been very reliable in the past, he gives you the same answer as before: you are again assuming that the future will resemble the past. Even if you merely say that it is highly probable that the future will resemble the past, he points out that this also begs the question in the same way, for in order to make that judgment you are implicitly putting a correspondingly lower a priori probability on the course of nature not changing than on it changing.

Hume did not have the apparatus of Bayesian probability at hand, but shortly afterwards Bayes had developed that apparatus to the point where it is easy to prove Hume's claim. Suppose that H and H′ are alternatives which explain some evidence E perfectly but which diverge in their future predictions. For example, we can represent the evidence as points in a suitable observation-space, and H and H′ could be any two of the infinitely many smooth curves which pass through those data points. Since they each explain E, we have $\text{Prob}(E|H) = \text{Prob}(E|H') = 1$. Substituting this value into equation (3) in Chapter 3 we obtain

$$\frac{\text{Prob}(H|E)}{\text{Prob}(H'|E)} = \frac{\text{Prob}(H)}{\text{Prob}(H')}$$

In words, *the posterior probabilities of H and* H′ *in the light of E remain in exactly the same ratio as their prior probabilities*, and it is only these priors

[21] David Hume, *An Enquiry Concerning Human Understanding* (Lasalle, IL: Open Court, 1988), section 4, part 2.

which therefore discriminate between them. Hume's prescient insight thus receives a simple formal proof.

Almost since it was first published, Hume's informal argument deservedly became a classic.[22] It has the astounding consequence that our fond belief that science rests *unambiguously* on observation and experiment is just wrong. What the consequences are for that belief, and how it should be adjusted in the light of Hume's devastating insight, would take too long to go into here in any depth. What does follow from its application to the present discussion is that when Swinburne infers that because simple theories have been mostly successful in the past, they are likely to be so in the future, he is implicitly putting a higher prior probability on the course of nature (at least in this respect) remaining the same. But he certainly cannot appeal without circularity to simplicity itself to order the priors in that way, even if that were possible, since the whole point of appealing to past evidence was to justify such an ordering. Do not think that this is an argument to the effect that one can in no circumstances use past experience to weight prior probabilities accordingly. It is not, and if any argument concluded that it would be wrong. The argument is that Hume (in effect) showed that you cannot eliminate prior probabilities when claiming that evidence supports some theory. Swinburne's claim that evidence supports a particular way of assigning prior probabilities thus begs the question.

Swinburne's claim that 'God exists' is a particularly simple hypothesis but is no less open to serious question. It may appear to be simple, but as we all know, appearances can be deceptive. With God defined as Swinburne defines him, as 'a person without a body (i.e. a spirit) who necessarily is eternal, perfectly free, omnipotent, omniscient, perfectly good, and the creator of all things',[23] the hypothesis that he exists *sounds* like a fairly simple sort of claim, granted a nodding acquaintance with the traditional language of theology. But delve a little deeper. God is credited by Swinburne and other theists with being omniscient but, as he (Swinburne) acknowledges, there is a vast amount of complexity in the universe.[24] If God knows everything, however, then all those bits of information must be stored

[22] Scores of philosophers have tried to expose a flaw in Hume's argument. In my book *Hume's Problem*, I argue that there is none, and I then examine what can be done to shore up our view that in some sense induction is a valid procedure.

[23] Swinburne, *The Existence of God*, p. 7.

[24] He includes in this the fact that all the elementary particles, atoms and molecules have identical powers wherever they are, but according to a standard interpretation of quantum field theory, what appear to be particles, 'real' as well as virtual, are excitation-states of relatively few quantum fields: electron fields, photon fields, etc.

in God, so God's simplicity would therefore seem to be a simplicity of name only, rather as 'uncomputable real number' is a simple name of a set of very complex entities.[25] Richard Dawkins attempts to show that in virtue of all this claimed explanatory power God would have to be extremely *improbable* rather than very probable, as Swinburne claims. I think Dawkins's argument fails, but I shall postpone saying why until Chapter 8.

These observations highlight a fundamental problem with appealing to simplicity that has nothing to do with probabilities. It is that the very notion is systematically ambiguous. 'Uncomputable real number', as we have just noted, is merely a simple name for a set of very non-simple things. An even simpler (!) example is 'London Telephone Directory'. The same objection applies to Swinburne's claims that zero and infinity are very simple numbers because 'there is a neatness about zero and infinity which particular finite numbers lack'.[26] Infinity when rendered in the familiar symbol ∞ may look simple enough, but mathematicians long ago abandoned attaching any genuine meaning to it because it does not denote a number (most now use it merely as shorthand for 'undefined'). At the end of the nineteenth century, however, the great German mathematician Georg Cantor revealed for the first time bewildering infinite hierarchies of authentically infinite *numbers*, the infinite ordinal numbers on the one hand and the infinite cardinal numbers on the other, each with a well-defined but very different arithmetic. This newly revealed infinity is anything but simple, and even the very basic conjectured property of the infinite cardinal numbers, that the cardinal number of the real numbers is the smallest cardinal number larger than the cardinal number of the integers (the smallest infinite cardinal), is not decided by the presently accepted axioms of set theory. Nor is it obvious that 'particular finite numbers' are necessarily any less simple than 0. There are things that you cannot do with 0, like dividing by it for example, which you can do with every other number. Moreover 1, π, e (the base of the natural logarithm), are all finite numbers which are very neat indeed if one considers the many simple and striking laws of mathematics in which they appear. All of them appear in possibly the simplest and most striking of all, Euler's equation: $e^{i\pi} = -1$.

[25] A computable real number is one all of whose decimal digits are computable (i.e. a suitably programmed computer can compute the nth digit, for each $n = 1, 2, 3, \ldots$). Since the set of computer programs is countably infinite (i.e. it can be indexed by the positive integers) and the set of all real numbers is not, there are uncountably many more uncomputable real numbers than computable. The familiar real irrational numbers, like π, e and so on, are computable.

[26] Swinburne, *The Existence of God*, p. 94.

5. SOUNDING A SCEPTICAL NOTE

But surely, I can hear a reader protesting, so many scientists all proclaiming the sterling virtues of simple theories can't all be wrong? Well, we have seen that there is a problem even with finding an unambiguous *concept* of simplicity. But even in simple Occam's Razor contexts it is certainly not the case that prior plausibility always pulls in the same direction as simplicity. The physicist E. T. Jaynes gives an imaginary example:

> Having observed some facts, what is the real criterion that leads us to prefer one explanation of them over another? Suppose that two explanations, A and B, could account for some proven historical facts equally well. But A makes four assumptions, each of which seems to us already highly plausible, while B makes only two assumptions, but they seem strained, far-fetched, and highly unlikely to be true. Every historian finds himself in situations like this, and he does not hesitate to adopt explanation A, although B is intuitively simpler. Thus our intuition asks, fundamentally, not how *simple* the hypotheses are, but rather how *plausible* they are.[27]

There are plenty of real examples as well. An excessively simple economic forecasting model would rightly be regarded as highly *implausible*: we know to our cost that there is often a multitude of variables whose effects are far from negligible.

None of this implies that Occam's Razor should be summarily thrown away. In fact, for a fairly large class of statistical hypotheses, as sample size increases the simpler ones can be shown to do better in terms of posterior probability among all those which fit the data equally well, where the measure of relative goodness-of-fit is given by what is called the maximum-likelihood ratio.[28] This result is often advanced as the ground for recommending a preference *in advance* for simpler models from that class, though there seems little warrant for taking a result valid only in the limit of large samples as justifying that recommendation. It is sometimes claimed, with even less justification, to ground a preference in general for simpler hypotheses. At any rate, the case for preferring simpler theories *in general*, in all informational contexts, has no warrant.

So what does have warrant? The quick and easy answer is the best guesses of scientists. The progress of science has been remarkable, not

[27] E. T. Jaynes, *Probability Theory: The Logic of Science* (Cambridge University Press, 2003), p. 606.

[28] It is quite difficult to give a vernacular translation of this and I will not even try, but simply refer the interested reader to the many accounts of the main result which can be found on the internet or in suitable statistics texts (look under *Bayesian Information Criterion*).

only in raising deeper and deeper questions, but also in being able to give good provisional answers to them. Signally not among these answers is 'God'. 'God' is in fact a very poor answer, because it is a hand-waving one: God can do everything, just like Santa of Chapter 3. I quoted earlier a famous remark of Laplace, to the effect that he didn't need the hypothesis of God to explain anything. Laplace added that 'indeed' that hypothesis explained everything, but from it we can actually predict nothing. This was simply a diplomatic way of saying – Laplace was after all speaking to Napoleon – that God doesn't *genuinely* explain anything at all.

6. A WALK ON THE WILD SIDE: THE ONTOLOGICAL ARGUMENT

I observed that Swinburne is unusual among theists in not regarding God's existence as a necessary truth, but merely one which, he claims, the rules of scientific inference themselves (i.e., in his opinion, the rules of probability combined with a simplicity postulate for ranking prior probabilities) would be forced to conclude to. I have said why I think that he is mistaken in that belief. If that verdict is correct it might seem to add cogency to the traditional theism according to which God terminates the otherwise endless cycle of 'Whys?' by not himself being a contingent existence but a necessary one. And it does seem at first sight that a grasp of God's defining properties makes a rigorous demonstration of that conclusion possible. Those 'omni' properties locate God as a sort of collection of maximum points on appropriate scales. In a decisive move in Christian theology these maxima were themselves seen as aspects of a single property of *superlativeness*, sheer unlimited, unfettered *greatness*. But as the medieval theologian St Anselm pointed out, in a flash of inspiration, *it is undeniably greater to exist than not to exist*. And there we have, in its luminously compelling simplicity, the famous a priori proof of the existence of God known as the *Ontological Argument*: God necessarily exists because he is the greatest thing which can be conceived to exist, and being existent is greater than not being existent. Hence existence is part of God's definition and so he necessarily exists. QED.

What a *coup*! Unfortunately for Rational Theology, two considerations stand in the way of the celebratory champagne. One is logical intuition, which says that nothing comes out of nothing, and one cannot in any valid way conjure existence, let alone necessary existence, out of pure thought. (On the other hand, that intuition is today's intuition; an earlier intuition seems not to have found a proof of necessary existence as in itself all that shocking.) A more considered objection was brought by the eighteenth/nineteenth-century philosopher Immanuel Kant, who pointed out that existence is not a predicate like, say, 'big', or 'foolish'. Anyone unfamiliar with this sort of language might not see why Kant's objection is as fatal as it actually is, so consider a simple example. A mathematician might go to a great deal of trouble to show that, say, some group with a specified number of symmetries exists (showing that things exist in mathematics might sound odd but it is in fact a very common procedure). Why not save him/her the trouble by just adding existence to its other defining properties? The answer is because that would still not show that the group as characterised *actually* exists – it might, for example, very well turn out to be an inconsistent notion. You have to *prove* that it exists, which may not be at all easy. And similarly with God. Being told that existence is implicit in his definition does not actually *make* him exist. In fact, as we shall see later, just like certain mathematical entities whose existence had been assumed, God as traditionally conceived turns out to be an inconsistent notion. Hence, far from existing necessarily, he necessarily doesn't exist.

That is not all (though it's surely more than enough). By a sort of photo-negative version of the same reasoning we can show that the Devil exists necessarily. Suppose we define that person as supremely awful. Well, something which sounds awful is even more awful if it exists than if it doesn't. *Hence the Devil exists necessarily by virtue of his own definition.* The seventeenth-century French philosopher and mathematician René Descartes presented his own version of Anselm's argument which looks like an attempt to evade that unwelcome consequence. In this, God is defined to be supremely *perfect*. But if Descartes thought he was on to a winner here he was wrong: the same photo-negative reasoning yields the conclusion that a supremely imperfect being exists. But we still haven't finished. The traditional ontological argument(s) also makes two assumptions which are far from being necessarily true. One is that there can be only one maximally great being, and the other is that a maximum exists at all. Neither is a logical truth or even a mathematical necessity, even on the doubtful assumption that any precise sense can be given to the notion of maximal greatness: for example, the set of real numbers contains no maximum, nor is it even bounded above.

Yet, despite its impressive catalogue of flaws, the ontological argument was, or so it appeared to some, given a new lease of life in the twentieth century as an alleged theorem (given a couple of supposedly innocuous premises) of a particular species of modal logic whose official name is S5. Modal logic typically contains two, dual, propositional qualifiers, 'necessarily' and 'possibly', where 'necessarily' under the so-called 'possible worlds' semantics is interpreted as 'is the case in all possible worlds accessible from the given one' and 'possibly' as 'is the case in at least one possible world accessible from the given one'. Many of the extant systems of modal logic, including the so-called Lewis systems (the S-systems) of which S5 is the strongest, have what logicians call sound and complete sets of rules of proof relative to the possible-worlds semantics: they differ in the constraints placed on the accessibility relation, which for S5 is that it be reflexive, transitive and symmetric, i.e. an equivalence relation. These technical details will not concern us, though. These and other modal systems have turned out to be very useful analytical tools in the investigation of fields of enquiry far removed from what the nebulous-sounding notion of a possible world might suggest, including computer science and the theory of provability.[29]

The same cannot be said for its enlistment in the cause of the ontological argument. The standard form of the modal ontological argument, of which Plantinga's well-known version[30] is an elaboration, has two premises. One is that if it is possible that God exists then it is possible that he exists necessarily. The other is that it is possible that God exists. The first premise is allegedly to be merely definitional: in Plantinga's version, God is defined to be 'maximally great', and this is defined as having 'maximal excellence' in all possible worlds which, so it is claimed, implies necessary existence in those worlds. From these two premises and the logical machinery of S5 there is a very simple proof that God *actually* exists.

The modal argument is, however, no more convincing than its informal forebears. Plantinga himself acknowledges that it is not a *proof* that God exists, but an argument which, he claims, is 'rationally acceptable' because the premise that God is merely *possible* is. Allow that, and through the tiny logical window of mere possibility squeezes Almighty Jove, with the assistance of S5, to fill heaven and earth with his refulgent glory. But we shouldn't allow that. Nor should we allow that the degree of rational acceptability of the conclusion depends only on the premise that God is possible. There are *two* non-logical premises, not one, and there is also the S5 logic itself. The crucial S5 rule that is employed, and exists in none of S1–S4, is that if for any proposition A it is possible that A is necessary,

29 Jordan Howard Sobel's excellent *Logic and Theism* (Cambridge University Press, 2005) gives a very thorough account of the formal modal arguments, including an unpublished one by Gödel.

30 In Alvin Plantinga, *The Nature of Necessity* (Oxford University Press, 1974).

then A is necessary (the distinctive feature of S5 is that for any string of modal prefixes to a proposition none but the last is significant). That rule itself might well count as a third, and far from obviously true, premise, since I suspect most people will not find very compelling the claim that if it is merely possible that a proposition is necessary, then it really is necessary. To be told that the rule, or more accurately S5 axiom, is valid in S5's semantics simply begs the question of why that should be accepted, and will certainly not convince anyone who already doubts that *possible* existence implies *actual* existence in a possible world.

Even more question-begging (at best) are the two explicit premises. The supposedly definitional premise that 'maximal excellence' implies necessary existence is just a variation on Anselm's argument, and just as that did it too falls victim to Kant's objection. The other premise, that God so defined is possible, is so far from being innocuous that it is *necessarily false*: the 'maximal excellence' Plantinga attributes to a possible God is just a list of the usual omni-properties, and the logical problems besetting omnipotence and, as we shall see in Chapter 8, omniscience, effectively slam the window of possibility firmly shut: God's existence is arguably just as impossible *in any world* as that of the round triangle.

We have already seen voodoo probability at work. This modal version of the ontological argument is *voodoo logic*. But of course we know, or should know, in advance that it would *have* to be voodoo logic. Considered, as it is almost uniformly considered today, as a set of principles of inference empty of substantive content, logic cannot or at any rate *should* not be able to produce an existent God out of nothing. It is true that modern classical deductive logic *does* prove some unconditional existence-statements, for example that something exists which is identical to itself, and it also proves that for any property Q there exists something which either has Q or does not. But these are no counterexamples to the general claim: they are classified as logical truths largely for the sake of a smooth technical development and can in principle be dropped without substantial loss (the result of doing so is called *free logic*).

There is nothing good to be said for the ontological argument. I say that without regret. It is at bottom just one more attempt to prove that something has a particular property by saying that the property in question is by definition in the nature of that thing, a strategy famously parodied by Molière in his play *Le Malade Imaginaire*: when asked why opium makes one sleep, the doctor replies (in Latin!) that it has a *virtus dormitiva*, i.e. a sleep-inducing power. But in this case the situation is even worse because the central assumption is inconsistent. 'Vain wisdom all and false philosophy'.[31]

7. SANTA REDUX

I have argued that the posterior odds on God relative to all the evidence should be set to zero, since the probability that if an all-powerful, all-knowing and all-good God existed he would not permit the evil that befalls innocent sufferers. That this conclusion continues to be denied by theologians is *not* evidence against it and should surprise no-one: as we noted in Chapter 2, people don't willingly give up positions which provide privilege and employment. What might surprise some people, however, is to learn that the *prior* odds against theism are also exactly zero, a situation for which the omni-properties of the theist's God are responsible. As we have noted, their function is to guarantee that God can explain everything that subsequently turns out to be the case. The problem is that in order to be a guarantee they have to be completely inclusive in their scope. It is as if someone is going to name a number at random, and we want to ensure that a number we are allowed to choose beforehand will always trump their choice: so, knowing that their choice is restricted to finite numbers, we choose ω, the smallest infinite ordinal (and cardinal: so called initial ordinals, like ω, are also cardinals, by definition). Both the theist and we have 'gone infinite', so to speak, knowing that we are thereby guaranteed to win. The difference is that in the theist's case the infinity has to be global, whereas there are still plenty of (infinite) numbers greater than ω. But the theist has to pay a severe cost for this pre-packed explanatory luxury: *inconsistency*. We have already witnessed it in the paradox of omnipotence, and as if that is not enough we shall witness it again with the concept of omniscience, in Chapter 8.

But it is not very satisfactory to be told that God cannot exist if it turns out not to be possible, as Swinburne and almost all theists tell us

31
> Others apart sat on a hill retir'd,
> In thoughts more elevate, and reason'd high,
> Of providence, foreknowledge, will, and fate,
> Fixed fate, free will, foreknowledge absolute,
> And found no end, in wand'ring mazes lost,
>
> . . . .
>
> Vain wisdom all, and false philosophy

(John Milton, *Paradise Lost*, 557–65). How little has changed.

it is not possible, to explain salient features of human existence, like the phenomena of consciousness, of susceptibility to moral commands, of an advanced cognitive ability (or so it pleases us to believe), and of a sensitivity to beauty that only a suitably intentioned creator could plausibly explain. Then we should have a paradox, the unwelcome position where extremely compelling evidence for is exactly balanced by extremely compelling evidence against. In the next two chapters I will show that – fortunately! – we are not faced with any such embarrassing situation.

EXERCISE

'Thus even the fool is convinced that something than which nothing greater can be conceived is in the understanding, since when he hears this, he understands it; and whatever is understood is in the understanding. And certainly that than which a greater cannot be conceived cannot be in the understanding alone. For if it is even in the understanding alone, it can be conceived to exist in reality also, which is greater. Thus if that than which a greater cannot be conceived is in the understanding alone, then that than which a greater cannot be conceived is itself that than which a greater can be conceived. But surely this cannot be. Thus without doubt something than which a greater cannot be conceived exists, both in the understanding and in reality.' Comment.

MAIN POINTS OF CHAPTER 5

- There is a potential infinite regress of explanations whose traditional stopping-point is God, considered as a self-necessitating explanatory principle.
- Many physicists would like to replace that terminus of explanation with a unified Theory of Everything satisfying various desiderata, like having no internal degrees of freedom (no adjustable parameters), subsuming gravity and quantum mechanics, having a suitable set of symmetries, and so on.
- Arguments by Paul Davies and others that such a theory must have a prior probability of zero are shown to be of the same species of spurious reasoning that was exposed in Chapter 4.
- A large majority of leading physicists reject the need to invoke God to explain the universe. They are not averse to dreams of a Final Theory, but such a theory is characterised in terms of entirely non-theistic criteria.

- Among the criteria are simplicity and beauty. Swinburne claims that it is the simplicity of the God hypothesis that, together with its explanatory power, renders theism a good scientific explanation.
- Simplicity cannot do the work Swinburne intends it to do, while his a posteriori argument for it is vulnerable to Hume's celebrated sceptical argument against induction.
- The chapter ends with a critical discussion of the Ontological Argument, arguing that it is no more than an elaborate form of question-begging.

APPENDIX

Let H_1 be the hypothesis that y is some quadratic function of x, i.e. that there are three parameters a, b and c, where $c \neq 0$ such that $y = a + bx + cx^2$. Let H_2 be the hypothesis that there are a, b with $b \neq 0$ such that $y = a + bx$. Finally, let H_3 be the hypothesis that there are parameters a, b, such that $y = a + bx + c'x^2$, where c' is some fixed nonzero number. H_3 and H_2 have exactly the same number of adjustable parameters (two) and so their degree of simplicity, and hence their prior probabilities, should be the same: $\text{Prob}(H_2) = \text{Prob}(H_3)$. But H_2 is simpler than H_1, having one fewer adjustable parameter, so $\text{Prob}(H_2) > \text{Prob}(H_1)$. H_3 entails H_1 because it is a special case of it, and so by the basic probability calculus $\text{Prob}(H_3) \leq \text{Prob}(H_1)$. Hence

$$\text{Prob}(H_3) = \text{Prob}(H_1) < \text{Prob}(H_2) = \text{Prob}(H_3),$$

which is a contradiction.

CHAPTER 6

Moral equilibrium

'ye shall be as gods, knowing good and evil.'[1]

1. GOD OF THE GAPS

Many theists are worried by an increasingly widespread perception that God is in headlong retreat from an advancing science, with the diminished function of simply filling in the explanatory gaps science has – so far – left open. As people have been quick to point out, invoking God in this sort of ad hoc role has obvious dangers. Apart from relegating him to a sort of *faute de mieux* status, and endowing that past bearer of grand titles (Lord of Hosts, King of Kings, Almighty God, etc.) with the less imposing sobriquet 'God of the Gaps', it makes him a hostage to fortune, never knowing when he is to be ejected from yet another piece of territory, and wondering if his shrinking fiefdom will soon cease to exist altogether. It may well have been with this apprehension that Stephen Jay Gould pre-emptively retired God altogether from an explanatory role. Science is still in its infancy (assuming – a big assumption – that the human race doesn't succeed in its apparent quest of prematurely wiping itself out), acquiring the technology to probe into conditions ever closer to the initial Big Bang and to unlock the brain's secrets, and one might well think that anyone with the temerity to claim that any of the current explanatory gaps will not at some point vanish should beware of putting their money where their mouth is.

To claim therefore, as some do, that some observable phenomenon or other is *intrinsically* or *in principle* inexplicable by scientific means seems even less likely to be a profitable undertaking. A priori arguments that this or that is in principle impossible have an unfortunate way of rebounding on their authors. The claim that the heavens were beyond the power of terrestrial science to predict and understand ended up by discrediting

[1] Genesis 3:5.

Aristotelian science even though there was still much that was valuable in it. Hegel demonstrated by a priori reasoning that there could be only seven planets shortly before an eighth was discovered, with the result that he became a joke-figure in the history of science.[2] People persisted in claiming that it was impossible a priori that life could be a property simply of a collection of molecules right up to the time when the evidence to the contrary became overwhelming and *vitalism* became a term of derision. The current Archbishop of Canterbury, Dr Rowan Williams, tells us that 'physics on its own will not settle the question of why there is something rather than nothing'. Undeterred, physics seems well on the way to doing what the Archbishop says it can't.

So much for a priori impossibility-proofs, one might think. But still people are arguing from first principles that various phenomena lie necessarily outside the reach of scientific explanation. A theistic philosopher and a theistic scientist, for example, are agreed that a class of phenomena relating specifically to human beings is of this type.[3] Principal among these are: consciousness; the recognition of the truth of objective moral law; acknowledging an intrinsic value to truth; and the appreciation of beauty. In the following two chapters I will examine the reasons which are alleged to support the claims, starting with those for the existence of what Francis Collins calls 'The Moral Law'.[4]

2. THE MORAL LAW

God and morality have always been a sort of conjugate pair for theists, who believe that you can't have one without the other. For non-theists any connection at all is less obvious. Over two centuries ago the great philosopher Immanuel Kant argued convincingly that there is very little of genuine morality in doing something simply because it is the will of a very powerful individual who is certain to pursue violations with condign punishment. Dante's *Inferno* gives a vivid idea of what the thirteenth-century mind could believe awaited sinners, with Hieronymus Bosch two centuries later supplying impressive video accompaniment. It is in essence a simple story: obedience is the price exacted by the Deity for salvation, much in the same way that a protection racket operates.

[2] There are claims in the literature that Hegel has been misunderstood, but the textual evidence is not very compelling.

[3] The scientist is Francis Collins and the philosopher is Richard Swinburne.

[4] Francis Collins, *The Language of God* (New York: Free Press, 2006), p. 216.

Kant's own theory postulated an authentic inner voice of obligation, and in this he was surely correct: most of us do heed what we take to be moral imperatives, without thought of penalty or reward. A more sophisticated theism acknowledges the innateness of some sort of moral imperative, but regards it as implanted by God. God gives us free will, according to this view, in order that we can compare good and evil as we see them in the light of this faculty, and freely choose to follow either. Following the good elicits God's approval, and evil his disapproval. St Thomas Aquinas argued that the existence of the moral faculty was therefore evidence for God, as have many since. Richard Swinburne tells us that 'If God is to give us significant choices he will ensure that we develop . . . moral awareness.'[5] Francis Collins gives a more personal rendering of the same message: 'After twenty-eight years as an unbeliever, the Moral Law stands out for me as the strongest signpost of God.'[6] Unsurprisingly, C. S. Lewis also believed that a moral sense was implanted in us by God.

Not everyone has believed in the innateness thesis, God-given or not, and more or less ingenious alternatives have been proposed. Two eminent twentieth-century thinkers declared morality merely a cover for something else less edifying and certainly non-innate, each offering a different choice. Marx saw it as an epiphenomenon of underlying 'relations of production', to use the quaint Marxian *patois*, while Freud saw it as an attempt to repress the dark urgings of a primordial Id. These reductive explanations have been discredited, probably rightly, while belief in the innateness of at least some moral dispositions has made a strong comeback. The obvious candidate for a purely naturalistic account is Darwinism, and it is increasingly enlisted in the explanation of widespread biological characteristics and dispositions. A good deal of recent research has focused, after Darwin himself first suggested it, on finding an evolutionary explanation of why certain types of behaviour are widely regarded as deserving of moral praise and emulation. One of the most morally praiseworthy species of human behaviour is altruism, and it also poses the biggest challenge to Darwinian theory since any trait which increases the fitness of others (and their genes) at the expense of oneself (and one's own) should, or so it would appear, eventually die out. Hence Francis Collins opines that 'selfless altruism presents a major challenge to the evolutionist'[7] – whereas (of course) it is to be expected under the hypothesis of theism.

[5] Richard Swinburne, *The Existence of God*, rev. edn (Oxford: Clarendon Press, 1991), p. 216.
[6] Collins, *The Language of God*, p. 218. [7] *Ibid.*, p. 27.

3. SELFISH ALTRUISM

One apparently very natural way of reconciling Darwin's theory with the maintenance of altruism, and one proposed by Darwin himself, is to invoke *group-selection*: groups of cooperative individuals who are ready to indulge in sacrificing their own good for others' will benefit at the expense of groups of less cooperative individuals. Thus will groups like the former be preferentially selected for, and hence their members too. This simple idea was shown to be untenable only much later, when it was pointed out that they would be eventually subverted by more selfish players of the game of life. But a remarkable insight of the eminent biologist and geneticist J. B. S. Haldane showed that selfish-gene Darwinism and at least some sorts of altruism are far from incompatible. Famously expressed in the observation that he would lay down his life for two brothers or eight cousins (on the average a sibling has 50 per cent of your own genetic material, assuming random mating in a diploid population, and a cousin 12.5 per cent), Haldane's insight opened the way to seeing one form of altruism, *kin-altruism*, as explicable in evolutionary terms. Later, in a seminal paper, or pair of seminal papers, published in the mid-1960s, the evolutionary biologist William Hamilton developed the idea systematically by showing that natural selection would favour a 'benevolent gene' just in case a simple inequality ($rb > c$) held between its and its companion gene's degree of relatedness (r), the benefactor's cost (c) and the benefactor's benefit (b), measured in terms of reproductive fitness.[8] We shall find an interesting echo of Hamilton's inequality later.

Hamilton was well aware that his ideas had echoes in game theory,[9] and it was the exploitation of the connection by him and others that produced a major new branch of science, *evolutionary game theory*, whose powerful techniques were immediately brought to bear on investigating how cooperation can evolve by natural selection, and indeed *whether* it can. A key assumption of game theory in its usual applications is that the players are rational beings, possibly boundedly rational, seeking to maximise their expected payoff. In the evolutionary–biological context it is often useful

[8] William Hamilton, 'The Genetical Evolution of Social Behaviour', I and II, *Journal of Theoretical Biology* 7 (1964), 1–16, 17–32. The degree of relatedness r is the probability that benefactor and benefactee share genes at a given locus which are copies of an ancestral gene.

[9] He made important contributions himself. One was to show how social enforcement diminishes defections in multi-player Prisoner's Dilemmas. William Hamilton, 'Innate Social Aptitudes of Man: An Approach from Evolutionary Genetics', in R. Fox (ed.), *Biosocial Anthropology* (New York: Wiley, 1975), pp. 133–53.

to measure the payoffs in terms of reproductive fitness of strategies in themselves, with successful strategies disseminated through the population by inheritance. This implies that were there to be any explanation in those terms of the emergence and preservation of moral strategies in human populations it should apply to any animal populations in which those strategies can be genetically encoded. As a matter of fact some striking instances of apparently altruistic behaviour have been reported in dolphins and among man's nearest genetic neighbours, the higher primates. A chimp in one cage may refuse to eat food given it in abundance when a chimp in a neighbouring cage is given nothing, and there are many other examples (the standard reference is Frans de Waal[10]). In addition, many examples of so-called *reciprocal altruism* have been discovered in animal populations. A striking example, discussed by the evolutionary game theorist Robert Trivers, concerns the parasitic fish found among coral reefs which clean the mouths and gills of larger fish to obtain the nourishment from the algae and other organisms found there: it is often observed that when predators on the host fish appear the latter will wait for the parasite fish to exit before fleeing.[11]

Pay no attention to the objection that any apparent altruism displayed in animal societies is not 'real' altruism, because it is not the outcome of some moral sort of deliberation. The objection begs the question and is anyway beside the point. If one can show that under conditions which simulate biological evolution a trait can become entrenched which seems to foster altruism then the hypothesis of a moral conscience given by God to humans is not necessary to account for the observed facts. The fact that animal populations also exemplify altruistic behaviour (and as we have seen they do) would then be a notable explanatory plus for any evolutionary model which incorporates no machinery for linguistic communication, as the simpler evolutionary game-theoretic models do not, especially in view of the fact that the Abrahamic religions assign no moral faculty, and thereby no moral rights, to animals. I shall return to this point later.

Can evolutionary game theory account for this sort of behaviour when 'ordinary' Darwinism seems to put a fitness premium on being selfish? More generally, can that theory account for *any* behavioural strategies present and maintained in populations when alternative strategies seem to offer greater

[10] *Good Natured: The Origins of Right and Wrong in Humans and Other Animals* (Cambridge, MA: Harvard University Press, 1996); *Chimpanzee Politics: Power and Sex among the Apes*, rev. edn (Baltimore, MD: Johns Hopkins University Press, 1998).

[11] This apparently altruistic behaviour is however compensated by the fact that the same or similar parasites will return in the future to discharge the same useful duty.

returns in fitness? It was just this question which caused Maynard Smith and Price, drawing on earlier work by Hamilton on 'unbeatable' evolutionary strategies (the idea, and one of the first results about them, goes back farther, to R. A. Fisher), to formulate the concept of an *evolutionary stable strategy*, now almost universally referred to acronymically as an ESS[12]. An ESS is one which will resist all mutant strategies invading a population of competing strategies if the mutants are sufficiently small in number (with a common upper bound). Since many if not most evolutionary game theorists are interested in trying to explain the evolution of cooperative behaviour, of which one is altruism, the focus of a good deal of work has been on how cooperative strategies fare against non-cooperative ones – including whether any is an ESS – in mathematical models in which the strategies themselves are the actors, competing against each other in sequences of strategic play.

4. THE PRISONER'S DILEMMA

Altruism is a form of cooperative behaviour. The classical game-theoretic model for investigating the strategic virtues of cooperation versus non-cooperation is the so-called *Prisoner's Dilemma.* This simple model has been especially fruitful in investigating the possibilities for altruistic strategies to emerge and be maintained in populations of players. Admittedly, the prospects seem unpropitious in the context of the so-called *one-shot Prisoner's Dilemma.* Formally, this is a type of payoff structure in a game between two players i and ii, who at each play are each given the choice of whether (in the established terminology of the game) to cooperate or defect without knowing what the other does. The payoff table below for i and ii is a Prisoner's Dilemma:

		ii	
	i/ii	cooperate	defect
i	cooperate	2/2	0/5
	defect	5/0	1/1

[12] John Maynard Smith and G. R. Price, 'The Logic of Animal Conflict', *Nature*, 246 (November 1973), 15–18. (An *unbeatable* strategy is one against which, in a population of competing strategies, no other can increase whatever its initial frequency.)

Examination of the payoff table quickly explains why the Prisoner's Dilemma quickly became an object of enormous interest – a despairing interest to many – for it shows in a particularly simple and striking way that the pursuit of rational self-interest can, and given an enormously large choice of payoffs necessarily will, result in a situation worse for all parties than one which could have been achieved by cooperation. On a single play, defecting is clearly the best strategy in ignorance of the other's move: neither can improve from that strategy whichever choice the other has made. Such a position is called a *Nash equilibrium* of the game after its discoverer, the American mathematician John Nash. There is only one such equilibrium in this game (a complicating factor in 'solving' other types of two-person game is that there may be more than one), and any payoff table with a unique Nash equilibrium at defect/defect is defined to be a Prisoner's Dilemma. Necessary and sufficient conditions for such an equilibrium are that two cooperators get more than two defectors, a defector against a cooperator gets the most and the cooperator against the defector least. There are infinitely many Prisoner's Dilemmas since clearly there are infinitely many sets of (four) numbers satisfying that condition.

It is of course precisely because that equilibrium is both unique and suboptimal – both players would obviously do better by cooperating – that the Prisoner's Dilemma graphically suggests a problematic drawback of rationality, under the modest assumption that rationality consists in choosing an optimal strategy where one exists. The message also looks bad for altruism, for it is easy to see that two players faced with the choice of whether to be reciprocally altruistic generates a Prisoner's Dilemma. Suppose I give you a benefit b at a cost c to myself. Now let us say that you and I are both cooperators if we give that benefit at that cost to each other, i.e. we are reciprocally altruistic, we are both defectors if we give each other nothing, and I am a cooperator (you are a defector) if I give you that benefit at that cost (you give me nothing); and vice versa. Then the payoff table for the strategies cooperate/defect as defined in this way satisfies the conditions for being a Prisoner's Dilemma.

People have tried various ways to circumvent the pessimistic directive of the Prisoner's Dilemma. In an influential book[13] David Gauthier argued that if either player is disposed to cooperate, and believes the other has a similar disposition, then he/she should cooperate. The problem with this idea, as many were quick to point out, is that the only equilibrium of

[13] David Gauthier, *Morals by Agreement* (Oxford University Press, 1986).

the game remains 'both defect'. Defecting strictly dominates cooperating, which means that *whatever the other does*, one does better by defecting. There is a large literature on Gauthier's theory, but I will not discuss it any further here because in any case the situation changes dramatically for iterations of the Prisoner's Dilemma where there is no certainty about the point at which the plays will end. More precisely, these are repetitions in which randomly chosen pairs of players play against each other at each round with a nonzero probability w of encountering each other in the future.[14] Since under this assumption there is no limit to the number of rounds, the set of all possible strategies is enormous: infinite even for pure, i.e. deterministic, strategies, and uncountably infinite for mixed ones (a mixed strategy is a probability distribution over pure strategies).[15] The players in this iterative scenario, or 'ecology', as it is often called in the evolutionary game-theory literature, can be identified with strategies, where the fitness of a strategy is defined to be the sum of its payoffs over all its players. As usual, fitness determines the 'reproductive rate' of the strategies: their frequencies are proportional to the cumulative scores.

The iterated Prisoner's Dilemma provides a reasonably natural way of modelling such reciprocally altruistic strategies as those in which the temptation to defect is compensated by an expectation of future benefit determined by the value of w, and also provides an evolutionary setting for investigating their stability and robustness[16] properties. A natural question to ask is whether any such strategy is an ESS. The conditionally cooperative strategy called *Tit for Tat* and characterised by the two rules (i) cooperate on the first round and (ii) in a successor round copy the opponent's move in the preceding one, was initially claimed to be one by Axelrod and Hamilton,[17] but it was later shown not only that it is not, but also that no pure strategy is an ESS for any value of w. It is in retrospect easy to see that Tit for Tat is not an ESS because the alternative strategy 'always cooperate' will never be eliminated, and in general this will be true for any strategy which only ever defects after an opponent's defection (such a strategy is called 'nice').

[14] If the number of repetitions is fixed and known to the players the situation is little different from the one-shot game, with the same sort of unique sub-optimal equilibrium.

[15] In the repeated Prisoner's Dilemma with just ten iterations the number of pure strategies available to each player is already enormous: $2^{349,525}$ (Ken Binmore, *Fun and Games: A Text on Game Theory* (Lexington, MA: D. C. Heath, 1992), p. 353).

[16] The robustness of a strategy is defined in terms of the number of invaders it can successfully resist: the larger the number, the more robust the strategy.

[17] Robert Axelrod and William Hamilton, 'The Evolution of Cooperation', *Science* 211 (March 1981), 1390–6.

Nevertheless Tit for Tat *is* a Nash equilibrium in the indefinitely repeated game: if all players use it none can do better by changing, so a form of reciprocal altruism can in principle gain a foothold. Moreover, the iterated Prisoner's Dilemma and its associated equilibrium strategies are relatively simple models (though the mathematics that needs to be employed for dealing with them often is not), which suggests that weaker but still recognisable criteria of stability, together with more complex cooperative strategies and the presence of noise, defined as the possibility of making a mistake, might be able to account better for the widespread existence of reciprocal altruism, and possibly even stronger forms, observed in human populations. There are some striking results that go some way to providing an affirmative answer to this question even without incorporating specifically human capacities, like the ability to engage in verbal communication, into the model, e.g. Hamilton himself had shown that an invading group of altruistic players can become established in a population of non-altruists, a result which Karl Sigmund, himself an outstanding contributor to the field, called 'arguably the most significant contribution of evolutionary game theory towards explaining the emergence of cooperation'.[18] I will mention one other major result. A strategy is called *nice* if it never defects first, *retaliatory* if it punishes a defection in the previous round and *nasty* if it never cooperates first (the terminology is that of Bendor and Swistak[19]). It has been shown that a nice but retaliatory strategy will be fitter than average as long as any non-nice strategy remains in the population, and will increase until all non-nice strategies have been eliminated. More generally, cooperative strategies are robust and have a very large basin of attraction in the evolutionary dynamics.[20]

So far so good. The models are still however a considerable way from the more complex situations arising in real strategic encounters. The next big step in the way of introducing more realistic constraints was to incorporate the possibility of communication, and in particular the possibility of storing and exchanging information between players. Trivers and another distinguished evolutionary biologist, R. D. Alexander, had both noted that a *reputation* for having evinced cooperative behaviour in the past might be a factor in inducing a suitably sympathetic, i.e. altruistic, response to

[18] Karl Sigmund, 'William D. Hamilton's Work in Evolutionary Game Theory', Interim Report IR-02-079, International Institute for Applied Systems Analysis.

[19] Jonathan Bendor and Piotr Swistak, 'Types of Evolutionary Stability and the Problem of Cooperation', *Proceedings of the National Academy of Sciences of the USA* 92 (1995), 3596–600.

[20] *Ibid.* The minimal stabilising frequency for any such strategy converges to 0.5 as the probability parameter w tends to 1 (Theorem 5, (ii), p. 3600), and the minimal stabilising frequency of any nasty strategy tends to 1 as w tends to 1 (Theorem 6)

the bearer of that reputation. Clearly, this type of altruism goes beyond both kin-altruism and reciprocal altruism, and intuitively it should be more resistant to a Darwinian explanation appealing only to mutation and natural selection. An examination of how cooperative strategies fare in a suitable elaboration of the iterated Prisoner's Dilemma shows that this is not true, however. In this, any pair of players interacts at most once with each other, and their possible strategies incorporate information about how other players have behaved in the past, i.e. altruistically or not. A specific model in which altruistic behaviour is shown to be sensitive to this sort of information is called a model of *indirect reciprocity*.

Such models have been extensively studied in the last fifteen or so years by Martin Nowak and Karl Sigmund. One of their models equipped players with scores which increase when the player cooperates with the co-player and decrease when they do not, placing the players into neighbourhood networks and assigning a fixed probability q to accurately assessing a co-player's score. Thus every cooperation brings a benefit b and every defection exacts a cost c. All scores start at 0. A striking and unexpected result emerged, an analogue of Hamilton's inequality for kin-altruism. This is another inequality, which states that manifestations of indirect reciprocity will emerge and be maintained so long as $q > c/b$ (recall that Hamilton's inequality is $r > c/b$ where r is the degree of relatedness between donor and recipient).[21]

5. THE LONG MARCH OF SCIENCE

These results are, I believe, an impressive example of the slow but steady erosion by scientific research of what had seemed once a bastion of scientific inexplicability. People (including most, but not all, religious people) who dislike what they call 'reductive' explanations of human behaviour are quick to point out that all these models are still over-simple compared with the 'richness' of human moral experience ('richness' is a word that never gets defined: too rich in meaning to be definable, presumably). This sort of ideologically inspired criticism is widespread, but it should not blind anyone to the significance of results like the ones we have seen. Initially altruism of any stripe had seemed to present an intractable problem for Darwin's theory. Then it was shown that kin-altruism could be explained, and after that various 'higher' levels of unselfish behaviour, from

[21] Martin Nowak and Karl Sigmund, 'The Evolution of Indirect Reciprocity', *Nature* 437 (2005), 1291–8.

reciprocally generous behaviour among biologically unrelated people under the assumption that they merely expect that they will meet again in the future, to altruistic behaviour when that assumption is itself relaxed and replaced by some form of socially accessible monitoring. Even very simple and crude models can be very useful in showing how little in the way of assumed structure need be required to reproduce salient features of behaviour.

But as we have seen, some of the more recent results obtained by evolutionary game theory go a long way beyond such a simple remit and, once additional factors like the possibility of communication and control are added to the models, an explanatory link is forged between evolutionary psychology and neuroscience. Novak collaborates with scientists from other relevant disciplines,[22] like Steven Pinker, Harvard Professor of Linguistics and well-known author of many works on the evolution of language and the mind, and the possibilities of fruitful interdisciplinary cooperation seem more promising than ever. In a recent survey of the literature on the evolution of indirect reciprocity (a literature to which they are of course probably the most prolific and distinguished contributors), Nowak and Sigmund point out that the evolution of cooperation by indirect reciprocity exploits a range of social, psychological and cognitive resources to whose further development it acts as a powerful evolutionary spur:

> Indirect reciprocity requires information storage and transfer as well as strategic thinking and has a pivotal role in the evolution of collaboration and communication. The possibilities for games of manipulation, coalition-building and betrayal are limitless. Indirect reciprocity may have provided the selective challenge driving the cerebral expansion in human evolution.[23]

That the evolution of the brain and in particular of its information-processing functions have played a crucial role in the biological evolution of a moral sense has been argued in a recent book by Marc Hauser.[24] Evolutionary game theory not only suggests a plausible evolutionary trigger

[22] And theologians. Nowak is a committed Christian who, besides being on the board of advisers of the Templeton Foundation, is also co-director of the Evolution and Theology of Cooperation programme at Harvard University. In Carl Zimmer's *New York Times* article about him (2007), he is reported as denying any conflict between science and religion, saying 'Like mathematics, many theological statements do not need scientific confirmation. Once you have the proof of Fermat's Last Theorem, it's not like we have to wait for the scientists to tell us if it's right.' The reader will be aware that my own view of theological claims is less charitable than Nowak's. His appeal to the indefeasibility of mathematical proof will be turned back on him in Chapter 8, where I will give one for God's non-existence.

[23] Nowak and Sigmund, 'The Evolution of Indirect Reciprocity', 1291–8.

[24] Marc Hauser, *Moral Minds: How Nature Designed our Universal Sense of Right and Wrong* (New York: Ecco, 2006).

for it to occur but also an explanation of how it resulted in the embedding and spreading of a specifically moral sense.

6. A VOTE AGAINST

For all his excellent credentials as a geneticist and advocate of evolutionary theory[25] Francis Collins nevertheless remains a resolute nay-sayer. It is not so much that he dismisses the evidence that types of altruistic behaviour are explicable in evolutionary terms, as that the explicable part is not true altruism:

> By altruism I do not mean the 'You scratch my back, I'll scratch yours' kind of behaviour that practices benevolence to others in direct expectation of reciprocal benefits. Altruism is more interesting: the truly selfless giving of oneself to others with absolutely no secondary motives.[26]

And he continues later: 'Agape, or selfless altruism, presents a major challenge to the evolutionist. It is quite frankly a scandal of reductionist reasoning.'[27] No it isn't. Collins is simply failing to acknowledge, or possibly even recognise, anything like the full range of alternative possibilities. (The same tendency is manifested later in his book when he endorses C. S. Lewis's trilemma of Christ's either being a liar, a lunatic or a truth-teller when Christ was supposed to have said that he was the son of God.[28]) To claim that the experience of 'agape' is 'a signpost to God', as Collins does,[29] is to fail to acknowledge plausible non-theistic possibilities which even an intelligent child could quite easily come up with. Here is one. Collins, like most people in western societies, inherited a transmitted culture based on Judaeo-Christian ethics in which assisting others plays a large role, even if neither the inheritors nor even their parents are of a religious bent. As everyone knows, it is very difficult to evade the promptings of an educational download which you receive, daily reinforced, from your very earliest childhood onwards. I think no more need, or should, be said about signposts to God being illuminated by the existence of generous impulses.

[25] He points out what compelling evidence the genetic distances between humans, chimpanzees, mice and chickens, measured by the chances of a human protein-coding piece of DNA being found in the others respectively provide is for the hypothesis of common descent (100%, 99% and 75% respectively, and for a piece of 'junk' DNA 98%, 40% and 4%). The probabilities for the junk item are more impressive than they might initially sound, since there would otherwise be no reason to expect a genetic relationship of this sort at all (Collins, *The Language of God*, p. 127).

[26] *Ibid.*, p. 25. [27] *Ibid.*, p. 27. [28] *Ibid.*, p. 224. [29] *Ibid.*, p. 25.

7. MORAL LAWS VS THE MORAL LAW

The moral norms to which people subscribe are not a unitary body of principles. Even a cursory inspection of the more universally acknowledged among them reveals some very different *types* of moral injunction. These seem to fall into three broad categories:

(i) those of generosity; in particular, altruism.
(ii) restrictive norms: the proscription of e.g. theft, murder, treachery, etc.
(iii) higher-order principles: in particular, equality of moral status.

Added to these are the more obviously culture-relative norms about which there's less unanimity: covering the head out of doors, sex before marriage, etc.

(i) and (ii) seem to be fairly invariant across societies and times. If the previous sections are correct then (i) has at least a partly evolutionary explanation, which the addition of plausible constraints to the model should improve. At any rate we have a good scientific theory which promises to explain aspects of behaviour that many had thought to require God to explain. But what about (ii) and (iii)?

Some people, impressed by the success of evolutionary explanations even outside biology, believe that moral norms and principles have not merely an evolutionary explanation but also an evolutionary *justification*. Denying that this is in principle possible is the famous argument of David Hume that I reported in Chapter 1, that moral obligations cannot arise by inference from any set of purely factual premises; and evolutionary theory is, logically speaking, just such a set. To take a topical example, Hume's argument denies that from the premise that evolution has endowed parents with the emotional and physical capacities to nurture and shelter their children until they pass the age of adolescence, you can validly infer a corresponding obligation. Substitute for the evolutionary premise any other factual claim you might think true: for example 'God wants me to do X', or 'To do X would result in the greatest happiness of the greatest number', or 'You or your ancestors were parties to a contract forbidding X', or . . . etc. Hume's claim is that from any such premise it is just as impossible to derive a moral obligation as it is from a premise describing human beings' evolutionary endowments. A simple corollary of Hume's argument is that moral utterances, whatever function they do perform,[30] *do not describe facts*; were they to do so, they *would* be able to stand in deductive relations with factual statements.

[30] Hume's view, shared by a large number of modern moral philosophers, is that they express particular types of personal attitudes and emotions; namely moral attitudes and emotions.

In a recent book whose central argument is that moral norms *can* be inferred from supposed evolutionary facts, and indeed are factual judgments themselves,[31] Larry Arnhart claims that Hume did *not* intend to show the impossibility of a valid derivation of norms from facts, citing the (textually correct) fact that Hume assimilated moral qualities to so-called 'secondary qualities', like those of colour, sound, etc. Granted that, and that 'This tomato is red' is a factual statement, Arnhart argues that Hume is implicitly committed to moral facts. But 'This tomato is red' is only a factual statement if 'is red' is understood as 'absorbs light outside the red part of the visual colour spectrum'. This is not what Hume meant by a 'secondary quality': he meant the *sensation* of redness, and 'I have a sensation of redness' does not follow from any fact about the wavelength of red light. Hume's so-called sceptical arguments, of which the no-ought-from-is argument is just one (others cast doubt on learning from experience, thinking that we have selves, and that there is a world external to us), typically have the remarkable property that attempts to refute them invariably illustrate clearly *why* they are valid – Arnhart's is no exception and I confidently predict the same outcome for all future attempts.

Prima facie more persuasive is another due to the philosopher John Searle. As presented by J. L. Mackie,[32] it is as follows:

(1) Jones uttered the words 'I hereby promise to pay you, Smith, five dollars.'
(2) Jones promised to pay Smith five dollars.
(3) Jones placed himself under (undertook) an obligation to pay Smith five dollars.
(4) Jones is under an obligation to pay Smith five dollars.
(5) Jones ought to pay Smith five dollars.

Mackie, who honours Hume's argument with the title 'Hume's Law', identifies the invalid step as that from (4) to (5), because he correctly sees an equivocation in the word 'obligation': it can either mean that *in fact* Jones entered into a recognised type of contract, or that Jones did really place himself under a *moral* obligation to pay Smith five dollars. But the second meaning does not in any way follow from the first without begging the question. The same thing could also be said about the first step, from

[31] For example: 'My judgment that this person is morally praiseworthy is true if this person's conduct is such as to induce a sentiment of approbation in normal human beings under standard conditions' (Larry Arnhart, *Darwinian Natural Right: The Biological Ethics of Human Nature* (State University of New York Press, 1998), p. 70).

[32] J. L. Mackie, *Ethics: Inventing Right and Wrong* (New York: Penguin, 1977).

(1) to (2): uttering a form of words does not entail a corresponding moral obligation. Either way, Hume seems to be vindicated.[33]

Hume's argument had a profound effect on moral theory. The twentieth-century philosopher P. H. Nowell-Smith described Hume's observation, an objection to eighteenth-century versions of naturalism just as much as to attempts to derive moral lessons from the existence of God, as 'crushing'.[34] The British philosopher G. E. Moore, more presciently than he knew, termed the fallacy Hume identified the '*Naturalistic Fallacy*'; presciently, because Moore wrote *avant la lettre*, before the term 'philosophical naturalism' had become part of the verbal currency of academic philosophy. I should add (philosophers are touchy about such things) that Moore was describing an inessential variant of Hume's fallacy, namely the belief that an ethical statement is equivalent to some factual one.

So where does the sense of moral obligation come from? The theist of course says that it is a specifically *human* faculty given by God. Hume was the first to offer a plausible and systematic naturalistic alternative. Whether it is all true is to some extent beside the point: the relevant fact is that it is a plausible naturalistic alternative, something theists deny can in principle exist. At any rate it is an account which, with a few qualifications which I think strengthen and extend it, I will endorse in the remainder of this chapter.

8. A MORAL THEORY FOR HUMEAN BEINGS

Hume believed that there are two sorts of moral virtues, one of which is an innate disposition which to some extent we share with animals, while the second of which is, in a sense I will describe shortly, acquired through strategic interaction with others. The latter therefore certainly doesn't need God to explain it, but what about the innate disposition? One example of this is the altruism displayed most strongly to family-members. It is open to anyone to say we are given this by God, but as the first half of this chapter relates, we now have at least a promising evolutionary explanation. Hume of course knew nothing of Darwin or genetics, so he knew nothing of the modern theory of kin-altruism, and could not have appreciated Haldane's

[33] There is a cottage-industry of attempts to refute Hume, and to review even the best of them would be a book-length undertaking. There is one however, due to another highly respected philosopher, A. N. Prior, which deserves mention because it is challenging and instructive, but I will reserve it to the Appendix to this chapter.

[34] Mackie, *Ethics*, pp. 36–7.

joke about laying down his life for x people whose degree of relatedness was 1/x. Or couldn't he?

> A man naturally loves his children better than his nephews, his nephews better than his cousins, his cousins better than strangers, where everything else is equal.[35]

Prescient in so many ways (we shall see some more in a moment), he now seems to have anticipated the evolutionary explanation of kin-altruism!

While that may be dismissed as a litttle *jeu d'esprit*,[36] Hume is widely acknowledged to have anticipated and to some extent laid the explanatory groundwork for another contemporary research programme employing the resources of evolutionary game theory: but now with the object of explaining the emergence and maintenance of the social norms I grouped under (ii) above, which Hume called 'norms of justice', against theft, murder, treachery and so on. For Hume these are no more than types of cooperative *equilibrium*. Hume called the associated norms 'artificial' because they are self-reinforcing *conventions*. That fundamental idea has been rediscovered by evolutionary game theorists, and the equilibria classified as Nash equilibria of multi-person strategies that reward cooperation and punish defection in indefinitely repeated games. Which games? You can probably guess the answer: Prisoner's Dilemma, and games closely related to it. But Hume's almost uncanny insight did not stop there, for he also provided the kernel of an explanation of one of the most fundamental moral principles of all: the sense we have that we are equal moral agents.

We shall come to all this in due course. As an introductory preamble we will temporarily elevate our thoughts heavenwards.

9. 'IF GOD DOES NOT EXIST, EVERYTHING IS PERMITTED'

Hume had very little time for God, except for philosophical target-practice and to be the butt of a good deal of sly humour – a dangerous practice at a time when atheists could still be tried and executed. He certainly wished to exclude God from being used to justify moral injunctions, and his 'no-ought-from-is' argument does that very effectively. Nevertheless, to concede that the source of moral authority is not the commands, or wishes, of God still seems to many to open the gate to moral anarchy.

[35] David Hume, *Treatise of Human Nature*, 2nd edn (Oxford: Clarendon Press, 1978), Book III, Part II, sect. I.

[36] Or it may not be: the plot is thickened by noting that Hume's ideas exercised a powerful influence on Darwin's grandfather, Erasmus Darwin, who was himself a seminal influence in the genesis of his grandson's theory!

Ivan Karamazov, one of the three brothers Karamazov in Dostoevsky's eponymous novel, was certainly of that opinion, which he (allegedly) expressed in the famous remark 'If God does not exist, everything is permitted.'[37] At a somewhat lower level we have another British newspaper columnist proclaiming, with no supporting evidence, '[w]ithout the Judaeo-Christian heritage there would be no morality and no true human rights'.[38]

Karamazov regarded his claim (or his author Dostoevsky regarded it), as a very large number of people still do, as a *reductio ad absurdum* of atheism via the syllogism 'If God does not exist, everything is permitted. It is not true that everything is permitted. Therefore God exists.' A slightly shorter version produced by William Lane Craig is 'We cannot be truly good without God. But if we can, in some measure, be good, then it follows that God exists.'[39] A public fed its moral views from the pulpit unfortunately has no difficulty in resonating with Karamazov's claim. But they have had the wool – or rather the cloth – pulled over their eyes. Besides running foul of Hume's objection, the major premise of that syllogism is rather obviously false. Anyone older than a year or so will know that what stops undesirable things being permitted is not God at all but an entire hierarchy of *people* invested by *other people* with the appropriate authority, including parents, schoolteachers, police, sergeant-majors, magistrates, the prison authorities and, in some countries, the public executioner – to say nothing of one's own conscience, which another famous fictional character remarked 'does make cowards of us all'. Ivan Karamazov, and the multitude of Ivan Karamazov think-alikes, simply fail to recognise what is in front of their eyes, an alternative source of moral authority to God: *ourselves*.

The realisation is slowly dawning, however. For the first time in my memory a leading British politician has publicly admitted to being an atheist, and when asked the (sadly, inevitable) question of whether he regretted having no faith to draw on, he replied 'No, because my belief comes from a set of values about the kind of society I believe in. It's a very strong part of who I am.'[40] But where, the religious objector might still ask, do those values themselves come from? That person will say that they are implanted in us by God. The Bayesian apparatus of Chapter 3 tells us

[37] I say 'allegedly'. It seems that nowhere in the novel does Ivan Karamazov actually say this (in Russian of course): the claim merely represents his views.

[38] Melanie Phillips, *Daily Mail*, 4 October 2010.

[39] *Can We Be Good Without God?* (video).

[40] Reported in the London *Evening Standard*, 31 August 2010. The politician is Edward Miliband, interviewed on the eve of the election for the Labour Party leadership (he won it).

that to accept that as an explanation means assigning some degree of prior credibility to the existence of God, and we have seen that there is already sufficiently much evidence against that hypothesis to cast comparable doubt on the explanation itself. In addition, evolutionary theory, which I shall take to include evolutionary game theory, seems to supply us with the framework for understanding why that most powerful of ethical impulses, that of altruism, needs no God to implant it in us.

As for the more civically directed moral principles, those prohibiting theft, murder, dishonesty, promise-breaking and so on, Aristotle provided at least the germ of the answer two millennia ago: it is not in our collective interest to condone these things because to do so would threaten the state and the civic state furnishes the optimal environment in which people can cultivate in freedom those activities that conduce to their well-being and develop their potentialities. One problem with invoking Aristotle in this way is, of course, that his ideas of morally acceptable behaviour do not always coincide with our own, to the extent that we rightly condemn some practices, like slavery, that he seems to have taken no serious exception to. But a more fundamental problem is to explain how, even if it would be in everyone's best interest to have contracts enforced, theft and murder punished, etc., (a) everyone would agree to establish institutions to do so and (b) norms which protect essentially self-serving interests should ever come to acquire *moral* status.

While it is fairly clear why (b) is a problem, it might be less obvious why (a) is. Re-enter Hume. He not only identified very clearly why (a) is a problem, but he used an idea very similar to one we are familiar with from the first half of this chapter to solve it. In addition he provided an answer to (b), and thereby, as we shall see, also an answer to the question of why we should object to slavery. The problem which Hume identified in (a) is essentially the problem of the Prisoner's Dilemma,[41] of self-interested individuals finding a reason to cooperate to their common benefit. Its serious implications for a range of modern environmental and strategic problems were illustrated by the game-theorist Garret Hardin in a famous parable, the *Tragedy of the Commons*.[42] The parable is of cattle-herders grazing their stock on common land, gaining new income with each additional animal, with the result that the pasture is eventually destroyed by overgrazing. Hardin used it to alert the public to the likely results of

[41] I have to say 'essentially' because of course Hume had never heard of the Prisoner's Dilemma.

[42] Garret Hardin, 'The Tragedy of the Commons', *Science* 162 (1968), 1243–8; Hardin refers to it as an n-person Prisoner's Dilemma.

overfishing, polluting the atmosphere, the arms-race and above all human overpopulation.[43]

But Hume had been presenting Prisoner's Dilemma and related parables two-and-a-half centuries before Hardin's. Here is one, often referred to as the *Farmer's Dilemma*:

> Your corn is ripe today; mine will be so tomorrow. 'Tis profitable for us both, that I shou'd labour with you today, and that you shou'd aid me tomorrow. I have no kindness for you, and know you have as little for me. I will not, therefore, take any pains on your account; and should I labour with you upon my own account, in expectation of a return, I know I shou'd be disappointed, and that I shou'd in vain depend upon your gratitude. Here then I leave you to labour alone: You treat me in the same manner. The seasons change; and both of us lose our harvests for want of mutual confidence and security.[44]

Though it is not a classical Prisoner's Dilemma because of its sequential moves, it is like it enough in that it is a two-player game with no cooperative equilibrium. The rational move for the first player is clearly to defect, since were he/she to cooperate today then, given the assumption of self-interest, the other would see only a disadvantage tomorrow in helping him/her, and would defect. Hence the first farmer decides that he/she should defect now.

We know, however, that the sting of the Prisoner's Dilemma is drawn by considering not one-shot plays but indefinite iterations, where the suboptimal unique equilibrium strategy in the one-shot game gives way to a number of cooperative equilibrium strategies (among others) in the iterated game where there is a high enough probability of its being repeated. Without ever having heard of the Prisoner's Dilemma or knowing anything about evolutionary game theory, Hume had grasped that changing the game to the indefinitely repeated version, and appealing to an appropriate retaliator strategy, was the solution to the cooperation problem:

> Hence I learn to do a service to another, without bearing him any real kindness; because I foresee, that he will return my service, in expectation of another of the same kind, and in order to maintain the same correspondence of good offices with me or with others. And accordingly, after I have serv'd him, and he is in possession of the advantage arising from my action, he is induc'd to perform his part, as foreseeing the consequences of his refusal.[45]

[43] It is common practice to dismiss the last item as Malthusian pessimism ignorant of the earth's apparently unlimited capacity to feed people. If only that were so. Ken Binmore explains why it is not in *Just Playing, Game Theory and the Social Contract – Vol.* 2 (Cambridge, MA: MIT Press, 1998), p. 151.

[44] Hume, *Treatise of Human Nature*, Book III, Part II, sect. V.

[45] *Ibid.*

It seems to be implicit in the way Hume words this account that the punishment is unlikely to be repealed, at any rate quickly. The strategy Hume describes is called a *trigger* strategy, because the first non-cooperative play acts as a trigger causing the other player to cease cooperating. Tit for Tat is a trigger strategy, but this one is not Tit for Tat but the variation of it consisting of ceasing to cooperate altogether after the trigger. For this reason it enjoys the name *Grim Trigger*.[46] It also is an equilibrium when played by both players.

Hume provides another illustration of his idea that mutually beneficial conventions can become established without explicit covenanting, this time with a so-called coordination game having *two* equilibria:

> When [a] common sense of interest is mutually express'd, and is known to both, it produces a suitable resolution and behaviour. And this may properly enough be call'd a convention or agreement betwixt [the players], tho' without the interposition of a promise; since the actions of each of [them] have a reference to those of the other, and are perform'd upon the supposition, that something is to be perform'd on the other part. Two men, who pull the oars of a boat, do it by an agreement or convention, tho' they have never given promises to each other.[47]

This coordination game is of a type called the *Stag Hunt* by game theorists, after a problem described by Rousseau[48] involving two (or possibly more) hunters deciding whether to hunt hare or stag. If both choose to hunt stag they both have a good dinner: if one decides to hunt hare and the other stag the first gets a less good dinner and the other gets nothing; if both hunt hare both get the less good dinner. The payoffs are the same up to a cardinal measure as in the boatmen case (deciding to row when the other does nothing is the worst outcome because it involves a fruitless expenditure of effort). Unlike the Prisoner's Dilemma this game has both a 'both defect' and a 'both cooperate' Nash equilibrium. However, while the latter is better for both than the former, playing it is risky, whereas the other equilibrium is not risky at all. Nevertheless, replies Hume, if both players know that they desire the optimal outcome then under suitable conditions they will coordinate on the cooperative equilibrium by an unspoken agreement.

What are those suitable conditions? Hume appealed to a gradual transition to equilibrium, initially among few players who can exchange information with each other, and in particular learn to recognise that other people

[46] A type of strategy is 'grim' in the language of game theory if it is the most severe of that type.

[47] Hume, *Treatise of Human Nature*, Book III, Part II, sect. V.

[48] J.-J. Rousseau, *Discours sur l'origine et les fondements de l'inégalité parmi les hommes*, vol. III of *Œuvres Complètes* (Paris: Gallimard, 1959).

have similar desires and dispositions. In such an environment conditionally cooperative strategies can flourish. It was in this way that he explained the evolution of the norm against theft:

> ... Nor is the rule concerning the stability of possession the less deriv'd from human conventions, that it arises gradually, and acquires force by a slow progression, and by our repeated experience of the inconveniences of transgressing it ... this experience assures us still more, that the sense of interest has become common to all our fellows, and gives us a confidence of the future regularity of their conduct: And 'tis only on the expectation of this, that our moderation and abstinence are founded. In like manner are languages gradually establish'd by human conventions without any promise.[49]

However, Hume did not believe that all conventions are likely to become established without the threat of retaliation being reinforced by some form of explicit covenanting, especially when, as in the Farmer's Dilemma, resources are committed (or not) *now* with the expectation of it being recompensed later. Hume felt that for the relevant 'foreseeing' and expectation to be justified there had to be an understanding between the parties that the obligation to return the service exists, and most importantly that a violation will be punished. And that requires some commonly accepted framework for registering such obligations. These are explicit *promises*:

> When a man says he promises any thing, he in effect expresses a resolution of performing it; and along with that, by making use of this form of words, subjects himself to the penalty of never being trusted again in case of failure. ... [Promises] are the conventions of men, which create a new motive, when experience has taught us, that human affairs wou'd be conducted much more for mutual advantage, were there certain symbols or signs instituted, by which we might give each other security of our conduct in any particular incident. After these signs are instituted, whoever uses them is immediately bound by his interest to execute his engagements, and must never expect to be trusted any more, if he refuse to perform what he promis'd.[50]

Promises, in other words, are the medium conveying the all-important information that defection will be the trigger for punishment. The Farmer's Dilemma is thus a curtain-raiser to Hume's explanation of how another convention, promise-keeping, emerges and is maintained.

[49] Hume, *Treatise of Human Nature*, Book III, Part II, sect. V. In his important book *Conventions: A Philosophical Study* (Cambridge University Press, 1969), David Lewis shows that the convention assigning *meanings* to signs and signals is a game equilibrium, crediting the insight to Hume.

[50] Hume, *Treatise of Human Nature*, Book III, Part II, sect. V.

10. FAST FORWARD

That Hume has been deploying, with great ingenuity, what are in effect sophisticated game-theoretic arguments two centuries before game theory itself was invented is remarkable enough, but even more remarkable is his anticipation, two-and-a-half centuries before *evolutionary* game theory emerged as a scientific discipline in its own right, of how appealing to indefinitely repeated games can explain how cooperative traits and institutions can become established as a by-product of agents – genes, people, replicators of whatever sort – pursuing their own ends. The strategy was greatly strengthened by the discovery that in repeated Prisoner's Dilemmas there exist infinitely many cooperative Nash equilibria.[51] It is small wonder so many leading game theorists assign Hume an honoured place in their pantheon.[52]

But their admiration is not blind either, and Hume's assumption that he has explained the emergence of the various norms of justice[53] by showing that they are cooperative equilibria has come in for a good deal of critical comment. Peter Vanderschraaf, one of those game theorists who acknowledge the depths of Hume's insights, points out that in an environment of mistrust promises will generally not be believed.[54] In a population most of whose members are promise-breakers, promise-keepers are very unlikely to maintain their numbers, let alone spread to dominate the population, so the 'all defect' strategy must also be considered as a possible equilibrium (Vanderschraaf cites a source[55] claiming that it became the actual equilibrium in the Italian corporate community). This leads Vanderschraaf to observe that there are a great number of equilibrium strategies in such repeated games, and Hume fails to provide an explanation of why the (Grim) Trigger should be the one selected rather than any of the others:

The problem Hume leaves unresolved is one of *equilibrium selection*. It is by no means obvious that the agents engaged in a particular game will follow any

[51] This is the so-called 'folk theorem' of evolutionary game theory.

[52] Binmore, *Fun and Games*, p. 21, calls Hume 'the true founding father of game theory', and Peter Vanderschraaf comments 'Hume did not know the technical vocabulary of game theory, but his analysis of convention in Part III of *A Treatise of Human Nature* contains a number of profound game-theoretical insights' ('Game Theory, Evolution and Justice', Technical Report No. CMU-PHIL-95 (1998) (Carnegie-Mellon University, Pittsburgh), p. 31 footnote 40).

[53] In calling them norms of 'justice' I am continuing to follow Hume's own somewhat idiosyncratic terminology.

[54] Peter Vanderschraaf, 'Hume's Game-Theoretic Business Ethics', *Business Ethics Quarterly* 9:1 (1999), 47–67.

[55] Arthur L. Kelly, 'Case Study – Italian Tax Mores', in T. Donaldson and P. Werhane (eds.), *Ethical Issues in Business* (Upper Saddle River, NJ: Prentice-Hall, 1979), pp. 37–9.

equilibrium at all, let alone a 'special' equilibrium like the all-Tr equilibrium of Hume's supergame.[56]

The objection is somewhat unfair, since Hume lacked the technical resources that have only recently been invented, and which even then raise substantial mathematical and conceptual problems. As Vanderschraaf himself points out: 'There is to date [1999] no generally accepted account of how patterns of cooperation emerge in the repeated Prisoner's Dilemma, which is less complicated than the game Hume was analyzing.'[57]

But what Hume did do, by fairly common consent, was fundamental: here is an eighteenth-century thinker who forged almost single-handed the conceptual tools that only over two centuries later would mathematicians recognise and develop into the most powerful and promising explanatory research programme that the social sciences have ever witnessed. Hume is a social-sciences Faraday, the profoundly innovative thinker whose idea of electric and magnetic fields needed Maxwell to formulate into the powerful mathematical theory that remains one of the foundations of modern physics.

I also do not think that Hume left the problem of equilibrium-selection quite as unresolved as Vanderschraaf claims. Hume would have agreed that accepting an obligation to be bound by promises will not work in an environment in which promising has become discredited (in fact he discusses a similar objection), but nevertheless claimed that people are far-sighted enough and good enough communicators to recognise its merits and augment that sense by endowing it with the status of a moral obligation. He would also have regarded it as a trite observation that sufficiently severe random shocks can disrupt any move to a cooperative equilibrium. But, again anticipating much later developments, he saw the ability to communicate and exchange information as the key to establishing cooperative conventions, and unsurprisingly, including such parameters into evolutionary game-theoretic models changes the situation dramatically.

There is a good deal of recent work modelling the reinforcing effects of communication and learning from experience. In one much-cited piece of work,[58] Skyrms and Pemantle constructed an interaction model in which a small group of mixed stag-hunters and hare-hunters initially interact at random, with payoffs depending on whether the interaction is with players of the same type: if it is the payoffs are bigger. These values are iteratively

[56] Vanderschraaf, 'Hume's Game-Theoretic Business Ethics', p. 62. [57] *Ibid.*

[58] Brian Skyrms and Robin Pemantle, 'A Dynamic Model of Social Network Formation', *Proceedings of the National Academy of Sciences of the USA* 97 (2000), 9340–6.

fed into the model, determining the probability at each stage of interacting with another of the same type.

> How do these interaction probabilities evolve? It can be shown, by simulation and analytically, that stag hunters will end up interacting with other stag hunters . . . If structure is fluid, and the learning dynamics for structure is fast relative to the strategy-revision dynamics, stag hunters will find each other and then imitation will slowly convert the hare hunters to stag hunters. That conclusion is robust to the addition of a little chance. Here, we finally have a model that can explain the institution of a modest social contract.[59]

These are impressive results, though I think that the authors probably go too far in claiming that a social contract, even a 'modest' one, has been explained by this or any other realistic model, for the simple reason that there is nothing contractual to be explained.[60] What has been explained is a dynamical evolution to a state of mutually beneficial cooperation much more along the lines suggested by Hume.

II. WHERE'S THE MORAL?

If the foregoing is true, and the game theorists themselves bear witness to it, Hume provided much of the conceptual basis of a novel explanation, two-and-a-half centuries in advance of its time, of how a community of self-interested agents can establish cooperative conventions which evade the objection posed by the Prisoner's Dilemma. So far, so good. But Hume's explanatory goal is still only half-achieved. It is one thing (although, as many evolutionary game theorists agree, also a major explanatory advance) to show how such conventions are likely to become established, and another to show why they, unlike the convention according to which people co-ordinate on a common language, or drive on one side of the road rather than another, acquire the character of *moral norms*. Where does their specifically *moral* colouring come from and why do other conventions lack it? Why, as Hume puts it, do 'we annex the idea of virtue to justice, and of vice to injustice'?[61]

To answer this question, he appeals to a new idea, *sympathy*. This, he claims, is the human tendency to see oneself as sharing in a common

59 Brian Skyrms, 'The Stag Hunt', Presidential Address to the Pacific Meeting of the American Philosophical Association, March 2001.

60 The idea that the legal and moral norms characterising a mature society receive their authority from a fictitious social *contract* is several centuries old. The fact that no such contract ever existed hasn't dimmed the enthusiasm of its advocates, from Rousseau onwards.

61 Hume, *Treatise of Human Nature*, Book III, Part II, sect. II.

humanity, identifying emotionally with it to the extent that we can feel its pleasures and pains reflected in us. Thus, in a widely dispersed society we still are moved to condemn a distant injustice, because we have an empathy with its proximate victim: 'We partake of their uneasiness by sympathy.' All such actions therefore evoke that sympathetic identification with the victims, attracting that peculiar type of emotional disapproval which Hume calls *moral disapprobation*, while their beneficial counterparts evoke a correspondingly contrary approval. These responses are then reinforced by education and 'the artifice of politicians', and acquiring the reputation of a person of good character confers a bonus of approval by one's fellows with, not to put too fine a point on it, corresponding benefits likely to accrue to oneself.[62] With this almost throwaway remark at the end of section II of Book III of the *Treatise*, Hume has now placed himself as an anticipator not only of the modern so-called 'folk theorems' of evolutionary game theory, but of Sigmund and Nowak's ideas of indirect reciprocity.

In heavily jocular vein, at the expense of his favourite target, Hume compares the way the norm of holding to promises acquires its moral patina with the way religious ritual acquires the odour of sanctity:

> I shall farther observe, that since every new promise imposes a new obligation of morality on the person who promises, and since this new obligation arises from his will; 'tis one of the most mysterious and incomprehensible operations that can possibly be imagin'd, and may even be compar'd to *transubstantiation*, or *holy orders*, where a certain form of words, along with a certain intention, changes entirely the nature of an external object, and even of a human nature.[63]

But modern readers of Hume might be excused for thinking that in investing what he himself called 'artificial virtues' with a moral character, he is actually trying to prove too much. Hume was politically no revolutionary, a cadet member of an aristocratic, landowning family, for whom property rights and the web of law and convention protecting them were fundamental. Almost a century later people of his class were fighting any attempt to reform Parliament in Britain because they feared – correctly – the eventual erosion of those rights. They were only persuaded to extend the franchise (still only to property-owners) in 1832 because the Duke of Wellington, pointing to the events in France between 1789 and 1793, persuaded them that to obstruct it would result in the total destruction of

[62] *Ibid.* [63] *Ibid.*

their class at the hands of the mob, who were already given to rioting in sufficiently large numbers to make the threat very apparent.

Today we are on the whole much less disposed to attach such an absolute moral character to the laws protecting property because we have a notion of distributive justice, absent entirely from Hume's discussion, according to which large disparities in the distribution of wealth are seen as unjust. But, as Hume himself acknowledges, from the point of view of explaining how and why these artificial conventions are maintained in large societies, he had in any case no need to invoke an additional norm of morality: as he points out, society – his society – sufficiently recognised the benefit to its members of maintaining the conventions that had become established in smaller societies where communication was relatively direct and the Trigger strategy effective. To that end, as Hume himself pointed out, less closely knit societies employed magistrates and a prosecuting authority to protect its interests – together, of course, with education and that 'artifice of politicians'.

This does not imply, however, that his concept of sympathy is explanatorily redundant. Far from it, as we shall see shortly: it merely explains something else, something which has a much closer relation than possibly Hume might have cared to acknowledge to distributive justice.

12. DAVID DRYASDUST?

Reading Hume, it is sometimes difficult to grasp what a seminal contribution to moral philosophy is being made. There is no obvious moral zeal, merely a dry, deflationary account of our moral sentiments that pays them few compliments. There is little that could be called rhapsodic about Hume's gently cadenced style, and its nearest approach to anything like moral elevation appears in his frequent eulogies of civic society. His were fairly typical eighteenth-century values, reflected in the music of Handel, the preference for fertile, drained pastures over rocky and heavily forested wildernesses, and the elegant, measured[64] poetry of Pope, which find little respondent echo today. His only rhetorical device, apart from an easy and elegant command of the language, is a mocking sarcasm. Some have found his astringent commentaries on human nature almost shocking, and he does himself few favours with such typical remarks as 'Here I learn to do

[64] Literally measured, in iambic pentameters.

a service to another, without bearing him any real kindness', and so on. That such a blinkered individual might prefer an explanation of moral principles which makes them a by-product of self-interest is only to be expected, one might think, and conclude that the author of *Hard Times*[65] could have taught the author of the *Treatise* more than a thing or two about human nature. Combined with Hume's apparently rather narrow moral compass, in which the rights of property seem to command a disproportionate amount of the discussion, this is enough for many people, even the non-religious, to dismiss Hume's account as false to the reality of our moral life.

This is wrong on two counts. Firstly, Hume may have been no Gandhi, and certainly no Christ, but he did allow that almost everyone inherits certain, what he calls 'natural', virtues, among which are generosity and a humane concern for others in distress from poverty, disease, etc. But he points out, which is surely true, that these virtues are typically limited ('confin'd') in extent, and they exist side by side with the desire to satisfy one's wants in an environment in which the means to do so are far from abundant. Were people inspired by a limitless love for each other, and nature to have supplied also every good in abundance – the state of affairs described, he ironically remarks, in 'the golden age of the poets' – then his so-called laws of justice would never need to emerge. But as a self-proclaimed scientist of human nature, Hume saw it as his task to observe humanity unsentimentally and without prejudice. If the structure of our social norms is better explained as the product of strategic interactions by individuals seeking to maximise utility than, say, by heeding the commands of The Word Made Flesh, then so be it.

Unfortunately, most people, even those not consciously religious, inherit a stock of presumptions and prejudices which lie very deep, often below the horizon of consciousness, that endows humanity with characteristics that are typically more wishful thinking than fact. Shakespeare knew better. My epigraph to Chapter 7, taken from 'Hamlet' – 'What a piece of work is a man! How noble in reason! How infinite in faculty!' – is usually thought to be an encomium on human nature. In fact it is anything but, a piece of pure irony: the play's principal features are murder, lust, revenge, fratricide, probable suicide, hypocrisy, cheating, procrastination, pointless war, moral cowardice, snooping, dissimulation, lying and the death by violence of all the protagonists save one, Horatio, who had essentially the role of a chorus,

[65] Charles Dickens.

and even he was only prevented from making the immolation total so that he could tell the story.

Secondly, self-interest is only one explanatory variable in Hume's moral theory. There are two. The other is responsible for explaining a fundamental feature of our moral outlook that I have not yet discussed, and it has some radical implications for how we regard the other inhabitants of this planet. Recall item (iii) in the typology I gave earlier of basic ethical principles. Item (iii) is the higher-order principle that all human beings have equality of moral status as a consequence of a shared humanity. It is taken as a fundamental moral principle, if not the fundamental moral principle, by all the major ethical theories, and rightly so. From it stems the important idea that justice is both blind and fair. As we shall now see, Hume's theory of human nature offers a novel, and I think compelling, explanation of its provenance.

13. MORAL SYMMETRY

Number (iii) in the list of moral principles displayed earlier, *equality of moral status*, is rather obviously a symmetry principle: it is a *moral symmetry principle*. From the point of view simply of your moral rights and obligations you are an arbitrary representative of *homo sapiens*: you are identical, *under that heading*, to every other person. Though the principle is rightly seen as fundamental, secular moral theories have not had an easy time explaining why it should be. Either they simply postulate that it is, or they resort to a variety of fictional devices, like Rawls's 'veil of ignorance', or the 'states of nature' and 'social contracts' beloved of seventeenth- and eighteenth-century moral philosophers. It is a great merit of Hume's moral theory that it can explain the principle by appeal to what is plausibly a *fact*: a fact of human psychology. The explanation proceeds via a concept in Hume's account with which we are already to some extent familiar: that of *sympathy*, the empathetic identification which most of us habitually make with another's happiness or unhappiness. The identification is made possible, indeed compelled, by recognising that, as Hume puts it, '[T]he minds of men are similar in their feelings and operations.' This is another symmetry principle, but rooted in a shared psychology.

The symmetry principle (iii) can now be explained in terms of the empirically based one. By the faculty of sympathy a recognition of others' happiness or pain becomes transferred imaginatively to ourselves. A violation of the norm protecting property in any particular case will cause pain to the victim, and indirectly, via our sympathy, to ourselves:

> Nay when the injustice is so distant from us, as no way to affect our interest, it still displeases us; because we consider it as prejudicial to human society, *and pernicious to every one that approaches the person guilty of it.* We partake of their uneasiness by sympathy.[66]

The influence of sympathy actually turns out to be more empirically based than Hume at the time had evidence to claim. He used an analogy, comparing human affections to tightened strings one of which will communicate its vibrations to the others.[67] A remarkable recent experiment by psychologists at the University of Birmingham not only bears out the claim that people feel painful emotions when witnessing the pain of others, but it strongly indicated that a substantial proportion *actually experience the pain themselves.* In the experiment 123 students were shown photos and videos of people experiencing pain: a footballer breaking a leg, a tennis player twisting an ankle, etc. All the subjects reported painful emotions and a third reported actually feeling pain, a report confirmed when fMRI imaging showed the pain centres of the brain activated in those subjects.[68]

Even more striking evidence is provided by fMRI scanning which reveals that on observing members of their own ethnic group performing actions, there is a group of neurons, so-called mirror-neurons, in each of the subject's motor-cortex that fires in exactly the same way as when they are performing the actions themselves. This may well be the evolutionary origin of empathy. Unfortunately, it may also be the root of racism. But that only goes to show that there is no question of Hume or anyone else deriving a *norm* from the observation of a fact. I have pointed out that Hume saw his task as a purely explanatory one, seeing himself as – if he were to be successful – the Isaac Newton of the science of human nature (Newton was his acknowledged model).

Hume was of course not aware of the extent to which recent research into the biological/neurological roots of ethical behaviour have given a scientific basis to his theory. That moral judgment is really the expression of

[66] Hume, *Treatise of Human Nature*, Book III, Part II, sect. II (my emphasis).
[67] *Ibid.*, Book III, Part III, sect. I.
[68] Jody Osborn and Stuart W. G. Derbyshire, 'Pain Sensation Evoked by Observing Injury in Others', *Pain* (11 December 2009). Online.

moral feeling is a cardinal element of it, and the involvement of the ancient limbic system in feelings of empathy/sympathy is now acknowledged. A highly significant discovery is that psychopaths are strongly deficient in such feelings, and a probable cause is a dysfunction of the amygdala, the gateway to the limbic system. In repeated experiments examining the response to words of 'negative valence', in the language of psychiatric research papers, those with reduced amygdala function scored lowest, and failed to process affective and neutral words differently.[69] There is also evidence that psychopaths have impaired processing of distress stimuli, exhibiting low galvanic skin response and little excitation of limbic centres.

But a good *explanation* of moral feelings, as I think Hume's is, or can be developed into, may not stop at merely explaining existing ones; it may well, and very likely will, suggest possible extensions – or restrictions – in the light of further relevant information. The 'no-ought-from-is' argument does not imply that the recognition of certain empirical facts should not *influence* moral feelings and injunctions. It obviously does. If I find out that the person to whom I have acknowledged a moral debt is an unscrupulous fraud my feeling of indebtedness will quickly vanish. If I find that my cat can experience sadness and fear but cannot articulate these emotions only because of an inherited physical architecture I shall no longer think of it as merely a sort of animated machine, my property to do with as I please. This feeling will be reinforced by learning that the brain-hardware and neurochemistry of cats are remarkably similar to those of human beings.

I believe that Hume's anchoring moral status in a sympathetic resonance with other beings' pleasures and pains is a fundamental moral and scientific insight. As our knowledge of other cultures and peoples grows, the class of beings to which we feel such a sympathetic attachment will grow also. Discovering that my cat is not merely an animated machine but has a brain structure like mine and has the capacity to experience authentic pain (and pleasure) just as I do will cause me to contemplate extending to it rights which were previously specifically human rights. Here we have a clear departure from a religiously based morality which, as far as the Abrahamic religions are concerned, excludes animals with similarly developed nervous systems from the ambit of moral concern, and in particular from the moral

[69] R. J. R. Blair, 'Neurobiological Basis of Psychopathy', *British Journal of Psychiatry* 182 (2003), 5–7; Kent A. Kiehl, 'A Cognitive Neuroscience Perspective on Psychopathy: Evidence of Paralimbic Dysfunction', *Psychiatry Research* 142 (2006), 107–28.

prohibition to harm them unnecessarily.[70] Unnecessary harming of course includes harm done to them for the sake simply of augmenting human welfare and providing food. Many people increasingly feel intuitively that the current exclusion is wrong, which no repetition of silly mantras like 'with rights come responsibilities' mitigates.[71] In the future we may even extend our moral compass to include types of intelligent machinery – or they may extend theirs to include us. Who knows?

Hume – probably unwittingly – has provided the foundation of a plausible moral theory based on a shared feeling of sympathy which explains why people increasingly feel that certain animals share the same fundamental right not to be gratuitously mistreated and harmed. This feeling should be reinforced by noting that primates other than human beings also appear to possess a faculty of sympathy. A recent study of a dying chimp in a Scottish safari park reports that when an elderly female chimp was dying she was tended and groomed with great care, and for weeks after she died the other chimps were visibly depressed and agitated.[72] The park keeper said that watching the dying hours of the chimp was one of the most moving experiences of his life, while a co-author of the study made this striking observation:

> We found it very difficult to avoid seeing parallels between how we know humans respond to losing a close companion or family member, and what the chimps were doing.

14. HUME AND ARISTOTLE

There is much in Hume's moral theory that is reminiscent of Aristotle's, and indeed agrees with Aristotle's. Aristotle eulogised the state. So did Hume. It is civilised society, he notes over and over again, which allows people to accumulate wealth, which in turn gives them or their descendants the leisure and education to develop their reflective powers and elevate their

[70] On the day of writing this (31 May 2010), I read a report in the British *Daily Telegraph* newspaper that a Malaysian minister (a Muslim) has defended a company's application to build an animal-testing laboratory in Malacca State, saying 'God created animals for the benefit of human beings. That's why he created rats and monkeys.' That well over a billion people in the twenty-first century have been brain-washed by their religion(s) into believing that there is nothing unremarkable in this preposterous claim is not only very sad, but also very frightening.

[71] Silly because apart from any other reason few people would advocate withdrawing legal protection from small children, the mentally ill or the severely disabled.

[72] James R. Anderson, Alasdair Gillies and Louise C. Lock, '*Pan* Thanatology', *Current Biology* 20:8 (27 April 2010). Online.

tastes.[73] And for civilised society to develop and flourish, the appurtenances of a state are required. In another passage which warms the hearts of game theorists, Hume considered the problem of two neighbours agreeing to drain a meadow in their common ownership. They can agree

> because 'tis easy for them to know each other's mind; and each must perceive, that the immediate consequence of his failing in his part, is, the abandoning the whole project. But 'tis very difficult, and indeed impossible, that a thousand persons shou'd agree in any such action; it being difficult for them to concert so complicated a design, and still more difficult for them to execute it; while each seeks a pretext to free himself of the trouble and expence, and would lay the whole burden on others. Political society easily remedies both these inconveniences. Magistrates find an immediate interest in the interest of any considerable part of their subjects. . . . Thus bridges are built; harbours open'd; ramparts rais'd; canals form'd; fleets equipp'd; and armies disciplin'd everywhere, by the care of government, which, tho' compos'd of men subject to all human infirmities, becomes, by one of the most subtle inventions imaginable, a composition, which is, in some measure, exempted from all these infirmities.[74]

It is not just its emphasis on the virtues of a law-based civic structure that cleaves Hume's moral and political philosophy to Aristotle's. There is an even more intimate connection. It is the emphasis on *happiness*. The capacity to experience happiness and pain and the moral value of assisting the one and placing obstacles in the path of the other are as central to Hume's account as they were to Aristotle's. Hume too was a *eudaimonist*. But his moral theory, or perhaps more accurately a moral theory based on his ideas, extends Aristotle's and points the way to a humane ethics based not only on the value it places on a fully developed happiness, but also on the right of other species to share it. It also provides another rationale for placing as few restrictions as possible on *freedom*. In the Judaeo-Christian ethic freedom has a value because it allows you to be rendered personally *culpable* for breaking God's law. In the eudaemonist ethic of Hume and Aristotle it receives the altogether less minatory rationale of providing the fullest scope possible for personal fulfilment. Sex for many Christians is something to be engaged in only for the sake of reproduction, and for all

[73] Of course not everyone was so fortunate. Boswell and Dr Johnson made a tour of the Hebrides (Boswell was Scottish, soon to become Lord Auchinleck), and Boswell's description of the pitiful state of the Scottish peasantry is dreadful to read. Throughout Europe at the time wealth, education and leisure existed side by side with illiteracy, squalor, disease and premature death. No doubt what we regard as the blandness of eighteenth-century aspirations was due to their close proximity to a much less tamed and pliant Nature.

[74] Hume, *Treatise of Human Nature*, Book III, Part II, sect. VII.

of them it is supposed to find its 'true expression' only in marriage. 'It is better to marry than to burn', St Paul told the Corinthians. The idea of purely recreational sexual activity remains anathema – in theory at least; in practice the officers of the various churches seem to have fewer inhibitions. A Humean ethics proposes none.

The moral sanity that Hume limned two-and-a-half centuries ago may eventually prevail, possibly in time to help prevent mankind from destroying itself in any of the various ways open to it and all currently being eagerly explored. But mankind must first wean itself off its comforting, but morally and intellectually debased and debilitating fairy stories, and grow up:

> When I was a child, I spake as a child, I understood as a child, I thought as a child: but when I became a man, I put away childish things.[75]

So must we.

EXERCISE

'Just as strong is the obvious reality that we are moral beings, capable of understanding the difference between right and wrong. There is no scientific route to such ethics.

Physics cannot inspire our concern for others, or the spirit of altruism that has existed in human societies since the dawn of time.

The existence of a common pool of moral values points to the existence of transcendent force beyond mere scientific laws. Indeed, the message of atheism has always been a curiously depressing one, portraying us as selfish creatures bent on nothing more than survival and self-gratification.' Comment.

MAIN POINTS OF CHAPTER 6

- Nearly all theists claim that our sense that we are subject to a moral law cannot be explained without reference to God. But science has been slowly claiming new ground in precisely that area.
- One of the most promising lines of scientific attack is to use evolutionary theory in combination with game theory, particularly the theory of equilibria in indefinitely repeated Prisoner's Dilemmas and related

[75] 1 Corinthians 13:12.

games. Where the payoffs are biological fitness, the results have been the successful theory of kin-altruism and reciprocal altruism.

- Where the payoffs are utility, similar equilibrium strategies were outlined with remarkable prescience by Hume.
- Hume's own moral theory based on his concept of sympathy forms the foundation of a secular, eudaimonistic theory that extends Aristotle's in a satisfying way, in particular allowing for moral growth and the extension of moral rights outside the class of human beings.
- There is much neuroscientific evidence for the existence of an inbuilt faculty of sympathy much as Hume described it. Moreover, many species of animal seem to share it.

APPENDIX: A. N. PRIOR'S ALLEGED COUNTEREXAMPLE TO HUME'S ARGUMENT

Consider the following two deductively valid arguments.

(I) Tea-drinking is common in England.

Therefore either tea-drinking is common in England or all New Zealanders ought to be shot [Prior was a New Zealander!].

(II) Tea-drinking is not common in England.

Either tea-drinking is common in England or all New Zealanders ought to be shot.

Therefore all New Zealanders ought to be shot.

It would seem that either the conclusion of (I), and the second premise of (II), is either an ethical statement or a non-ethical one. If it is ethical then (I) is a valid inference of an ethical conclusion from a non-ethical premise. If it is non-ethical then (II) is a valid inference of an ethical conclusion from two non-ethical premises. In either case we have a valid inference of an ethical conclusion from non-ethical premises, and Hume was wrong. Yes?

No. Prior's counterexample is no counterexample, since being ethical and being non-ethical do not exhaust the possibilities, as 'Either tea-drinking is common in England or all New Zealanders ought to be shot' actually shows. That sentence is a compound, called by logicians a *truth-functional compound*, of an ethical and a non-ethical statement, which is most accurately classified as neither. As with any seminal contribution to thought, Hume's argument has occasioned a vast literature, some of which is quite demanding. I myself believe that it withstands all attempts to undermine it (though to my mind Prior's is far and away the best), and direct the reader who wants to see what a very good contemporary logician makes of the situation, and who can bear some technical argument, to Gerhard Schurz's book.[76]

[76] Gerhard Schurz, *The Is-Ought Problem: An Investigation in Philosophical Logic* (Boston: Kluwer Academic, 1997).

CHAPTER 7

What is life without Thee?

'What a piece of work is a man! How noble in reason! How infinite in faculty!'[1]

1. THE WATCHMAKER'S RETURN

William Paley's celestial Watchmaker seems to have returned after an absence of two centuries, to mixed fortunes. One of the recent arguments from design, that based on the so-called fine-tuning life of some fundamental physical constants, founders on the following objections: an extremely small prior probability merited by the God of theism in the light – if that is the right word – of the Problem of Evil; the fact that it is not obviously unreasonable to place a substantial probability on the hypothesis that a future theory will fix those values; and the sheer incoherence of computations of the 'chances' of fine-tuning were there no fine-tuner. But where what is to be explained is the existence of life, where even the assembling of atoms into amino acids is a highly complex affair, it is not clear that comparable objections achieve so much purchase. Put simply, the only eligible explanatory theory would be evolutionary biology, but that theory is in principle incapable of doing the job – or so it is claimed even by people having no obvious axe to grind on behalf of God.

Is that charge true? The answer boils down to determining whether evolutionary biology really is as incapable as is claimed of explaining the data in question. On examination it seems to be not complexity as such that is the problem, but a certain kind of holistic property in which the component parts of a biological system must exhibit a strong co-dependence in order for the system to perform its function at all. Even in such an apparently simple mechanism as blood-clotting, the removal or alteration of a single member of an extensive chain of chemical reactions will

[1] *Hamlet.*

cause the whole process to fail. The eye is another much-touted example. The all-or-nothing character of such systems seems therefore to be at odds with the standard Darwinian account, since there would be no selective pressure for any particular bit of a highly integrated biological system to evolve without all the others being present at the same time. But if it's not evolution which has produced these marvels of biological engineering, what is it? Re-enter Paley, to applause.

Such in essence is the argument expounded vigorously by Michael Behe.[2] Is it correct? The answer seems quite decisively to be no. According to quite standard evolutionary biology, so standard that it is accepted by the vast number of working biologists, mutations may be selected for within existing systems to produce a novel adaptation, which is then fixed in the population until another mutation occurs adapting the first, and so on culminating possibly in some quite novel emergent biological system. The evolving system, in other words, gets where it does not all at once but by taking successive steps along an evolutionary pathway which may terminate with a radically different type of organism or process. As the biologist H. Allen Orr comments in a review of Behe's book:

> An irreducibly complex system can be built gradually by adding parts that, while initially just advantageous, become – because of later changes – essential. The logic is very simple. Some part (A) initially does some job (and not very well, perhaps). Another part (B) later gets added because it helps A. This new part isn't essential, it merely improves things. But later on, A (or something else) may change in a way that B now becomes essential. This process continues as further parts get added to the system. And at the end of the day many parts may be required.[3]

Indeed, almost immediately after Behe claimed that the development of complex biological systems is inexplicable by standard evolutionary theory he was dramatically refuted. A study by Nilsson and Pelger in 1994 presented a model of a possible evolutionary pathway to a fish-like eye from light-sensitive cells (these had been around long before there were eyes), and found that with even a pessimistic estimate of the parameters involved it took an upper limit of only a few hundred thousands of years for a weak selection process to produce an eye, or something functionally resembling an eye, which in terms of evolutionary time is almost no time at all.[4]

[2] Michael Behe, *Darwin's Black Box: The Biochemical Challenge to Evolution*, Tenth Anniversary edition (New York: Free Press, 2006).

[3] H. Allen Orr, 'Darwin v. Intelligent Design (Again)', *Boston Review* 21 (December 1996/January 1997).

[4] D.-E. Nilsson and S. Pelger, 'A Pessimistic Estimate of the Time Required for an Eye to Evolve', *Proceedings of the Royal Society of London, B. Biological Sciences* 256 (1994), 53–8.

Needless to say, US Creationists were quick to denounce Nilsson and Pelger's simulation as trickery. One of their favourite responses, which they also used against Dawkins's well-known simple computer-simulations of evolution,[5] is that the selection-process was deliberately designed to select appropriate 'mutations', whereas in nature, according to evolutionists, there is no such purpose. There are two things independently fallacious in this objection. I will leave the reader to find them.

Not only do the eye and other human organs and biological processes not require an explanation in terms of intelligent design, they frequently defy one. Steven Weinberg, reviewing the structure of the genetic code, points out that it defies basic principles of simplicity and efficiency:

> The genetic code is pretty much a mess; some amino acids are called for by more than one triplet of base pairs, and some triplets produce nothing at all. The genetic code is not as bad as a randomly chosen code, which suggests that it has been somewhat improved by evolution, but any communications engineer could design a better code. The reason of course is that the genetic code was *not* designed.[6]

Francis Collins, himself a geneticist and a Christian as we know, is also strongly dismissive of Behe's claim that the eye is the product of intelligent design:

> [T]he design of the eye does not appear on close inspection to be completely ideal. The rods and cones that sense light are the bottom layer of the retina, and light has to pass through the nerves and blood vessels to reach them. Similar imperfections of the human spine (not optimally designed for vertical support), wisdom teeth, and the curious persistence of the human appendix also seem to many anatomists to defy the existence of truly intelligent planning.[7]

Collins might be the perpetrator of some not very good arguments for God but he is very good on his own science, as one might expect, giving a masterful account of the compelling genetic and other evidence for evolution. And it is not just Behe to whom he gives short shrift. He quotes another prominent Intelligent Design advocate, William Dembski, to devastating effect. Dembski wrote:

> If it could be shown that biological systems that are wonderfully complex, elegant and integrated – such as the bacterial flagellum – could have been formed by a gradual Darwinian process (and thus that their specified complexity is an illusion), then Intelligent Design would be refuted on the general grounds that one does

[5] Richard Dawkins, *The Blind Watchmaker* (New York: Norton, 1987), chapter 3.
[6] Steven Weinberg, *Dreams of a Final Theory* (New York: Pantheon Books, 1992), p. 163.
[7] Francis Collins, *The Language of God* (New York: Free Press, 2006), p. 191.

not invoke intelligent causes when undirected natural causes will do. In that case, Occam's razor would finish off Intelligent Design quite nicely.[8]

Collins is quick to grasp the proffered gift, showing that what Dembski is implicitly claiming has not and cannot be achieved actually has been: components of the flagellum have been shown to have evolved for a quite different purpose than that of bacterial locomotion, refuting the claim that the parts of the whole assembly could not have evolved piecewise in accordance with Darwinian evolution.

2. STARTING OUT

As many of the more intelligent scientists who believe in God have done before him, Collins warns those who use the 'God of the gaps' strategy of invoking God to fill the gaps in scientific knowledge that it is a dangerous game, which threatens to leave their position dangerously exposed when the gaps become filled by the growth of science itself – not, as I noted earlier, that this warning has prevented Collins himself from using that very strategy when it suited him. Much the same goes for that other gap, the origin of life itself. It is true that right now there is no account of how life actually started on earth that does not involve unsubstantiated guesses. It may genuinely be a stupendous coincidence (recall Hoyle and Wickramasinghe's calculation that the probability of the 2,000 or so enzymes assembling themselves by chance was a mere $10^{-40,000}$, a pretty small number), or there may be some systematic cause. For example, Hoyle and Wickramasinghe's own claim that life here was seeded by interstellar comets[9] has recently been partially corroborated with the discovery that some material gathered by the Stardust probe from the comet Wild 2 contained an amino acid, glycine, one of the amino acids used to manufacture protein in the cell. Of course, glycine is just one of the many amino acids required, but where there is one there may well be others. Moreover, comets also contain abundant quantities of water in the form of ice.

At the cost of being unduly repetitive, we know that the fact that there is no currently accepted explanation of the origin of life, on earth or anywhere else, is no reason whatever to suppose that there never will be one. We can imagine a sort of metric in logical space which measures the explanatory

[8] William Dembski, *The Design Revolution: Answering the Toughest Questions about Intelligent Design* (Downer's Grove, IL: Intervarsity Press, 2004), p. 282.

[9] Fred Hoyle and Chandra Wickramasinghe, *Evolution From Space* (London: J. M. Dent & Sons, 1981).

distance from the body of current science to a piece of data which by assumption is not included in it. If a computer of its own accord one day printed out 'I am the resurrection and the life', and minute examination revealed no good reason why it had done so, we might well think that piece of data a long way away from current or any other science, and correspondingly rather close to the hypothesis of theism (it would, as they say, be a miracle). We already know that some amino acids are transported to earth from space, and it therefore doesn't seem too audacious to put some prior probability on this being the origin of life on earth. To the objection that one still has to think of a reason why life should have originated at all, anywhere, one can only reply 'One thing at a time.'

3. THE 'PROBLEM OF CONSCIOUSNESS'

The self-styled 'highest' species of organism in the evolutionary tree, i.e. us, has properties that have always seemed remarkable and resistant to any physical/evolutionary explanation. Pre-eminent among these are our 'private' inner experiences, including an innate respect for truth, for beauty and for morally praiseworthy behaviour (there are of course apparent deviations in every human population, but these might be explained as resulting from preponderating environmental influences). And, to cap it all, there is the mysterious fact of consciousness itself. Richard Swinburne and other theists claim that these faculties are easily explained if there is a God, and point to their apparent inexplicability by science as powerful evidence for that hypothesis. How apparent and how real is that inexplicability? Let us start with the most problematic of those properties listed, consciousness. Why is this so widely thought to be impossible to explain *in principle* in physicalistic terms?

The crucial question was posed in its classic formulation by the seventeenth-century French philosopher-scientist-mathematician Descartes: How can an apparently quite immaterial thing, the conscious mind, have a causal effect on something undeniably material, the body? That it does seems to be beyond question: we think of things we want to do, and lo, they are done, even if not always with the consequences intended. How? Descartes' answer was to suggest that a small body situated in the neighbourhood of the brain, the pineal gland, mediates the interaction, but his answer was never fully accepted and has long been discarded. It was only in the twentieth century that some progress seemed to be made, with the discovery of the neuronal structure of the brain and the mapping of causal pathways within it which allow certain chemical substances to affect mood and cognition.

But the central problem remains, or seems to remain: on the one hand there are purely physical phenomena and on the other an apparently immaterial inner and personal display of feelings and thoughts, and the latter systematically appear to interfere causally with the former by causing bodily actions (the modifier 'appear to' is deliberate and the reason for it will be seen later). Firings of brain-neurons are certainly physical events, and the way these stimulate muscular actions is reasonably well understood. But what is not understood at all (yet) is the nature of the relation between conscious thoughts and feelings, and neurons firing. Philosophers and many scientists are agreed in calling this the '*hard problem*' of consciousness. Possibly it is hard, possibly even, ultimately, inexplicable by science. It may, of course, just be a matter of these being early days yet. As we observed earlier (more times than I care to calculate), the growth of science is not ours to see from the vantage point of the present, and one day's puzzle is typically the next day's (or century's) familiarity. Isaac Newton was perplexed by his own theory of gravitation which seemed to demand instantaneous action at a distance. Field theory supplied the resolution of that problem, long after Newton's death. Wave-particle duality, so incomprehensible at one time, has been rendered comprehensible by attributing the wave character to probabilities. But that problem has only given way to others that seem just as incomprehensible as that once did. And so it will doubtless go on.

Swinburne believes that consciousness, together with our moral sense, our appreciation of beauty and truth, will *never* fall into the category of solved scientific problems. This is not to say that they are not explicable according to him. They are, but only *theologically*. Noting that in the history of science there has been a reduction of many pre-scientific properties, like force, heat, weight, work, speed, colour and so on – even spin – to scientific quantities admitting precise definition and measurement, he points out that each reduction has been precisely that, a reduction, and with each one something has got lost: *felt* heat, *felt* weight, *seen* colour, etc.[10] In other words, to bring these qualities within the realm of science it seems that a significant aspect of reality has had to be abandoned, and that what has been abandoned in each and every case is our *conscious* experience of reality. And it is, of course, that conscious experience of reality which in combination

[10] Philosophers have traditionally called these 'secondary qualities': their measurable counterparts are primary qualities.

with our desires drives our actions. Thus, Swinburne observes, apparently justly:

> the existence of the most novel and striking features of animals and above all of humans [the causal connection between the mental and the physical] seems to lie utterly beyond the range of successful scientific explanation.[11]

Plausible though it may sound, I believe that Swinburne's conclusion is question-begging, if not demonstrably false. It is certainly not true that science is unable to discover causal explanations linking physical and mental. Already a good deal is known about the 'mental' relata of selective electrical or chemical stimulation of various parts of the brain. Brain-imaging techniques have come a long way in the last score or so of years and the results are surprising and impressive. Not only are different patterns of neural activity routinely witnessed when the subject is seeing or hearing stimuli, or feeling various emotions, but these patterns turn out to be fairly reliable predictors of the accompanying mental sensations: researchers can now frequently tell *which* pictures and *which* faces subjects are seeing on the basis of the observed neural activity. To say that these are merely acausal correlations is, I think, being ostrich-like. Such a strategy, systematically applied, would have denied us access to all our rich causal understanding of the world.

Ah yes, it might be replied, but the fact remains that the content of our mental experiences can never *in principle* be exhausted by any set of statements about neurons being excited and firing. What is necessarily omitted in any attempted reduction of that type is, to use another favourite word of the philosophers, *intentionality*, which roughly translates as 'meaning'. Not only is intentionality omitted, but there is also the purely qualitative and private experience consisting in my registering, for example, the colours of a flower, or a sequence of musical notes as pleasing. It is true that one could describe the colours of the flower in terms of the wavelengths of electromagnetic radiation in the visible part of the spectrum, but that would not enable anyone never having had those sensations to understand fully what I had experienced. Such conscious but (so far) scientifically unanalysable experiences are denoted by another favourite term of philosophers, *qualia*. No amount of scientific analysis of the wave-structure of light and sound

[11] Richard Swinburne, *The Existence of God*, rev. edn (Oxford: Clarendon Press, 1991), p. 209. As far as Swinburne is concerned, of course, '[t]here is available a personal explanation: God being omnipotent, he is able to join souls to bodies. He can cause there to be the particular brain-event-mental-event connections that there are' (*ibid.*).

will reproduce the qualia associated with listening to a piece of music or seeing a flower.

So it seems that intentionality and qualia, though in an obvious sense the most important part of our reality, can never be captured in a purely physical, or more broadly, scientific, language. 'May God us keep', wrote the English poet William Blake, a fervent opponent even then (the late eighteenth century) of what he saw as scientific reductionism, 'From single vision and Newton's sleep'. 'Newton's sleep' was Blake's dismissive way of referring to what he saw as the blindness of science to the richness of visual experience, typified for him by Newton's great advances in the scientific analysis of light (on the basis of several beautiful experiments Newton had advanced the theory, part of which survives to this day, that light is a corpuscular phenomenon[12]).

4. TRUE BELIEF

For theists, God will have known in advance that the complex structure of human and possibly some animal brains would generate mental properties allowing the possibility of rational, investigative thought, a precondition of which is the ability to develop true mental representations of an external world, at first visual and then, with increasing sophistication, mathematical. With the aid of such representations, including the ability to consider a range of alternative possibilities, purposive action can be planned and performed with an enhanced likelihood of success. Swinburne endorses an argument due to Alvin Plantinga[13] that no such ability could have evolved by purely evolutionary means, since on a purely physicalistic view the causal determinants of action would have to be brain-events alone, and cognitively rich beliefs would be mere epiphenomena having no causal status.[14] Thus, concludes Swinburne–Plantinga, on the hypothesis of physicalism there is no selective advantage in having true beliefs as opposed to false ones.

This argument succeeds only in begging the question, namely that a belief *cannot* be a physical encoding which can be accessed and processed, and having communication-channels to the motor centres. But why should

[12] Richard Feynman believed that light is wholly corpuscular, and had no wave-like character at all, an idea he thought only betrayed a misunderstanding of quantum theory.

[13] In J. Beilby (ed.), *Naturalism Defeated? Essays on Plantinga's Evolutionary Argument against Naturalism* (Ithaca, NY: Cornell University Press, 2002). There are other parts to Plantinga's complete argument, but this seems to me to be the only remotely challenging one. It is of course open to anyone to disagree.

[14] Swinburne, *The Existence of God*, p. 351.

it not be? It would still remain just as advantageous to have true beliefs as it would on any non-physicalistic account. Such an account, if successful, would also solve the Cartesian problem of how something that is by nature non-physical can interact with something physical. Moreover, it seems that there is already a ready-made model. The brain is an information-processor containing 100 billion or so neurons firing in a network. It receives inputs from an external environment, processes them and then outputs some command or response. Can we not simply conclude, then, that the mind is merely a sophisticated type of program running on a biological, but still digital, computer? Called *the computational theory of mind*, it inspired an imaginary experiment devised by the celebrated British mathematician Alan Turing, who was one of the first to give a simple mathematical description of a general-purpose computer (now called a Universal Turing Machine[15]). In what is now called the *Turing Test*, a computer program is 'tested' by seeing whether, when run on a computer, the program-plus-computer can answer all questions put to it in a way that is indistinguishable from the way in which an average human being might answer them. If it can, then according to Turing we have as much right to ascribe intelligence and understanding to the program-plus-machine as we do to a human being.[16]

5. THE CHINESE ROOM

The computational theory of mind theory was, however, subjected to a famous onslaught by John Searle. The root of Searle's objection is intentionality, a quality necessarily lacking, claimed Searle, in any digital computer, however powerful. His ingenious counterexample, called *the Chinese Room*, processes suitably coded inputs and produces appropriate outputs in the following way. A person, who knows English but not Chinese, is shut in a room in which there is a list of all the Chinese characters, together with a manual for arranging them such that any question put in Chinese to him/her can be 'answered' by him/her. We are told to disregard the staggering complexity involved in doing this: it is a thought-experiment, no more. *Surely*, no-one could believe that the person-plus-room actually understands Chinese. Since a digital computer is also a purely 'mechanical' processor with a program for carrying out simple operations on appropriate

15 'Universal' because it can take as input the program of any other computer and compute it. An ordinary laptop is a universal computer.

16 Alan Turing, 'Computing Machinery and Intelligence', *Mind* 59 (1950), 433–60.

inputs, Searle's clever example strongly suggests no digital computer-plus-program can ever be said to *understand* what it is doing. So it seems to refute Turing's thesis.

Searle's example has become a classic of modern philosophy. It has generated more responses than any other single contribution to the literature on mind and artificial intelligence, with the possible exception of Turing's own. But it remains a very clever piece of *trompe l'œil* nevertheless, for the simple 'flat' structure of the Chinese Room is less a model than a parody, and a deliberate parody, of the complex architecture that might model the computational structure of the brain. It may well be that all sorts of unlikely physical devices can simulate the embodied input–output function that is a computer, any digital computer. The key word here is 'simulate'. The sort of computational model that Searle was discussing was based on what is still standard computing: a stored program run serially on general-purpose circuits. As such, it is a very poor model of massively distributed parallel processing, which is what the brain does. When more sophisticated computational models designed to work broadly in the same way are considered, the Chinese Room will seem even more obviously a parody.

Another consideration to bear in mind is that physical structures can and do have so-called *emergent properties*, or properties that seem irreducible to any properties the parts individually might possess. *Life* is an emergent property of the complex electro-chemical machines called animal bodies. The Chinese Room is not obviously a counterexample to the hypothesis that consciousness and understanding are also emergent properties of purely physical structures, and that those structures are – essentially – universal computers. But Searle had what he considered to be an effective counter to that claim. A computer program, however complex the machine that implements it, is just a *syntax* for manipulating symbols and hence is an embodied formal system deprived of a semantic interpretation. But this reply begs the question in that it simply *assumes* that meaning cannot be implicit in any formal structure. The Chinese Room does not prove this true, because the Chinese Room is a caricature. In fact, there is a good reason to think Searle's counterclaim false. One of the great discoveries of mathematical logic in the twentieth century is that the criteria of *consistency* and *validity*, which determine that truth flows faithfully down chains of reasoning, can be encoded as formal constraints that a deterministic computer can follow. Indeed, Gödel showed that they can be encoded within the syntax of whole-number arithmetic, which is simply another, disembodied, form of computer (the number-coding the key to proving his famous incompleteness theorems). Of course, we have to prove that those rules are faithful to the transmission of truth, but the proof that they are faithful (called a *soundness theorem*) appeals to the same rules at a higher level. Arguably, *semantic meaning itself is an emergent property of syntax.*

But in a further dramatic development the Gödel theorems themselves have been made the basis of another well-known argument claiming to refute the computational theory of mind. Due to the philosopher John Lucas and elaborated by Roger Penrose, it not only acknowledges those facts about the representative capacity of purely formal systems, but actually uses them to arrive at the conclusion that the human mind is more than a program run on a biochemical digital machine. However, because the argument (a) requires a certain amount of background information about technical logic, and (b) is in my opinion anyway incorrect, I have relegated its discussion to an Appendix to this chapter. I can only ask the reader at this point to provisionally accept my own verdict.

6. WHITHER NOW?

Perhaps surprisingly, Searle himself did not regard his own argument as establishing that understanding and consciousness may not be emergent properties of a physical system. On the contrary, he believed that they are, and that the physical system is the brain:

> [M]ental phenomena are as much a result of electrochemical processes in the brain as digestion is a result of chemical processes going on in the stomach and the rest of the digestive tract.[17]

What he did not believe, because of his Chinese Room argument, is that the brain is a digital computer. For the reasons I have given, I don't think the Chinese Room argument actually does lead to that conclusion. But in any event, we can agree with Searle that consciousness and all the apparatus of understanding may be emergent properties of the brain whether or not the brain is a computer.

Now the brain is an exceedingly complex structure, with its 100 billion neurons linked by neural pathways in a vast hyper-network. One of the hypotheses currently most favoured by neuroscientists is that consciousness is an emergent property of sufficiently complex systems, and therefore that it is the brain's complexity that generates consciousness. The corollary is

[17] John Searle, 'Minds and Brains without Programs', in Colin Blakemore and Susan Greenfield (eds.), *Mindwaves: Thoughts on Identity, Intelligence, and Consciousness* (Oxford: B. Blackwell, 1987), pp. 209–33.

that if the brain's physical architecture could be replicated in inorganic materials then the replication should also experience consciousness. Even were that so, and work has already begun on the project in several AI laboratories, what would still be lacking, at any rate for the present, is any obvious causal/explanatory pathway from the physical structure of the brain to that emergent property. But as we have seen, many neuroscientists certainly put a nonzero prior probability on there being one. Nor is it only neuroscientists and atheists who do so. Some theists are quite happy to do so too, among them John Polkinghorne:

> As these entities [quarks, electrons, etc.] combine into systems of greater and greater complexity, new possibilities come into being, exhibiting properties (such as life or consciousness) that were unforeseeable in terms of the simpler constituents out of which they were made, while only being realizable through the potentialities with which those same entities were endowed.[18]

I will end this discussion with a prediction: in fact two predictions. Given the progress in machine intelligence already, it is I think reasonable to believe that at some point a descendant of the current generation of universal computers will pass as rigorous a Turing Test as can be devised. My second prediction is that at that point we will accept that we have a thinking machine. It is of course always open to anyone to doubt whether a machine like that can *really* think, just as it is open for anyone to doubt that light *really* is electromagnetic radiation, or that heat *really* is kinetic energy, or that gravity *really* is space-time curvature. Eventually the doubters die out and the question is answered by default. So my second prediction is that the question of whether a machine can think and understand will one day no longer be thought worth asking.

7. VARIETIES OF RELIGIOUS EXPERIENCE

Personal epiphanies of God have been one of the strongest factors in religious conversion, from St Paul's famous blinding by the Light on the road to Damascus to the present day. Since then many people have claimed to have had an overpoweringly direct experience of God. St Teresa of Avila was immortalised (in the only way that seems at all likely) by Bernini with his extraordinarily beautiful sculpture of her religious – or sexual – ecstasy.

[18] John Polkinghorne, *Science and Creation: The Search for Understanding* (Philadelphia: Templeton Foundation Press, 2006), p. 46; one can suppose that they were not unforeseeable to God, however.

A less ecstatic but very moving account of coming face to face with God was given by the French poet Paul Claudel, who experienced his epiphany listening to Vespers on Christmas Day 1886:

I was standing in the crowd, by the second pillar at the entry to the choir, to the right of the sacristy. It was then that the event occurred which dominates my whole life. In an instant my heart was touched and *I believed.* I believed, with such force, with such an uplifting of my entire being, with a conviction so powerful, with such certitude leaving no room for any sort of doubt, that since then no books, no reasoning, nothing in a hectic life have been able to shake my faith, nor, truth to tell, affect it at all. I experienced all at once the heart-rending sense of innocence, of the eternal child-likeness of God, an unspeakable revelation. In trying, as I often have, to reconstruct the moments following that extraordinary instant, I have remarked the following elements which however make up a single enlightening, a single weapon which divine Providence employs for at last opening the heart of a poor desperate child: 'Let those who believe be happy! But is it true? *It is true!* God exists, he is there, as much a person as me. He loves me, he calls me.'[19]

Such experiences, we are told by many believers, are beyond the remit of science to explain or comprehend: those who experience them are in some realm of cognition outside the phenomenal experience of space and time, in a direct apprehension of God.

But there is an obvious answer to this, which is that the part of the previous sentence immediately following the colon is an interpretation of a personal experience, or experiences, that not only lacks any independent support, but for which there are more mundane explanations which do have independent support. In the case of St Teresa of Avila this might be that she was suffering from a pathological condition like schizophrenia. Hearing voices as if they were real, and interpreting them as emanating from God, is a common feature of that malady, though without the subject herself there to undergo tests one can't of course be definite about such a diagnosis. Another possibility is that without normal nourishment people commonly suffer hallucinatory experiences, and the mortification of the flesh (and poor personal hygiene) was strongly encouraged among the early saints as a way to induce such experiences – though the interpretation put on them was, of course, that they were divinely inspired visions. Thus when the philosopher Gary Gutting asks the following rhetorical question we should have the salt-cellar ready (again):

[19] Paul Claudel, *Contacts et Circonstances* (Paris: Gallimard, 1947) (my translation).

Through experiences of, for example, natural beauty, moral obligation, or loving and being loved, we may develop an abiding sense of the reality of an extraordinarily good and powerful being who cares about us. Who is to say that such experiences do not give reason for belief in God as much as parallel (though different) experiences give reason for belief in reliable knowledge of the past and future and of other human minds?[20]

C. S. Lewis deftly reintroduces the Prosecutor's Fallacy into the discussion:

Creatures are not born with desires unless satisfaction for those desires exists. A baby feels hunger: well, there is such a thing as food. A duckling wants to swim: well, there is such a thing as water. Men [sic] feel sexual desire: well, there is such a thing as sex. If I find in myself a desire which no experience in this world can satisfy, the most probable explanation is that I was made for another world.[21]

Lewis says that his being made for another world is the most probable explanation of a trait for which he is adapted but where the adaptation is not one favoured by natural selection. What he meant is that Prob(E|H) is large; but it is just as easy to read 'the most probable explanation' as referring to Prob(H|E). Notice, incidentally, how ordinary language itself conspires in the identification of Prob(E|H) with Prob(H|E).

8. VARIETIES OF MATHEMATICAL EXPERIENCE

When it comes to the capacities and complexities of organisms, evolutionary theory is of course the principal explanatory competitor of theism and, an increasingly large number of scientifically oriented people believe, is almost certain to be the ultimately victorious one. I say 'ultimately' because of course there are still many things in that area, like consciousness, that still lack any sort of complete scientific explanation. The gaps are nevertheless being filled, if slowly. But still some people, preponderantly theists, insist that there will always remain enclaves resistant to scientific explanation. The Moral Law, as Francis Collins calls it, may seem to be gradually giving way to the combined forces of biology and game theory but for some, implicit in the seemingly remorseless advance of science, is notice of an ultimate failure. Why? Because the tools increasingly employed with such apparent success are *mathematical*, and some of the mathematics, particularly in physics, is of a highly sophisticated kind, so sophisticated that it now pushes on the boundaries of pure mathematics, and even more

[20] Gary Gutting, 'The Opinionator', *New York Times*, 1 August 2010.
[21] C. S. Lewis, *Mere Christianity*, rev. and enlarged edn (London: Collins, 1955), p. 115.

amazingly, sometimes beyond. To take a very striking recent example, string theory has supplied the answer to an outstanding mathematical problem, that of determining for each integer d, the number of rational curves of degree d contained are contained in what is called a quintic 3fold. Solutions had been obtained for certain values of d, but *physical ideas* arising in string theory allowed the problem to be solved *for all d*. Some physicists, like Max Tegmark, believe that ultimately physics and pure mathematics will cease to be distinct disciplines at all.

But if this fruit of our intellects is ultimately the product of evolution then, many allege, a very hard question is faced. For in the final stages of human evolution that shaped us as we are today there could have been no conceivable selective advantage in possessing a brain capable of inventing and using so effectively such highly abstract mathematical tools as, say, algebraic topology, M-theory, etc. John Polkinghorne tells us that he can't believe that 'Dirac's ability to invent [quantum field] theory, or Einstein's ability to invent the general theory of relativity, is a sort of spin-off from our ancestors having to dodge sabre-toothed tigers.'[22] On the other hand, if God has wished us to be able to appreciate at least part of the exquisite theoretical webs that are His laws of nature then we would naturally be endowed with just such capacities.

Polkinghorne has erected a straw-man, if one can describe a sabre-toothed tiger as a straw-man. Being able to dodge those terrifying predators may well not have stimulated mathematical thoughts, but being able to predict the recurrence of broadly similar seasons, with their corresponding possibilities for finding or catching or – eventually – growing food certainly conferred an evolutionary advantage. The ancient star-gazers observed that every 365 days the Dog-star appeared in the same position in the heavens, and the calendar was born. Of course, one needs numbers to mark the significant parts of the year and count the time needed to seed the ground before crops appear, and so forth. But this amounts in the first instance to assigning canonical status to easily identifiable tokens that have the right properties. Our ancestors will have had their own store of these, possibly simple tally-marks like I, II, III, IIII, IIIII, etc., which they could map in a one-to-one way onto other collections, for example herds, crops and so on. The basic computational rules of addition and multiplication, are also very basic and simple: two non-negative whole numbers are added by finding two collections of things of the respective sizes with no members

[22] John Polkinghorne, 'Religion in an Age of Science', *McNair Lecture*, University of North Carolina, March 1993.

in common, merging them, and tallying the result (set theorists call this cardinal addition), while multiplication is just repeated addition. The invention of special symbols for 10, 20, . . . 100, 1,000 enabled sophisticated computations to be performed with large numbers, including numbers so large that they corresponded to no known collections of things. Thus was abstract mathematics born.

It is, of course, still a very long way to the calculus, and an even longer one to the mathematics of twenty-first-century science, but these distances were traversed in small piecemeal steps, with language playing an indispensable assisting role by allowing notations to be developed which facilitated the construction of simple algorithms. Developments in styles of living also played their role in stimulating new mathematical developments. Measuring the lengths and areas of cultivated land became of great importance, and the mathematics of fractional numbers makes its historical appearance. The necessity of going beyond even these eventually became apparent in a dramatic and celebrated way: *the hypotenuse of a right-angled triangle with two equal sides of one length-unit each cannot be measured using fractional numbers.* The length of the hypotenuse is equal to the square root of two, and this is an entirely new type of number, a so-called 'irrational' number (this means that it can't be expressed as a ratio, not that it's somehow stupid!) and implicitly – though this was only recognised 2,000 years later – a vastly larger set of numbers than the integers and rationals. The real-number continuum was born.

The discovery of the irrationality of root two, which was invested with deep mystical significance by Pythagoras and his followers, illustrates the important fact that implicit in even the simplest arithmetic assumptions there can be sometimes very unexpected and abstruse consequences. It is this relatively elementary *logical* fact, and not some mysterious feature of our mental apparatus that cannot be explained in evolutionary terms, that is responsible for our having at our disposal the mathematical tools to construct physical theories which we cannot fully comprehend, like quantum mechanics. In fact, much of the mathematics in modern physics was not originally invented for its current purpose at all. Brane theory is a ten-dimensional theory. We cannot easily, if at all, visualise ten physical dimensions, but we can work sensibly with them, or even a hundred dimensions, because we are using mathematical tools, constructed from a simple basic tool-kit, that do nearly all the visualising for us. Here is another example: in Hawking-Hartle cosmology there is a so-called imaginary time dimension. An imaginary number is a real number multiplied by i, the square root of minus one. Intuitively, negative numbers don't have square roots, but we have simple rules for manipulating imaginary numbers, and the larger class of complex numbers of the form $a + ib$, where a and b are real, that originally arose in the sixteenth century in the context of trying to solve algebraic equations of relatively low degree. Quantum mechanics makes essential use of complex numbers. Group theory, the other mathematical foundation of modern physics, also originally arose in the same area of enquiry, finding the roots of algebraic equations. God doesn't come into it.

9. AND BEAUTY TOO?

Richard Dawkins dismisses personal revelations of the divine with his customary briskness,[23] to which I have nothing to add. That section in Dawkins's book is preceded by an equally brisk discussion of another phenomenon frequently alleged to be evidence of God and our central role in his creation: our sense of beauty, for it is in beauty that it is often claimed that we see God in some sort of direct apprehension. One such recipient of that beatific vision is our old friend Francis Collins:

> On a beautiful Fall day, as I was hiking in the Cascade Mountains . . . the majesty and beauty of God's creation overwhelmed my resistance. As I rounded a corner and saw a beautiful and unexpected frozen waterfall, hundreds of feet high, I knew the search was over.[24]

This is a curious argument. Unless you already give some belief to the idea that God created this natural beauty, and created in us a faculty of experiencing it, it would seem that there is no good reason to interpret it as a sign of God's presence. Yet Collins tells us that he was a committed atheist until he experienced his epiphany.

His argument is thus perilously circular. By contrast, there is some reason to believe that evolution has endowed us with a positive emotional response to various types of beauty. A keen appreciation of a salubrious landscape, fresh air and an abundant presence of fast-flowing water might well be expected on this view, and high places and waterfalls clearly come under that head. Then there is an appreciation of human beauty which is very plausibly linked to considerations of reproductive fitness: principal among such characteristics are symmetry in human physiology and the ideal types of masculine and feminine beauty celebrated

[23] Richard Dawkins, *The God Delusion* (London: Bantam Books, 2006), pp. 112–17.
[24] Collins, *The Language of God*, p. 225.

by the Renaissance (and classical Greek) artists and sculptors. There is in addition a type of glorious extravagance to which many organisms seem susceptible that might at first glance appear to diminish fitness. The classic example is the peacock's tail, an apparently gratuitous encumbrance diminishing mobility and therefore survival potential. But survival potential is not the same as fitness, and we now know that it is just one manifestation of the mechanism, if that is the right word, of sexual selection. Such splendid violations of nature's sumptuary laws increase fitness by attracting mates already attuned to the appreciation of such excesses.

There has been a good deal of research into the neurological components of appreciating beauty, in art, in music and in nature itself. Recent empirical studies in the experiencing of western tonal music confirm an old suspicion, that it is the regularity of tonal structure that is linked to its enjoyment. Regularity and predictability are of course two sides of the same coin, and predictability most certainly has survival value. There is also evidence that the same neurological mechanisms are involved in language-processing, according to Anirrudh Patel, Esther J. Burnham Fellow of the Neurosciences Institute in San Diego, USA, whose laboratory was one of the first to investigate the neurological relationship between language and music. There is a grammatical structure to music, in the rules of harmony, and there are more familiar rules of grammar in language, and Patel and his team found that aphasia with respect to the one is highly correlated to aphasia with respect to the other: in fact, brain-responses to errors in both were indistinguishable. Patel also found that rhythm is recognised in humans in a deep, i.e. very old, centre of the brain, the basal ganglia, which controls motor activity. Music, it is gradually being revealed by such studies, is processed in a variety of brain regions known to be involved in other important human activities. The idea that somehow the appreciation of beauty should be completely distinct from the neurological mechanisms that facilitate our interactions with our environment is already implausible; in Bayesian terms it has rather small prior odds. In addition, with every discovery of such a link we see a corresponding increase in the likelihood ratio in favour of an evolutionary basis, and thereby a corresponding augmentation of the posterior odds.

10. POOR GOD

It is not only in the positive experiences of visual (and musical) beauty that people have claimed to discern God's presence, but, curiously, also in the reverse: in the depths of ugliness, anguish and despair – in a word, in *pathos*. Many who have 'felt' the presence of the holy in such situations see God himself as a sort of victim too. It is not uncommon to hear believers claim that some of the nasty things people do to others on earth causes God to shed celestial tears.[25] T. S. Eliot expressed that feeling in the beautiful lines:

> I am moved by fancies that are curled
> Around these images, and cling:
> The notion of some infinitely gentle
> Infinitely suffering thing.[26]

This suggests that for many people, God is not the omnipotent power of the theists but someone or something who still shares in the sufferings of his people but is powerless to abate them.

Though the expressions of this touching faith may be noble, like Eliot's, they are in effect a convenient way to let God off the terrible hook he would otherwise be impaled on, of having the power to prevent these atrocities and yet not doing so. I noted earlier that many Jews at the beginning of the Common Era had abandoned belief in the omnipotence of God because of the prevalence of arbitrary suffering, visited on good and bad alike, a state of affairs of which they felt that a joint dominion of the world, shared by God and the Devil, offered a better explanation. But it won't wash now. God's omnipotence wasn't just a later add-on by theologians, but a necessary attribute of the Creator of the heavens and earth, and more, a creative origin which must at all costs block the potentially infinite regress of questions 'And what caused that?' And the only way it can block it is by God being responsible for absolutely everything, including himself. It is precisely this unboundedness that formed the basis of that argument for God's *necessary* existence, the Ontological Argument, that drifts in and out of intellectual history and whose acquaintance we made earlier. But now escape is impossible. If the Creator is all-powerful and all-knowing He cannot shelter behind the excuses that he didn't know or that he was powerless to do anything. But he is done for anyway: in the next chapter, I will reinforce the argument that he is a shade too powerful for his own good by showing that

[25] Hence the common Anglo-Saxon expletive 'Jesus wept'. I noted in Chapter 1 that a survivor of Auschwitz believed that he heard God weeping there.

[26] *Preludes*.

he also knows too much for his own good. God will be hoist on his own petard.

EXERCISE

'Hawking, like so many other critics of religion, wants us to believe we are nothing but a random collection of molecules, the end product of a mindless process.

This, if true, would undermine the very rationality we need to study science. If the brain were really the result of an unguided process, then there is no reason to believe in its capacity to tell us the truth.' Comment.

MAIN POINTS OF CHAPTER 7

- A recent design argument based on biological systems claims that a type of holistic complexity defies any explanation, in principle, by evolutionary theory.
- These claims have been largely exploded, but there remain features of human life, namely consciousness, understanding, respect for truth as such and the appreciation of beauty, that are held by many, not only theists, to resist in principle scientific explanation.
- Given the neuronal structure of the brain, a natural theory is that it functions like a very large digital computer, of which consciousness is an emergent property.
- The philosopher John Searle opposed this with the famous Chinese Room argument, and Lucas and Penrose with an argument from Gödel's incompleteness theorems.
- Both arguments are shown to beg the question. So far, nothing rules out the possibility of *some* explanation of mind and consciousness as emergent properties of a purely physical system. Showing the mere possibility is enough to destroy the argument that no such explanation is in principle possible.
- The supposed evolutionary inexplicability of our ability to do advanced mathematics is shown to rest on a misappreciation of the simplicity of its basic conceptual structure and on a failure to understand the elementary logical fact that simple axioms may have very recondite consequences.
- That the appreciation of truth and beauty has to be some God-given gift is also shown to be based on a failure to understand the resources of modern science, and in particular growth in neurobiology.

APPENDIX: KNOWING WHAT THE MACHINE CAN'T KNOW: THE LUCAS–PENROSE ARGUMENT

I will present an amalgam of the Lucas's and Penrose's argument, taking the Gödel theorems as the point of departure. The first of those theorems states that if *any* formal axiom system S merely strong enough to be able to represent whole-number arithmetic (i.e. the arithmetic of the so-called natural numbers 0, 1, 2, . . . , n, . . .) is consistent, then there will be a sentence in the language of S that is neither provable nor refutable within S. For any such S Gödel showed how to encode sentences and also proofs in S as whole numbers, and also how to construct a sentence, call it G, which is neither provable or refutable in S. In fact, G encodes the statement that G itself is not provable in S. To round off the *tour de force*, Gödel showed that the sentence 'If S is consistent then G is true' can also be encoded as an arithmetical sentence, and that sentence is a theorem of S. So S itself can prove that if it is consistent then G is true (I am not going to go into more details here; they can be found in intermediate logic texts[27]).

So far, even stevens. We can prove that if S is consistent then G is true, but so can S too. What S cannot do, however, on pain of *inconsistency*, is prove its own consistency. That is the content of Gödel's second incompleteness theorem. In fact, what the theorem actually states is that if S is consistent then any proof of its consistency *will require stronger axioms than those of S itself.* According to the Lucas–Penrose argument, however, there are systems S which *we* can show to be consistent by noting that its axioms are all true in the natural numbers, and that the rules of inference used are all truth-preserving. One of the simplest such systems is called First Order Peano Arithmetic, PA for short, after the mathematician Giuseppe Peano. Everything we know about the natural numbers implies that the axioms of PA must be true: these express such truisms as, among others, that if two numbers differ, so do their successors; that 0 is not the successor of any natural number; and most importantly, the induction principle, that if 0 satisfies some arithmetical condition A(x), and if whenever A(n) is true so is A(n + 1), then every natural number satisfies that condition. The induction principle says no more than that all the natural numbers are either equal to 0 or to some descendant of 0 obtained by adding 1 finitely many times. We arguably would not have any coherent conception

[27] For example, Moshé Machover, *Set Theory, Logic and their Limitations* (Cambridge University Press, 1996).

of natural number arithmetic were this not true. Hence for such a system we have shown that G is true *unconditionally*, which S cannot do. Hence, the argument concludes, the deductive capacities of our minds are not computer programs run on computer-brains.

This reasoning may sound very plausible, but – alas – there is no avoiding the limitation imposed by Gödel's second theorem: if we think we have proved the consistency of PA then we have, whether we realise it or not, used stronger assumptions than those available in PA – which, of course, a suitably programmed computer could also do. The argument above for the truth of PA's axioms is itself an argument which can be formalised in a suitable theory of truth. But since truth implies consistency that theory will prove the consistency of PA. Hence by Gödel's second theorem we know that *this theory must be stronger than PA*. To underline the fact, there are unsolved problems in mathematics whose truth would be implied by a demonstration of PA's consistency, as Gödel pointed out.[28] So it cannot be the case that in any genuine sense of the word 'demonstrate' we can demonstrate PA's consistency, or G's absolute truth.

So much for the Lucas–Penrose argument. There is a further interesting feature of the Gödel sentence. It has the form of what is called a Π_1^0 sentence, and all such sentences have the property that if they are false then there is a proof in Peano Arithmetic, or any extension of it, that they are false. But if, like the Gödel sentence, they are undecidable then they cannot be proved true (the reader might like to show how this fact, combined with Gödel's first incompleteness theorem, provides a proof that if Peano Arithmetic is consistent then the Gödel sentence is true). Of course you may never know whether a particular Π_1^0 sentence is or is not provable: the Goldbach conjecture, that every even positive integer greater than 2 (1 is not a prime number!) is the sum of two prime numbers, is a Π_1^0 sentence which may turn out to be undecidable. Thus the mathematician is faced with a situation in which, if the sentence he/she is considering is an undecidable Π_1^0 sentence, it can be falsified if it is false, but never shown to be true if it is true. This is the epistemological quandary faced by scientists in general when they try to assess the evidence bearing on a general hypothesis, and which the philosopher (Sir) Karl Popper made the foundation of his falsificationist philosophy of empirical science. It shows, I believe, that there is little methodological difference between mathematics and empirical science,

[28] For further discussion see Alasdair Urquhart, 'Metatheory', in D. Jacquette (ed.), *A Companion to Philosophical Logic* (Malden, MA: Blackwell, 2002), pp. 307–18.

and that the same principles of evidence and inference apply to both. I argued in Chapter 3 that the falsificationist theory is inadequate, and that the Bayesian theory is *the* logic of scientific inference. In that case the same Bayesian theory should extend to mathematics.[29]

[29] I argue this in my book *Hume's Problem: Induction and the Justification of Belief* (Oxford University Press, 2000).

CHAPTER 8

It necessarily ain't so

'You can't know everything.'

1. THE ULTIMATE SANTA CLAUS

In Chapter 2 I pointed out that the omni-properties of the God of theism are there for a purpose, to allow God to have enough explanatory power to be able to account for everything that goes on in the universe. Swinburne tells us that being omnipotent, God can do whatever he wants to do, this side of logical possibility:

> clearly, whatever e [e stands for 'evidence'] is, God, being omnipotent, has the power to bring about e. He will do so, if he chooses to do so.[1]

Earlier (Chapter 3, section 4), I cited as an example of an incredible ad hoc 'explanation' the hypothesis that the observed outcome of a sequence of coin-tosses happened as it did because Santa Claus willed it to, and that whatever Santa wills happens. In order to fulfil his diverse explanatory and regulatory duties, the God of theism is endowed with very similar powers. We are told that God created the universe. How could he do that? Easily: *he can do anything he wants, and he wanted to create the universe*. He has to create the conditions necessary for life and give a certainty of intelligent life emerging. How could he do that? Easily: *he can do anything he wants, and he wanted to create the conditions for life to emerge*. He can tell when any of us sins. How? Easily: *he knows everything*. God *is the Ultimate Santa Claus hypothesis*.

Clearly, such explanations are no more than a 'cheap fix', as Adolf Grünbaum neatly puts it in a discussion of appeals to God's powers and wishes in cosmological explanation.[2] Moreover, when the cheap fix has

[1] Richard Swinburne, *The Existence of God*, rev. edn (Oxford: Clarendon Press, 1991), p. 109.

[2] Adolf Grünbaum, 'The Poverty of Theistic Cosmology', *British Journal for the Philosophy of Science* 55 (2004), 561–615.

to be as versatile as God supposedly is, it comes at a very high price: loading up such unlimited explanatory power is only achieved at the cost of inconsistency. The association between the two was first noticed by the medieval theologians who failed however to grasp fully its potentially lethal character. Modern logicians, on the other hand, know that increasing logical strength gets us closer to the limit of inconsistency.[3] God in his infinite knowledge, infinite power and infinite goodness is well over the consistency-limit. We have already seen omnipotence inculpated. Later in this chapter I will show that omniscience is too.

In *The God Delusion* Richard Dawkins also identifies God's presumably vast explanatory power as the means of convicting him, not of deductive inconsistency – which as we saw earlier Dawkins believed, incorrectly, to be impossible in principle – but of something like probabilistic inconsistency. Given that the conclusion of Dawkins's argument is weaker than a demonstrative proof of non-existence, it might be thought easier to prove and less liable to error than an argument claiming necessity for its conclusion. As we shall see in what follows, however, the proof of God's necessary non-existence is relatively straightforward, while Dawkins's argument is incorrect.

2. THE ULTIMATE 747

Set out in the chapter of Dawkins's book audaciously headed 'Why God Almost Certainly Does Not Exist', the argument commences with Dawkins reporting Chandra Wickramasinghe reporting an observation of Fred Hoyle:

> Hoyle said that the probability of life originating on earth is no greater than the chance that a hurricane, sweeping through a scrapyard, would have the luck to assemble a Boeing 747.[4]

Though not a theist, Hoyle concluded that it was therefore so unlikely that life could have originated spontaneously on earth that the possibility could be discounted, and in a book written with Wickramasinghe he advanced the alternative hypothesis that life was seeded here by comets.[4] Earlier, when faced with an equally amazing 'coincidence' enabling the production

[3] From an inconsistent set of premises *everything* follows deductively.

[4] Richard Dawkins, *The God Delusion* (London: Bantam Books, 2006).

[5] Fred Hoyle and Chandra Wickramasinghe, *Evolution From Space* (London: J. M. Dent & Sons: 1981).

of carbon in the early universe, Hoyle had already concluded that the universe itself is, in his words, 'a put-up job'.

But it may well be that life starting on earth simply was an enormous coincidence. We are aware that coincidences of such improbability occur all the time if the assumptions of current physical, biological and social theory are true. We are told time and again that very small probabilities, very large coincidences, 'cry out' for explanation, but that is usually because the people who hear the cry are unwittingly committing the Prosecutor's Fallacy and inferring that because evidence E has a negligible probability given hypothesis H (say, the hypothesis that E was generated by chance) then H has a negligible probability given E. As we noted in Chapter 3, that need not be the case. It is entirely possible that H has a probability close to 1 given E. It all depends, and we know from Bayes's Theorem just what it depends on: the prior probability of H and the probability of E supposing some other cause than H is responsible. The latter probability depends on the prior probabilities of each of the possible alternatives to H, as we saw in Chapter 3, and if these are small enough the probability of E on the assumption that H is not the cause may be very much smaller than the probability of E given H. In this case the likelihood ratio λ will be very small and the posterior odds on H proportionately large. For example, if E describes the configuration of all the molecules in the air in my room at a specified moment then E will be immensely improbable on the hypothesis of random generation, yet that is exactly the hypothesis that current statistical physics tell us is the most likely to be true. Hence that hypothesis has a very substantial prior probability and the probability of E on the assumption that some other cause is responsible is very much smaller than the probability of E given H.

Dawkins himself is worried by the informal calculations of the improbability of life being spontaneously generated on earth. For the reasons I gave at the end of Chapter 4, arriving at any value of that improbability, on the assumption that it is due to 'chance', is a highly questionable procedure, and any claim that the improbability is overwhelming must be treated with a good deal of scepticism. Random generation is of course not the only alternative to God: there is a potential infinity, among them Hoyle and Wickramasinghe's hypothesis that life was seeded by comets, a hypothesis that is increasingly seen as not so very unlikely. Dawkins himself believes that the Anthropic Principle is the best scientific alternative which, in the role of an 'observer selection effect', explains why we shouldn't be surprised that life appeared on earth even if the odds against it occurring on any given planet are many billions to one against. As we saw, however, adding the tautology 'If there weren't life here we wouldn't be around to see it' doesn't shorten the odds at all on life originating on this planet. 'Anthropic reasoning' doesn't cut the mustard.

Nevertheless, having – at any rate to his own satisfaction – disposed of the problem, Dawkins then turned his critical attention to the Creationists' favourite argument for design, namely that the probability of any complex biological system evolving by random mutations in the time-scale of the earth's existence is simply too small. Dawkins himself was a pioneer in pointing out that the claim is simply mistaken, and that the progress of evolution from very simple to quite complex organisms can be surprisingly fast, and easily within the time allowed. Not content even with that, in Chapter 4 of *The God Delusion* he sought to turn the argument from improbability back on the Design advocates with a *reductio* argument. 'Properly deployed', he claims, the argument from improbability which is alleged to *support* an argument from design is easily turned into one *against* it, and one so powerful as in effect to amount almost to a *disproof* of God's existence. Dawkins's argument, he claims 'demonstrates that God, though not technically disprovable, is very very improbable indeed'.[6] It proceeds as follows:

> Some observed phenomenon . . . is correctly extolled as statistically improbable. Sometimes the language of information theory is used: the Darwinian is challenged to explain the source of all the information in living matter, in the technical sense of information content as a measure of improbability or 'surprise value'. . . . [But] [t]he argument from statistical improbability, properly deployed, comes close to proving that God does *not* exist. My name for the statistical demonstration that God does not exist is the Ultimate 747 gambit . . . *However statistically improbable the entity you seek to explain by invoking a designer, the designer himself has got to be at least as improbable.* God is the Ultimate 747.[7]

To paraphrase Dawkins's argument: given the complexity in the universe that God is supposed to be the author of, he must be at least as improbable as it is, which is very great indeed. Think of how many bits of information are needed to specify everything that happens, down to the finest detail, from the dawn of the universe to its dying final crunch (if it dies). Information theory equates complexity with statistical improbability (to be precise, it equates it with negative entropy, which is minus the logarithm of the probability). If that complexity is implicit in God himself, as it must be by assumption, and if that is very improbable then God can't be less so.

[6] Dawkins, *The God Delusion*, p. 136. [7] *Ibid.*, p. 139 (my emphasis).

It sounds very neat, and Dawkins himself is certainly in no doubt that it does the job thoroughly, quoting the philosopher Daniel Dennett's supporting verdict that it is 'an unrebuttable refutation'.[8] Unfortunately, Dawkins and Dennett are both wrong. The argument is as fallacious as the one it attempts to refute. A warning note is sounded in its pivotal assumption that '[h]owever statistically improbable the entity you seek to explain by invoking a designer, the designer himself has got to be at least as improbable'. To say that some event – Dawkins's examples are biologically complex systems – is statistically improbable is to say that it is improbable *conditional on* the hypothesis of random generation. This conditional improbability is then contrasted, in the probabilistic arguments for design that Dawkins is attacking and we are familiar with from Chapter 4, with the probability of that event on the hypothesis of a life-friendly God. In other words, God and random generation are two mutually inconsistent *rival explanations*, so to claim that God must be at least as 'statistically improbable' as life, or fine-tuning, is nonsensical. My friend Nicholas Beale has called Dawkins's 'Ultimate 747 Argument' 'magnificently confused',[9] and so it is. There is thus an unconscious irony in Dawkins's comment:

> I have yet to hear a theologian give a convincing answer despite numerous opportunities and invitations to do so.[10]

Several of the published criticisms of Dawkins's argument[11] have, curiously, attacked the one assumption he makes that is valid, that if an improbable event is entailed by some hypothesis then the entailing hypothesis is at least as improbable. The argument those critics use against him is that simple generating mechanisms can generate very complex behaviour, indeed *chaotic* behaviour, which is certainly true. A classic example is the *logistic map*

$$x_{n+1} = rx_n(1 - x_n)$$

where $n \geq 0$, $0 \leq x_i \leq 1$ and r is a positive constant. Although the equation is a simple quadratic function, when r is close to 4 the successive values of x_n become very erratic, and for $r = 4$ we have chaos: minute variations in the initial value of x_0 generate wildly divergent behaviour in the trajectory of x_n (the map can be used as a random number generator). In other words, a simple deterministic generating mechanism can simulate *random*

[8] *Ibid.*, p. 187. [9] Unpublished manuscript.
[10] Dawkins, *The God Delusion*, p. 187. [11] I have yet to see a correct one.

behaviour (it is called *pseudo-random* because it is not really random). Hence, these critics argue, Dawkins was wrong to say that God must be as 'statistically improbable' as the details of his design.

But the critics are wrong. Dawkins was certainly not denying (as far as I am aware) that apparently simple mechanisms are capable of generating very complex behaviour. He merely claimed, which is perfectly correct, that *the hypothesis* that the data are generated by a specified generating mechanism must be at least as improbable as the *consequences* of that hypothesis, on whatever basis you are calculating the probabilities. It will help to use the standard probabilistic symbolism I introduced in Chapter 3 to see what is going on. Let E describe some observed data which is identical to a segment of the output of the logistic map for $r = 4$. Let C be the hypothesis that this complex data is due to chance, and L the hypothesis that it is indeed generated by a deterministic source using the logistic map. Assume that $\mathrm{Prob}(E|C)$ is very small. Because L entails E, it follows from the probability calculus that $\mathrm{Prob}(L|C) \leq \mathrm{Prob}(E|C)$. Hence $\mathrm{Prob}(L|C)$ cannot be any greater. Let L now be the God hypothesis and E be the description of some complex biological system and we have Dawkins's attempted *reductio*. But as I said in the previous paragraph, it is nonsense because L and C are mutually inconsistent alternatives and $\mathrm{Prob}(L|C)$ is therefore trivially equal to 0 in any case.

Dawkins disparages the probabilistic apparatus but it is only *logic*, the logic we need for arguing from the data to the odds on various possible explanatory hypotheses being true. Even more ironically, it would have given him, *validly*, the answer he wanted: the posterior odds on the theistic God, given that evidence, are at most negligible. This is very simply because the God of theism is inconsistent with the facts of innocent suffering. In fact, the probabilistic argument adds nothing more to the demonstrative argument that the God of theism is *inconsistent* with the reported facts of innocent suffering: inconsistent, that is, unless you become a logical contortionist (or, I am tempted to add, a theologian) and deny the usual meanings to ordinary words.

Not only is there arguably a demonstrative argument from the facts to the non-existence of the sort of God theists postulate, but there is also a demonstrative proof that God's own properties *by themselves*, without any appeal to external bodies of facts, are sufficient to entail his non-existence. I observed in the opening paragraphs of this book that capitalism did not, as Marx predicted it would, perish through its internal contradictions. In fact, we can conclude from the failure of Marx's prediction of its necessary demise that capitalism isn't internally inconsistent. For quite a long time, however, people have suspected, with horror if they were theologians, less unhappily if they are atheists, that the God of theism himself suffers from internal problems of a logical nature which, at the very least, imperil his existence. The so-called omnipotence paradox, I pointed out earlier, either is or can easily be turned into a demonstration of inconsistency. I am going to end this chapter, and the book, with what I believe is a rigorous demonstration that an *omniscient* God cannot possibly exist. If it is correct, and I think it is, then God really perished quite a long time ago, of fatal internal injuries. God is indeed dead (if his meme lives on). Nietzsche was right, if for the wrong reason.

3. THE LIAR

The sentence 'This sentence is not true' has a peculiar and unsettling property. It seems to generate a contradiction out of nothing. Let us go over the steps. Assume that the sentence is true or not true, according to a law of deductive logic of ancient pedigree known as the *law of excluded middle*. If it is true then, since it says that it is not true, it must be not true. That may sound bad, and it is, but it is not yet a contradiction: it merely implies that the sentence is not true. Now comes the nasty part. If it is not true then, given that that is what it claims, it must therefore be true. Hence it is true. But by another hallowed law of deductive logic, known as the *law of non-contradiction*, no sentence under a uniform interpretation of its referring terms can be both true and not true (this rules out spurious counterexamples like 'It is snowing here now' and 'It is not snowing here now', where 'here' and 'now' refer respectively to different times or/and places).

This is the famous *Paradox of the Liar*, sometimes also known as *the Epimenides paradox*, because of a passage in St Paul's epistle to Titus, *a propos* the sixth-century BCE Cretan poet and prophet Epimenides. In the course of an ill-natured condemnation of his Cretan ex-hosts, Paul wrote: 'One of themselves, even a prophet of their own, said, "The Cretians are always liars, evil beasts, slow bellies."'[12] The joke was on St Paul, however, who failed to spot the implication that Epimenides must himself be lying, for he added 'This witness is true'! Epimenides's claim is not outrightly paradoxical, however, since while its falsity follows from assuming its truth, from its falsity follows only the logically unproblematic conclusion that

[12] Titus 1:12.

Cretans sometimes do not lie. 'This sentence is false', on the other hand, generates a genuine paradox because it forces us into a contradiction.

This raises a number of questions. Firstly, I said that every meaningful declarative sentence is either true or false (not true), but why should we accept as meaningful the sentence 'This sentence is not true'? The sentence, if sentence it really is, is obviously problematic because it is far from clear that there is a genuine sentence that the denoting phrase 'This sentence' could refer to, genuine in the sense that it asserts a definite-enough assertion to have truth or falsity ascribed to it. Indeed, the sentence is something like a Möbius strip embedded in three-dimensional space, where it seems that you are on both the outside and the inside (in fact it doesn't have an outside and an inside: it has only one side). Secondly, even granted that some definite sense can be made of that sentence, what does the paradox have to do with the idea of an omniscient God?

As an *entrée* to answering both these questions I will introduce you to a very quick and neat paradox generated from God's omniscience, invented by the philosopher Patrick Grim.[13] Like the Liar paradox it involves the notion of truth and is directly self-referential. It is obtained almost immediately from the following sentence:

(1) God doesn't believe that (1) is true.

As Grim points out, if (1) is true then God doesn't believe it and since God is omniscient (1) is therefore false. Hence (1) is false (using a standard law of deductive logic). Hence God believes that (1) is true and since he is omniscient (1) must therefore be true. *Contradiction.*

(1) is a sentence that says something directly about itself, and there are still many people who (wrongly) think that, like the Liar paradox itself, it must therefore be meaningless. It also involves the rather opaque and apparently very subjective notion of belief, which is apt to arouse mistrust in certain quarters. But the charge that self-referential statements are meaningless is easily shown to be untenable: 'This sentence is in English', for example, is not only meaningful but *true.* And Gödel proved a very deep theorem of logic by exploiting a sentence that declared itself unprovable (Gödel's sentence is discussed further in the Appendix to Chapter 7). With belief there is more possibility of doubt – possibly! – so to demonstrate beyond any reasonable doubt that omniscience really is inconsistent in its own right and not by dint of any logically dubious manoeuvres with vague

[13] Patrick Grim, 'Logic and Limits of Knowledge and Truth', in Michael Martin and Ricki Monnier (eds.), *The Impossibility of God* (Amherst, NY: Prometheus Books, 2003), pp. 381–408.

propositions I shall show how that conclusion follows fairly directly from considering the following possible capacities of a possible reasoning system:

(i) The ability to encode information in some way, including the notion of truth.
(ii) The ability to refer to itself and its own properties.
(iii) The ability to discriminate with perfect accuracy between truth and non-truth.

These are surely absolutely minimal capacities of an omniscient God. It might be objected, however, that God, being absolutely omniscient, has no need to encode information at all. According to much of Indian and Chinese religion, for instance, and mystics generally, the whole truth is ineffable, beyond words. But God is nonetheless truthful (necessarily so), and truth is the concordance between factual claims and the facts themselves. So there must be some informational encoding, even at the level of God's thoughts, and the structure of his universe. If the universe was planned by God, as the main religions tell us it was, then necessarily there was a *plan* whose details were faithfully followed. It is just *incoherent* to say that the universe was planned by God yet there is no informational structure embodying that plan. It may be that he can see at a glance, so to speak, the information contained therein, but information contained therein there must be.

So let us proceed. (i)–(iii) may seem innocuous yet, as we shall see, the Liar paradox implies that (i)–(iii) are jointly unsatisfiable. How it does this is via the theorem of Tarski described below, which implies that any well-defined language-system L which is minimally expressive in the sense of (ii) cannot also satisfy (i) and (iii). The proof is little more than a formalisation of the Liar paradox, proceeding in the following steps. (I) Suppose that L contains the predicate 'is true', as a predicate which will or will not hold of any sentence of L. (II) If L has more than fairly minimal descriptive resources it is possible to construct a sentence of the form 'Sentence A is not true', where A represents a referring term in L naming that same sentence. Depending on the particular structure of L the self-reference may be slightly more oblique. Even if L talks about things very unlike linguistic utterances the construction can still usually go ahead. Gödel showed that it is possible in a language ostensibly discussing whole-number arithmetic to encode statements about its own sentences and the deductive relations holding between them. (III) We now proceed as above with the dilemma of the Liar paradox: either sentence A is true or it is not, and in either case we infer to the contradictory of the supposition that it is true or that it is not true. Thus we infer that (i)–(iii) are jointly unsatisfiable.

We have in effect proved, in an informal way, a famous theorem in logic proved in the late 1920s by the logician and mathematician Alfred Tarski and now usually known as Tarski's Undefinability of Truth Theorem.[14] The theorem is very deep: it can be shown to imply the two incompleteness theorems of Gödel. It is in fact a sort of semantic analogue of the second incompleteness theorem, which states that no consistent theory T can prove its own consistency; Tarski's theorem states that no language L can contain a predicate which applies to, i.e. is true of, all and only its own true sentences. That theorem doesn't imply that we can't discuss consistently the truth and falsity of L's sentences. Of course we can: it's just that we have to do so in a language which contains L but *in addition* has the semantic resources to discuss L's truth and falsity. This transcending language is called a *metalanguage* for L.

The implications for an omniscient God are not difficult to discern. An omniscient God is one for whom truth is coextensive with his own knowledge: in effect, 'God knows X' is equivalent to 'X is true'. So God's knowledge states transcend God: he can't faithfully describe them. But statements about these knowledge states, just as statements about truth, are themselves either true or false. For example, if it is raining today in Toronto then 'It is raining today in Toronto' is in the extension of the predicate true, and hence it is true that it is true that it is raining today in Toronto. And one can iterate this 'It is true that . . . ' indefinitely starting from any factually true statement. Tarski's theorem proves that God can't know them. But the principle that God is omniscient entails that God does know them: according to it, the domain of God's knowledge is absolutely universal: nothing in principle escapes God. But in that case the principle of God's omniscience is necessarily false. God can claim that he knows everything, but the Liar lurks and the result will be inconsistency: God will be enmeshed in the Liar paradox.

Now let us consider some objections. One, for long regarded as very powerful, is that the Liar sentence is meaningless because there is no genuine reference for 'this sentence' in 'this sentence is false': there is just an unending loop. But one of the most useful functions of the sort of formalisation that logic and mathematics underwent in the first half of the twentieth century was that it could furnish a sort of precise, well-defined experimental laboratory for testing claims like that. And this one was proved to be false by Kurt Gödel in the course of developing the technical machinery required to prove his incompleteness theorems. Gödel's

[14] Saul Kripke, 'Outline of a Theory of Truth', *Journal of Philosophy* 72 (1975), 690–716.

test-bed, so to speak, was the language of formal arithmetic, call it LA, and he showed that (i) a device now known as Gödel numbering allowing the syntax of LA to be coded as numbers; and (ii) that an adequate set of axioms for the arithmetic of the whole numbers, e.g. the system PA described in the Appendix to Chapter 7, imply that for every property P(x) definable in LA, there exists a sentence S in LA equivalent to $P(S^{\#})$, where $S^{\#}$ is the code of S (S is called a 'fixed point' of P(x)). Loosely speaking, S 'says' that it has the property P. Gödel's own interest was in showing that there was a predicate Q(x) definable in LA which under the numerical coding is interpreted as 'x is the number of a formula of LA which is unprovable from PA'. But we might add to LA a new predicate 'True(x)', and it will then follow from Gödel's fixed-point theorem that then there is a fixed point, call it $B^{\#}$, of 'not-True(x)'. Hence in PA B is provably equivalent to not-True($B^{\#}$): *B is a Liar sentence of LA*. This technical result should remove any doubt on the score of whether 'This sentence is not true' is in principle ill-formed or senseless.

Another possible objection is that the predicate 'is true' can be sensibly and consistently used as long as certain statements, like the Liar statement, are avoided. That is all very well, but it is not a solution for a would-be omniscient God. A much more interesting objection is that we used the law of excluded middle to generate the Liar paradox: if the Liar sentence is true, then it is false, and if it is false, then it is true. There is no third possibility. *But there is* if we deny that true and false are exhaustive possibilities, and there are certainly sentences of English where that bivalence seems to fail: 'The present King of France is bald', is one (this is a famous example of Bertrand Russell's, though he tried to force a truth-value on it, namely 'false'). And there is another natural candidate: there is no matter of fact which could determine the truth or falsity of the Liar sentence, so we seem to have good grounds for denying that it has a determinate truth-value. There has in fact been a long tradition of considering the possibility of three (and sometimes more)-valued logics, where 'indeterminate' is a third value. In the twentieth century formalisms were developed for many-valued logics, but until the 1970s no-one had attempted to develop a systematic truth-value-gap theory which would explain in a systematic, non-ad hoc way why the Liar sentence should lack a truth-value. In 1975, in a characteristically brief sketch, the logician Saul Kripke provided such a systematic theory, in which it can actually be *proved* that no basic matter of fact assigns the Liar sentence a determinate truth-value (in his terminology the sentence is *ungrounded*), or for that matter the more benign 'This sentence is true' one either. Both are indeed like loops in logical space, and their ungroundedness is a nice explanation of why we find them both prima facie suspicious. Moreover, it can also be proved in Kripke's theory that while 'This sentence is true' can consistently be assigned (arbitrarily) the value either 'true' or 'false', the Liar sentence never can.

The technical details of Kripke's theory are beyond the scope of this discussion,[15] but it was and still is regarded as a highly significant contribution to modern logic, and has inspired a very large literature. The question we need answered is whether it allows an omniscient God to crawl back through the truth-value gaps (a God of the gaps of a slightly different type!). Though he did not see himself addressing that question, the answer was nevertheless provided by Kripke himself, and is in effect 'no'. The reason is very simple. By restricting the sense of the negation 'not' so that 'true' and 'not true' are not exhaustive but permit a third possibility, indeterminate,[16] there remains a broader sense of 'not' such that a sentence which is neither true nor not true in the restricted sense is still *not* true in the broader sense of 'neither indeterminate nor definitely true': this inclusive sense of negation is not, however, even definable at all in Kripke's theory, since otherwise it would let the Liar paradox back in (if not through the back door, one might say, then through the 'inclusive-not' gate). Letting God back in through truth-value gaps is a strategy bought therefore at the cost of truncating the body of authentic truths that God can know, so that in particular God cannot know that the Liar sentence is not true in a system with truth-value gaps.

Kripke himself didn't discuss God in the context of his theory, but acknowledged that the gap-solution of the Liar paradox has the consequence that the intuitive truth that the Liar sentence is not true can only be asserted outside the language L. But taking the God's-eye view, so to speak, there can be no language outside God's own language, for that would in itself be enough to limit God's omniscience. But then the notion of truth for that language turns out to be unutterable within it, as Tarski showed. In either case there will be truths that God cannot know or say.

4. GOD IS GREAT! – AND THEN SOME

When the doctrine of an absolute, unlimited God was first promulgated it must have seemed like a wonderful theological theory-of-everything that satisfied the need for an all-encompassing, final explanation of the cosmos

[15] There is a more extended but still relatively informal discussion of it in my book *Logic with Trees* (New York: Routledge, 1997).

[16] The three-valued logic that Kripke adopted for his valuation scheme is called Kleene's *strong three-valued logic*, after the logician/mathematician Stephen Kleene; Kleene himself employed it for a quite different purpose to do with computability.

that evaded the regress problem by disallowing by definition anything prior or external to that individual. As we noted in Chapter 5, God became a sort of limit-point along multiple axes – of power, understanding, compassion, etc. – whose necessary existence was duly guaranteed by the Ontological Argument. This sort of procedure can be harmless enough if suitably restricted, but if it is sufficiently global in its scope we know how easily it can lead to just the sort of trouble we have been witnessing.[17] One of the most striking examples arose in mathematics at the turn of the nineteenth and twentieth centuries, during the attempt to make set theory into a truly universal mathematical theory, universal in the sense that all mathematical concepts could be defined in terms of abstract sets, and all truths about them proved from self-evident principles of set-hood. One such self-evident truth is that since there are sets of this, that and the other then there must be a set of *all* sets, call it V. But the mathematician Georg Cantor, to whom the mathematical theory of sets was largely due, had shown that if S is any set, then the set of all subsets of S must be strictly greater in size than S, in a sense of 'strictly greater' that could be made precise. So the set *P*(V) of all subsets of V[18] must be strictly greater in size than V. But *P*(V) is of course a subset of V, and by another theorem of Cantor it can be at most as big as V; contradiction. Nor was that all. The set ω of so-called ordinal numbers is a transfinite set, and it itself has the structure of an ordinal number. But it can be shown that it must exceed in size all the ordinal numbers within it, yet since ω is – in effect – an ordinal number itself it must therefore be bigger than it is. Contradiction.

The similarity between rational theology and what, in our wiser days, is now called *naive set theory*, is quite startling when it is first noticed, and it bears witness to the penalties attendant on making the naive assumption that a concept in which there is implicit a notion of degree can always be extended to some postulated maximum. Set theory has learned its lesson and now all sets are regarded as being built up from below by well-tested methods of limited extension.[19] Rational theology has still to learn its lesson.

[17] For another couple of 'paradoxes' associated with God's presumptive properties see Matt McCormick, 'The Paradox of Divine Agency' and 'Why God Cannot Think', in Martin and Monnier (eds.), *The Impossibility of God*, pp. 313–23 and 258–74 respectively.

[18] The set *P*(S) of all subsets of S is called the *power set* of S, so called because if S is finite, with n members, *P*(S) has 2^n members.

[19] The interested reader can learn more about the way set theory – and mathematics – evolved to meet the challenges of these set-theoretical paradoxes in Michael Hallett's book *Cantorian Set Theory and Limitation of Size* (Oxford University Press, 1984).

5. SO WHAT?

The physicist Victor Stenger has written a number of very good books on the scientific evidence for God, concluding that there is none whatever. I have no wish to question this verdict (I agree with it), or most of the contrary arguments he marshalls: nearly all are skilfully presented, admirably supported by evidence and highly compelling. But in a recent book,[20] he downplays the arguments which claim to show that the omni-properties, omniscience, omnipotence and omnibenevolence, are inconsistent jointly, and some even individually. His response is not to question the inconsistency, but to claim that the reasoning which demonstrates it has doubtful effectiveness because '[w]ays out of purely logical arguments can always be found, simply by relaxing one or more of the premises'. Indeed, he claims, the assumption of omnibenevolence can simply be dropped without theological loss, on the ground that it is actually *inconsistent* with what holy writ tells us. Thus:

> the God of the more conservative elements of Judaism, Christianity, and Islam that take their scriptures literally can hardly be called omnibenevolent. No-one reading the Bible or Qur'an literally can possibly describe the God described therein as all-good . . . the reader is invited to simply pick up an Old Testament or Qur'an, open to a random page, and read for a while. It will not take you long to find an act or statement of God that you find inconsistent with your own concepts of what is good.[21]

Now it is certainly true that one would have to be using the word 'good' in a very unusual way to describe as good what the holy books of Judaism, Islam and Christianity tell us about God's actions and even more his motives: 'petty, vindictive, tyrannical, sadistic and cruel' might well seem more apposite descriptions. But Stenger's blanket assessment of 'purely logical arguments' as easily defeatable, because all one has to do to avoid their conclusions is to drop some of the premises, is far too optimistic in many cases and certainly in the present one, for the good theological reasons we noted in Chapter 2, that they are essential to the theistic picture of God, and for that matter of the God of Abraham himself. It is precisely because the omni-properties are essential properties and can't be dropped at will

[20] Victor Stenger, *God: The Failed Hypothesis: How Science Shows that God Does Not Exist* (Amherst, NY: Prometheus Books, 2007).

[21] *Ibid.*, p. 34. Stenger also correctly points out that much in the gospel is hardly what we would ordinarily describe as good either; some of Christ's admonitions are threateningly unpleasant.

that the paradox of omnipotence arose and was taken very seriously by theologians.[22]

Philosophers ancient and modern endorse this view. Spinoza, the most rigorous and theologically minded of the great seventeenth-century Rationalist philosophers, founded his entire philosophy on a God *necessarily* free of any a priori restriction:

> By God I mean an absolutely infinite being, that is, substance consisting of infinite attributes, each of which expresses eternal and infinite essence,[23]

and he explains that what he means by infinite 'is the *unqualified existence* of some nature'.[24] The language is quaint, but the meaning is clear: nothing contingent can bound God's nature and powers. Richard Swinburne puts it in more up-to-date language: God is bounded only by logical consistency.[25] Well, we have seen that on pain of inconsistency there is no being who can know all and only truths. But that implies that the traditional theistic *notion* of an omniscient God, one who *can* express all and only truths – is an impossible one to instantiate. The God everyone has been talking about for centuries, and has tried from time to time to prove *must* exist out of his sheer illimitable perfection, just does not and *cannot* exist. Do not, by the way, take consistency as a limitation that a fully omnipotent God should be able to overcome. Some did, and had to be put right on the matter by St Augustine. Tertullian said that he believed the impossible, but it was a thoughtless remark. We have seen Kant point out *à propos* the Ontological Argument that existence is not a property that things may or may not have: if they are things, they necessarily have it; if they do not have it they are not things. Logical possibility similarly is not a property things may or may not have: as things, they necessarily have it; if they do not have it, they are not things. God does not have it.

6. FINALE

As his defenders rightly point out, God has been responsible for inspiring much of sublime beauty in art, architecture, literature and music. He has

[22] Stenger makes the further curious claim that *since* the God of the monotheistic scriptures is *in fact* not omnibenevolent (supposing the scriptural reports are understood in a straightforward sense, though as we have seen we are usually counselled against doing this), he is therefore 'not ruled out by logical inconsistency'. But this is just a logical mistake, since the very same scripture says that he is.

[23] B. Spinoza, *The Ethics*, Edwin Curley (ed. and trans.) (London: Penguin, 1996), Part I, 'Concerning God', Definition 6.

[24] Spinoza, *Ethics*, Scholium I to Proposition 8 (my emphasis).

[25] Swinburne, *The Existence of God*, p. 7.

also inspired more than 2,000 years of subtle argumentation that contains its own glories. But He has also been responsible for suffering on an enormous scale. And even when every rational reason to believe in him has been cut away, He still obstinately stands there, blocking to the best of his ability a more enlightened vision of the world and its creatures. It is time to complete the Copernican revolution and replace Him by his creature, mankind, as the moral centre of our world, and so bid Him – *adieu.*

CODA

This book opened with a poem in which Matthew Arnold made the ebbing tide on Dover Beach emblematic of the decline of religious faith. I shall close with another poem, in which the sight of the ocean inspires a very different thought, and a very different emotion:

> For instance, I stand on the sea-shore,
> alone, and start to think.
> There are rushing waves . . .
> mountains of molecules,
>
> -
>
> Deep in the sea, all molecules repeat the patterns
> Of one another till complex new ones are formed.
> They make others like themselves . . . and a new dance starts.
> Growing in size and complexity . . .
> Living things, masses of atoms, DNA, protein . . .
> Dancing a pattern ever more intricate.
> Out of the cradle onto the dry land
> Here it is standing . . . atoms with consciousness
> Matter with curiosity.
> Stands at the sea . . . Wonders at wondering
> I . . . a universe of atoms . . . an atom in the universe.

This may not have the art of Matthew Arnold, but it is every bit as moving as 'Dover Beach'. Its author was Richard Feynman.[26]

EXERCISE

'My little children, let us not love in word, neither in tongue; but in deed and truth. And hereby we know that we are of the truth, and shall assure

[26] It is quoted in J. Mehra, *The Beat of a Different Drum: The Life and Science of Richard Feynman* (Oxford University Press, 1994).

our hearts before him. For if our heart condemn us, God is greater than our heart, and knoweth all things.' Comment.

MAIN POINTS OF CHAPTER 8

- Richard Dawkins has recently attempted to prove that God's existence is extremely improbable: he claims to have demonstrated that God almost certainly doesn't exist.
- To prove that requires at least as strong probabilistic premises, which Dawkins claims are provided by the extreme 'statistical improbability' of life.
- This is a confusion, since that last probability is the probability conditional on the hypothesis of chance, so the most Dawkins can have shown is that God's existence is at least as improbable *given that hypothesis*, which should surprise no-one.
- But a demonstration of the impossibility of omniscience, and hence of the God of theism, is possible, and it is provided using Tarski's indefinability of truth theorem.

Bibliography

Abdel Haleem, M. A. S. (trans. and ed.), *The Qu'ran* (Oxford University Press, 2004)
Abdennour, B., 'La lapidation, preuve extréme de la logique de violence de l'Islam', *Le Monde*, 31 August 2010
Adams, F. C., 'Stars in Other Universes: Stellar Structure with Different Fundamental Constants of Nature', *Journal of Cosmology and Astroparticle Physics* 8 (2008), 010
Ali, A. H., *Nomad* (Toronto: Knopf Canada, 2010)
Anderson, J. R., A. Gillies and L. C. Lock, '*Pan* Thanatology', *Current Biology* 20:8 (27 April 2010)
Anderson, P., 'The Reverend Thomas Bayes, Needles in Haystacks, and the Fifth Force', *Physics Today* 45:1 (January 1992), 9–11
Arnold, M., *Culture and Anarchy* (London: John Murray, 1924)
Poems (London: Macmillan, 1923)
Aristotle, *Nicomachean Ethics*, Christopher Rowe (trans.) (Oxford University Press, 2002)
Arnhart, L., *Darwinian Natural Right: The Biological Ethics of Human Nature* (State University of New York Press, 1998)
Axelrod, R. and W. Hamilton, 'The Evolution of Cooperation', *Science* 211 (March 1981), 1390–6
Barnes, J., *Aristotle* (London: Oxford University Press, 1982)
The Constants of Nature: From Alpha to Omega (London: Jonathan Cape, 2002)
Behe, M., *Darwin's Black Box: The Biochemical Challenge to Evolution*, 10th Anniversary edn (New York: Free Press, 2006)
Beilby, J. (ed.), *Naturalism Defeated? Essays on Plantinga's Evolutionary Argument against Naturalism* (Ithaca, NY: Cornell University Press, 2002)
Bendor, J. and P. Swistak, 'Types of Evolutionary Stability and the Problem of Cooperation', *Proceedings of the National Academy of Sciences of the USA* 92 (1995), 3596–600
Binmore, K., *Fun and Games: A Text on Game Theory* (Lexington, MA: D. C. Heath, 1992)
Just Playing, Game Theory and the Social Contract – Vol. 2 (Cambridge, MA: MIT Press, 1998)

Blackmore, S., *The Meme Machine* (Oxford University Press, 1999)
Blair, R. J. R., 'Neurobiological Basis of Psychopathy', *British Journal of Psychiatry* 182 (2003), 5–7
Boyer, P., *Religion Explained: The Evolutionary Origins of Religious Thought* (New York: Basic Books, 2001)
Carse, J. P., *The Religious Case Against Belief* (London: Penguin, 2008)
Claudel, P., *Contacts et Circonstances* (Paris: Gallimard, 1947)
Clough, A. H., *Poems* (London: Macmillan, 1903)
Collins, F., *The Language of God* (New York: Free Press, 2006)
Collins, R., 'Our Evidence for Fine-Tuning', in N. Manson (ed.), *God and Design: The Teleological Argument and Modern Science* (New York: Routledge, 2003), pp. 178–99
Davies, P., *The Goldilocks Enigma: Why is the Universe Just Right for Life?* (London: Allen Lane, 2006)
Dawkins, R., *The Blind Watchmaker* (New York: Norton, 1987)
The God Delusion (London: Bantam Books, 2006)
The Selfish Gene, 30th Anniversary edn (New York: Oxford University Press, 2006)
'Is Science a Religion?', *The Humanist* 57 (1989), 26–9
de Waal, F., *Chimpanzee Politics: Power and Sex among the Apes*, rev. edn (Baltimore, MD: Johns Hopkins University Press, 1998)
Good Natured: The Origins of Right and Wrong in Humans and Other Animals (Cambridge, MA: Harvard University Press, 1996)
Dembski, W., *The Design Inference: Eliminating Chance Through Small Probabilities* (Cambridge University Press, 1998)
The Design Revolution: Answering the Toughest Questions about Intelligent Design (Downer's Grove, IL: Intervarsity Press, 2004)
Dennett, D. C., *Breaking the Spell: Religion as a Natural Phenomenon* (London: Allen Lane, 2006)
Donoghue, J. F., 'The Fine-tuning Problems of Particle Physics and Anthropic Mechanisms', arXiv:0710.4080v1 [hep-ph], 22 October 2007
Douglas, N., *Old Calabria* (London: Martin Secker, 1915)
Dyson, F., *Disturbing the Universe* (New York: Harper and Row, 1979)
Eliot, T. S., *Collected Poems* (London: Faber, 1974)
Empson, W., *Collected Poems* (London: Chatto and Windus, 1977)
Feynman, R., 'The Relation of Science to Religion', *Engineering and Science* (June 1956)
Fisher, R. A., *Statistical Methods for Research Workers* (Edinburgh: Oliver and Boyd, 1932)
Frazer, J., *The Golden Bough* (New York: Macmillan, 1922)
Gauthier, D., *Morals by Agreement* (Oxford University Press, 1986)
Good, I. J., *Probability and the Weighing of Evidence* (London: Griffin, 1950)
Gould, S. J., *Rocks of Ages: Science and Religion in the Fullness of Life* (New York: Ballantine Books, 1999)

Grim, P., 'Logic and Limits of Knowledge and Truth', in Michael Martin and Ricki Monnier (eds.), *The Impossibility of God* (Amherst, NY: Prometheus Books, 2003), pp. 381–408

Grünbaum, A., 'The Poverty of Theistic Cosmology', *British Journal for the Philosophy of Science* 55 (2004), 561–615

Gryn, H., *Chasing Shadows* (London: Penguin, 2001)

Gutting, G., 'The Opinionator', *New York Times*, 1 August 2010

Hallett, M., *Cantorian Set Theory and Limitation of Size* (Oxford University Press, 1984)

Hamilton, W., 'The Genetical Evolution of Social Behaviour', I and II, *Journal of Theoretical Biology* 7 (1964), 1–16, 17–32

'Innate Social Aptitudes of Man: An Approach from Evolutionary Genetics', in R. Fox (ed.), *Biosocial Anthropology* (New York: Wiley, 1975), pp. 133–53

Hardin, G., 'The Tragedy of the Commons', *Science* 162 (1968), 1243–8

Hawking, S., *A Brief History of Time: From the Big Bang to Black Holes* (New York: Bantam Books, 1990)

Hawking, S. and L. Mlodinow, *The Grand Design* (New York: Bantam Books, 2010)

Hauser, M., *Moral Minds: How Nature Designed our Universal Sense of Right and Wrong* (New York: Ecco, 2006)

Herrnstein Smith, B., *Natural Reflections: Human Cognition at the Nexus of Science and Religion* (New Haven, CT: Yale University Press, 2009)

Hitchens, C., *Thomas Jefferson: Author of America* (New York: Atlas Books/Harper Collins, 2005)

Howard, D. and J. Stachel (eds.), *Einstein: The Formative Years, 1879–1909* (Boston: Birkhauser, 1998)

Howson, C., *Hume's Problem: Induction and the Justification of Belief* (Oxford University Press, 2000).

Logic with Trees (New York: Routledge, 1997)

'Popper's Solution to the Problem of Induction', *Philosophical Quarterly* 34 (1984), 143–7

Howson, C. and P. Urbach, *Scientific Reasoning: The Bayesian Approach*, 3rd edn (Lasalle, IL: Open Court, 2006)

Hoyle, F. and C. Wickramasinghe, *Evolution from Space* (London: J. M. Dent & Sons, 1981)

Hume, D., *An Enquiry Concerning Human Understanding* (Open Court: Lasalle, IL, 1988)

Treatise of Human Nature, 2nd edn (Oxford: Clarendon Press, 1978)

Humphrey, N., *Leaps of Faith: Science, Miracles and the Search for the Supernatural* (New York: Copernicus, 1999)

Jastrow, R., *God and the Astronomers* (New York: Norton, 1978)

Jaynes, E. T., *Probability Theory: The Logic of Science* (Cambridge University Press, 2003)

Jeffreys, H., *Theory of Probability*, 3rd edn (Oxford: Clarendon Press, 1961)

Kac, M. and S. Ulam, *Mathematics and Logic* (New York: Praeger, 1968)
Kahneman, D. and A. Tversky, 'Judgement Under Uncertainty: Heuristics and Biases', *Science* 185 (1974), 1124–31
Kelly, A. L., 'Case Study – Italian Tax Mores', in T. Donaldson and P. Werhane (eds.), *Ethical Issues in Business* (Upper Saddle River, NJ: Prentice-Hall, 1979), pp. 37–9
Kiehl, K. A., 'A Cognitive Neuroscience Perspective on Psychopathy: Evidence of Paralimbic Dysfunction', *Psychiatry Research* 142 (2006), 107–28
Kripke, S., 'Outline of a Theory of Truth', *Journal of Philosophy* 72 (1975), 690–716
Lane Craig, W., *Reasonable Faith: Christian Truth and Apologetics*, 3rd edn (Wheaton, IL: Crossway Books, 2008)
Can We Be Good Without God? (video)
Lane Craig, W. and Q. Smith, *Theism, Atheism, and Big Bang Cosmology* (Oxford: Clarendon Press, 1993)
Lane Fox, R., *The Unauthorized Version: Truth and Fiction in the Bible* (London: Viking, 1991)
Laplace, P., *A Philosophical Essay on Probabilities*, Frederick Wilson Truscott and Frederick Lincoln Emory (ed. and trans.) (New York: Dover Publications, 1951)
Leibniz, G. W., 'On the Ultimate Origination of Things', in G. H. R. Parkinson (ed.), Mary Morris and G. H. R. Parkinson (trans.) *Philosophical Writings* (London: Dent, 1995), pp. 136–44
Leslie, J., *Universes* (New York: Routledge, 1989)
Lewis, C. S., *Mere Christianity*, rev. and enlarged edn (London: Collins, 1955)
The Problem of Pain (New York: Macmillan, 1962)
Lewis, D., *Conventions: A Philosophical Study* (Cambridge University Press, 1969)
Machover, M., *Set Theory, Logic and their Limitations* (Cambridge University Press, 1996)
Mackie, J. L., *Ethics: Inventing Right and Wrong* (New York: Penguin, 1977)
'Evil and Omnipotence', *Mind* 64 (1955), 200–12
Martel, H., P. Shapiro and S. Weinberg, 'Likely Values of the Cosmological Constant', *Astrophysics Journal* 492 (1998), 1–57
Martin, M. and R. Monnier (eds.), *The Impossibility of God* (Amherst, NY: Prometheus Books, 2003)
Maynard Smith, J. and Price, G. R., 'The Logic of Animal Conflict', *Nature*, 246 (1973), 15–18.
McCormick, M., *The Case Against Christ: Why Believing is No Longer Reasonable* (Amherst, NY: Prometheus Books, forthcoming)
'The Paradox of Divine Agency', in Michael Martin and Ricki Monnier (eds.), *The Impossibility of God* (Amherst, NY: Prometheus Books, 2003), pp. 313–23
'Why God Cannot Think', in Michael Martin and Ricki Monnier (eds.), *The Impossibility of God* (Amherst, NY: Prometheus Books, 2003), pp. 258–74
Mehra, J., *The Beat of a Different Drum: The Life and Science of Richard Feynman* (Oxford University Press, 1994)

Mendelson, E., *Introduction to Mathematical Logic*, 3rd edn (Monterey, CA: Wadsworth and Brooks, 1987)
Nilsson, D.-E. and S. Pelger, 'A Pessimistic Estimate of the Time Required for an Eye to Evolve', *Proceedings of the Royal Society of London, B. Biological Sciences* 256 (1994), 53–8
Nowak, M. and K. Sigmund, 'Evolution of Indirect Reciprocity', *Nature* 437 (2005), 1291–8
Onfray, M., *In Defense of Atheism: A Case against Christianity, Judaism, and Islam*, Jeremy Leggat (trans.) (Toronto: Viking Canada, 2007)
Orr, H. A., 'Darwin v. Intelligent Design (Again)', *Boston Review* 21 (December 1996/January 1997)
Orwell, G., *1984* (London: Penguin, 2003)
Osborn, J. and S. W. G. Derbyshire, 'Pain Sensation Evoked by Observing Injury in Others', *Pain* (11 December 2009). Online.
Pascal, B., *Pensées*, Roger Ariew (ed. and trans.) (Indianapolis, IN: Hackett, 2005)
Penrose, R., *The Road to Reality: A Complete Guide to the Laws of the Universe* (London: Vintage, 2005)
Plantinga, A., *God and Other Minds* (Ithaca, NY: Cornell University Press, 1967)
The Nature of Necessity (Oxford University Press, 1974)
Polkinghorne, J., *Science and Creation: The Search for Understanding* (Philadelphia: Templeton Foundation Press, 2006)
'Religion in an Age of Science', *McNair Lecture*, University of North Carolina, March 1993
Popper, K. R., *The Logic of Scientific Discovery* (New York: Harper & Row, 1968)
'Probability Magic, or Knowledge out of Ignorance', *Dialectica* 11 (1957), 354–72
Redhead, M. L. G., 'Review: W. L. Craig and Q. Smith: Theism, atheism, and Big Bang Cosmology', *British Journal for the Philosophy of Science* 47:1 (1996), 133–6
Redmond, G., *Science and Asian Spiritual Traditions* (Westport, CT: Greenwood Press, 2008)
Rousseau, J.-J., *Discours sur l'origine et les fondements de l'inégalité parmi les hommes*, vol. III of *Oeuvres Complètes* (Paris: Gallimard, 1959)
Samuels, R., 'Evolutionary Psychology and the Massive Modularity Hypothesis', *British Journal for the Philosophy of Science* 49 (1998), 575–603
Savage, L. J., *The Foundations of Statistics* (New York: Dover Publications, 1954)
Schurz, G., *The Is-Ought Problem: An Investigation in Philosophical Logic* (Boston: Kluwer Academic, 1997)
Searle, J., 'Minds and Brains without Programs', in C. Blakemore and S. Greenfield (eds.), *Mindwaves: Thoughts on Identity, Intelligence, and Consciousness* (Oxford: Blackwell, 1987), pp. 203–33
Sigmund, K., 'William D. Hamilton's Work in Evolutionary Game Theory', Interim Report IR-02-079, International Institute for Applied Systems Analysis
Skyrms, B., 'The Stag Hunt', Presidential Address to the Pacific Meeting of the American Philosophical Association, March 2001

Skyrms, B. and R. Pemantle, 'A Dynamic Model of Social Network Formation', *Proceedings of the National Academy of Sciences of the USA* 97 (2000), 9340–6
Smith, Q., 'Review of *Universes*, by John Leslie', *Nous* 28 (1994), 262–9
Smolin, L., *Three Roads to Quantum Gravity* (New York: Basic Books, 2001)
Sobel, J. H., *Logic and Theism* (Cambridge University Press, 2005)
Spinoza, B., *The Ethics*, Edwin Curley (ed. and trans.) (London: Penguin, 1996)
Steinhardt, P. and N. Turok, *Endless Universe: Beyond the Big Bang – Rewriting Cosmic History* (New York: Doubleday, 2007)
'The Cyclic Model Simplified', *New Astronomy Reviews* 49 (2005), 43–57
Stenger, V., *God: The Failed Hypothesis: How Science Shows that God Does Not Exist* (Amherst, NY: Prometheus Books, 2007)
Has Science Found God? The Latest Results in the Search for Purpose in the Universe (Amherst, NY: Prometheus Books, 2003)
Susskind, L., *The Cosmic Landscape* (New York: Little, Brown and Co., 2006)
Swinburne, R., *The Existence of God*, rev. edn (Oxford: Clarendon Press, 1991)
Tegmark, M., 'Is "The Theory of Everything" Merely the Ultimate Ensemble Theory?', *Annals of Physics* 270 (1998), 1–51
'Parallel Universes', in J. D. Barrow, P. C. W. Davies and C. L. Harper (eds.), *Science and Ultimate Reality: From Quantum to Cosmos* (Cambridge University Press, 2003), pp. 459–92
Turing, A., 'Computing Machinery and Intelligence', *Mind* 59 (1950), 433–60
Urquhart, A., 'Metatheory', in D. Jacquette (ed.), *A Companion to Philosophical Logic* (Malden, MA: Blackwell, 2002), 307–18
van Inwagen, P., 'Why is There Anything at All?', *Proceedings of the Aristotelian Society Supplementary Volumes* 70 (1996), 95–120
Vanderschraaf, P., 'Game Theory, Evolution and Justice', Technical Report No. CMU-PHIL-95 (1998) (Carnegie-Mellon University, Pittsburgh), 1–59
'Hume's Game-Theoretic Business Ethics', *Business Ethics Quarterly* 9 (1999), 47–67
Vermes, G., *The Authentic Gospel of Jesus* (London: Penguin, 2004)
Ward, K., *God, Chance and Necessity* (Oxford: Oneworld, 1996)
Weinberg, S., *Dreams of a Final Theory* (New York: Pantheon Books, 1992)
The First Three Minutes: A Modern View of the Origin of the Universe, updated edn (New York: Basic Books, 1988)
Wells, G. A., *The Historical Evidence for Jesus* (Buffalo, NY: Prometheus Books, 1992)
Yeats, W. B., *Collected Poems* (New York: Macmillan, 1967)

Index